EDITORIAL
At Home in Modernism

Text: Anh-Linh Ngo

Architecture and urban planning have always been instruments of identity construction. Not only does this apply to the reconstruction of lost historical buildings and city ensembles— much of which is currently being undertaken in Europe with underlying right-wing agendas— it also applies in a special way to the epoch of modernity. The vision of an ideal past and the design of a better future are two sides of the same coin. This political context serves as the backdrop for this issue's understanding of architectural modernisms in Cambodia, Indonesia, Myanmar, and Singapore as an expression of these societies' struggle for a postcolonial future.

Taking a political angle opens up this topic to more than purely architectural and historical considerations, bringing it into the present-day discourse. Indeed, the relevance of this issue is that it reminds us, in our encounters with Southeast Asian modernisms, how closely architecture and ideology are intertwined, for better or worse. For worse, because modernism has been used, top-down, by rulers of various stripes to advance their nationalist interests. For the better, because designing the future was always associated with some progressive notion of society. Given the triumph of the depoliticized International Style in the wake of the Second World War, it is exciting to discover just how politically charged modernism was in Southeast Asia.

But to view architecture solely from the perspective of ideological superstructures would be to overlook the decisive aspect of its agency. That would mean, as Indonesian curator Setiadi Sopandi aptly notes in this issue, "reducing the complexity of architecture to a mere representational function." Among all human cultural products, architecture stands out in that it is an embodiment of both the ideological superstructure *and* the economic base, as Marxist architectural theorist Douglas Spencer pointed out in ARCH+, *The Property Issue* (p. 130). Not only does it shape our thinking as a social narrative, it also intervenes as a substructure—as the material basis of everyday life, in the reality of the lives of the people who live and work within it. Because of this dual nature, architecture is able to transcend not only ideologies but cultural boundaries as well. The original invention, interpretations, and adaptations of modernism in Cambodia, Indonesia, Myanmar, and Singapore, which are presented and critically discussed in this issue, impressively illustrate this balancing act.

Finally, the examination of Southeast Asian modernisms reminds us, once again, that the modern movement was not an exclusively Western development, but multivoiced, multilayered, and globally integrated. However, this is not about the cultural appropriation of stylistic features alone, but also, and even more importantly, about the openness of modernism to adaptation in order to meet the life-styles of its users and inhabitants. Architecture only becomes effective on a local level if it enriches people's lives from the bottom up. This insight—which is not at all new—also makes clear what task still lies ahead of us: balancing the tension between universalist claims and specific social contexts. Only then can we become at home in modernism.

PS: As we wrap up this issue, democratic protests in Myanmar are being brutally put down by the military. The struggle for an emancipatory future continues. In shedding light on a hitherto little-known side of the country—the struggle for a local modernism—we express our respect and solidarity with the people of Myanmar.

ACKNOWLEDGEMENTS

This issue owes much to the pioneering work of the *Encounters with Southeast Asian Modernism* project by Sally Below, Moritz Henning, Christian Hiller, and Eduard Kögel, who initiated and curated the project in 2019 to explore the many important voices and perspectives on modernism(s) in Southeast Asia as part of the Bauhaus centenary. I would like to thank them, as well as all the contributors, for their fruitful collaboration as guest editors. A big thank you also goes to the ARCH+ team for transforming this body of knowledge into an exceptional issue, first and foremost Mirko Gatti (project manager), Nora Dünser (managing editor), Max Kaldenhoff (creative director), Melissa Koch (editor), as well as Julius Grambow and Leonie Hartung (editorial assistants).

© Giovanna Silva

Page 26

ARCH+
features

© Manuel Oka

Page 124

ARCH+ TEAM OF THIS ISSUE:
Anh-Linh Ngo, Mirko Gatti (project leader), Max Kaldenhoff (creative direction), Nora Dünser, Christian Hiller, and Melissa Koch (editors), Julius Grambow and Leonie Hartung (editorial assistants).

GUEST EDITORS:
Sally Below (SB), Moritz Henning (MH), Christian Hiller (CH), Eduard Kögel (EK).

COVER:
Stéphane Janin: Capitol Cinema by Vann Molyvann, Phnom Penh 1992
© Stéphane Janin

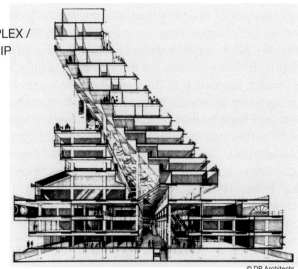

Page 178

© DP Architects

ENCOUNTERS WITH AND DISCUSSIONS ABOUT ARCHITECTURAL MODERNISM IN SOUTHEAST ASIA

Text: Sally Below, Moritz Henning,
Christian Hiller, Eduard Kögel

I. Encounters with Southeast Asian Modernism

A History of Architecture by Banister Fletcher Sr. and Jr., a worldwide classic of 20th century architectural education, was first published in 1896. According to Johannes Widodo, who teaches architecture and urban history in Singapore, this book illustrates the West's ignorance about the architecture of entire regions of the world—a condition that persists to this day. For years, Widodo has been promoting the work of various efforts in Asia—such as the mASEANa (modern ASEAN architecture) Project, founded in 2015—which are helping to rewrite history by reappraising Southeast Asian architectural modernism in particular. Fletcher's book focuses on European architecture from the Romanesque to the Renaissance, but also mentions the buildings of the British colonies and the United States as "historical styles." The architecture of India, China, and Japan, on the other hand, is classified as "non-historical styles." He visualized this limited and strongly colonialist perspective in 1905 with a family tree of architecture, where the superior European building culture is located in the lush treetop, while the architectures of the rest of the world are depicted on dead side shoots (see Johannes Widodo's article in this issue).

Fletcher's position is not an isolated one; the list could be extended at will to standard works of the late 20th century—such as Kenneth Frampton's *Modern Architecture. A Critical History* from 1980 or Leonardo Benevolo's *History of the City* from 1980—which, while claiming a global, universalist perspective, utterly ignore the Southeast Asian region.

Johannes Widodo presented his critique in August 2019 at the symposium *Encounters with Southeast Asian Modernism* in Berlin, where he was joined by a number of other architects, historians, artists, and curators from Southeast Asia, who accepted our invitation to discuss the treatment of architectural modernism in Germany and Southeast Asia, and how it relates to global and local political and social developments. The symposium was the kick-off of our multiyear exhibition, event, and research project, which, as the project title suggests, we developed as actual encounters, together with our curatorial partners in Jakarta, Indonesia; Phnom Penh, Cambodia; Singapore; and Yangon, Myanmar. From October to December 2019, the project provided a platform for exchange between local professionals and interested parties in the four cities mentioned above. But why did we, having dealt with the region and/or subject matter in various ways for quite some time, initiate this project in the first place?

As the Bauhaus centenary in 2019 drew near, we saw an opportunity to advance what we see as an equally fascinating and long overdue exploration of architectural modernism in Southeast Asia, and to share this with a wider audience. In the countries of Southeast Asia themselves, postcolonial architectural modernism is, in some circles, a hotly debated topic. In Germany and the rest of Europe, on the other hand, it is barely present. It is important to close this gap, not least because discussions about the architectural heritage of modernism are currently being conducted both here and there in a in surprisingly similar ways.

The question of how to position oneself as a Western European in a project seeking to address colonialism and postcolonialism in Southeast Asia without reproducing hierarchies is subject to constant reflection within the team. This does not always go smoothly. At the *Encounters* symposium, Farid Rakun, part of the curatorial team from Jakarta, offered concrete approaches for a new kind of collaborative practice. In his presentation, "De-Modernizing the School in Practice," he spoke about the ideas developed by the ruangrupa collective and the Gudskul initiative they cofounded. Rakun explained how they are collectively managed like "ecosystems" and seek to deconstruct established thought structures in order to enable new insights (see ARCH+ features 104 inside this issue).

In conjunction with the 100th anniversary of the Bauhaus, several projects, such as *bauhaus imaginista* and *projekt bauhaus* (see ARCH+ 222, 230, 234), had already shaken up the established narrative of an architectural modernism that began its worldwide triumphant march from the West. *Encounters with Southeast Asian Modernism* took its own approach. Instead of focusing on the lives of students, famous Bauhaus teachers, or their artistic and architectural legacy, we looked to political and social upheaval as catalysts for change. This can be observed in Germany, both in the example of the Bauhaus during the Weimar Republic and in the period of reconstruction in both German states after the Second World War. It is also evident in many countries of Southeast Asia: when the colonies and protectorates of France, Great Britain, and the Netherlands gained their independence, these upheavals led to new ideas about structure and form. In this historical situation, the young nations were faced with the task of establishing themselves in the international arena, and this was often accompanied by a desire to express their new beginnings through architecture and urban planning. In the architectural language of international modernism, many countries found a form that reflected their hopes for progress and prosperity and at the same time signaled their emancipation from former colonial rule.

During the tour that followed the *Encounters* symposium, the experts from Southeast Asia were less impressed by the icons of modernism in Dessau and Berlin than by their encounters with activists and initiatives that, for various reasons, are committed to the preservation and revival of postwar modernism in particular. One place that made a particularly strong impression was Haus der Statistik at Alexanderplatz in Berlin, where the exhibition *Contested Modernities* is planned for 2021.

Haus der Statistik (House of Statistics) establishes a direct thematic link to the architectural, artistic, and activist approaches of our project partners in Jakarta, Phnom Penh, Yangon, and Singapore. Built around 1970 in what was the heart of East Berlin, it originally served as a representative administrative building for the East German government. After German reunification it stood empty for many years and was pegged for demolition. But thanks to civic engagement and open-minded allies in politics and the city administration, the building could be saved, and is currently being used for exhibitions and events. In the future, this model project will combine art, culture, social services, education, affordable housing, as well as a new town hall and public administrative uses. The building's history and future development offer exemplary approaches to exchanging knowledge and practices between the initiatives working in Southeast Asia for the preservation and reprogramming of modernist buildings.

II. Phnom Penh, Jakarta, Yangon, Singapore

Each of the curatorial teams involved in *Encounters with Southeast Asian Modernism* explored the significance and preservation of modernist architecture in different ways. The program kicked off in Southeast Asia in September 2019 in Phnom Penh, Cambodia, with the exhibition *Folding Concrete* curated by Vuth Lyno and Pen Sereypagna. The title refers to three aspects of Cambodian modernism: the new design possibilities opened up by building techniques imported from the West in the 1960s; the multiple "folded" building elements that have become a kind of emblem of Cambodian modernist architecture; and less linear, more polyphonic approaches that emerged from the meeting of tradition and modernism. The transdisciplinary concept of the exhibition is prototypical for *Encounters,* and also manifests itself in this issue.

In addition to artistic works, research projects, and surveys of modernist buildings, a central theme was the so-called White Building in Phnom Penh, an apartment building from the 1960s whose history somewhat parallels that of Haus der Statistik in Berlin. It was built in a political system that no longer exists, and its demolition was long debated. But unlike Haus der Statistik, the voices of protest by its residents and numerous architects and artists were not heeded, and the building was knocked down in 2017. Vuth Lyno and Pen Sereypagna curated community-based projects in the White Building for many years, which in turn gave rise to other initiatives.

Occupying Modernism in Jakarta, Indonesia, curated by Avianti Armand, Setiadi Sopandi, and Rifandi S. Nugroho, was also based on artistic research: a comic artist, a graphic designer, a product designer, and a painter/publicist/writer were invited to take a subjective look at how people in Indonesia have appropriated modernist structures. According to Sopandi, this approach made it possible to bypass the usual confrontations in architectural discourse. In his speech at the exhibition's opening, he posited that architectural history (in Indonesia) has always been written in terms of dualisms: modern vs. traditional, colonial vs. non-colonial, left vs. right, urban vs. rural, national vs. foreign (see Setiadi Sopandi's article in this issue). This binary thinking runs throughout history, at least since the exoticization of local building methods by Dutch colonial exhibitions. But it could also be felt in the struggle for independence, when colonial architecture was attacked. While these dualisms subsided in the first years after independence under President Sukarno, they reemerged under the authoritarian New Order regime of Suharto in the late 1960s.

A parallel project was launched at Gudskul in Jakarta by Farid Rakun, JJ Adibrata, and Grace Samboh with Hyphen –. Under the title *From, by, and for whom?* it examined the interdependence of politics, art, architecture, and design, using dioramas by artist Edhi Sunarso depicting key scenes from Indonesian history as a starting point. Found at monuments and museums, Sunarso's dioramas play a key role in educating the public, and disseminating an idealized and politicized version of national history. This is also true of the dioramas at the National Monument on Merdeka Square in Jakarta, which had been commissioned by Sukarno. After Suharto came to power, Edhi Sunarso continued his work on the dioramas, although now according to the guidelines dictated by the New Order regime. To this day, the dioramas are an integral part of the visitors program aimed at school groups, families, and tourists. As part of a seminar led by Grace Samboh, students developed podcasts that reveal the political dimensions of the dioramas and discuss them in reference to contemporary issues (see Hyphen –'s article in this issue).

The realization of the exhibition *Synthesis of Myanmar Modernity* in Yangon, Myanmar, was influenced by a complex political situation even before the events currently taking place in the country. For decades—as explained by the curatorial partners Pwint, professor at the Faculty of Architecture of Yangon University of Technology, and Win Thant Win Shwin, an architect and planner in Mandalay and Yangon—the discourse on modernist architecture and urban planning in Myanmar was relatively dormant. Since the pro-democracy political reforms in the country began in 2011, however, interest in the modernist era and its architecture has been growing. A younger generation has been asking about the historical significance and current value of this architectural heritage. But in a multiethnic society, with a population that speaks hundreds of different dialects, renegotiating modern architecture is hardly a simple task.

Despite the challenging situation, Pwint and Win Thant Win Shwin made it possible for us to visit buildings in Myanmar that are seldom accessible to outsiders, and which, until now, have not been discussed in the context of national or international architectural history. However, the promising developments that began to emerge during our project suffered a tragic setback with the unexpected death of Pwint in January 2020. And with the military seizing power again in a coup on February 1, 2021, the already fragile development of democracy is once again at stake. The future is uncertain, and at the time of writing it is completely uncertain whether and how this fruitful collaboration can be continued. For it is clear that the discussion of some of the buildings featured here in this issue, as well as the interviews with two Myanmar architects captured by filmmaker Christopher Chan Nyein as part of the 2019 project and reprinted here, can only provide a first glimpse into the country's complex architectural history, in the hope of inspiring further research.

In Singapore, the curatorial team was led by Johannes Widodo and Nikhil Joshi and headed by Ho Puay-Peng, all from the National University of Singapore. Their focus in the exhibition *Housing Modernities* was on early modernist settlements and multifunctional complexes, such as the People's Park Complex and the Golden Mile Complex, both of whose future is uncertain. Since the early 1960s, when the Housing and Development Board (HDB) was established under the leadership of the People's Action Party, the economic ascent of the city-state has been flanked by public housing programs. The goal of providing adequate housing for the entire population was quickly achieved. However, a process of displacement has been underway for years, with early neighborhoods and iconic buildings threatened with demolition.

In addition to the focus on *Housing Modernities,* the concluding symposium that took place at the NTU Centre for Contemporary Art (CCA) in Singapore addressed current perspectives on the narrative of modernity that the exhibition curators had developed and presented for discussion.

Tay Kheng Soon (see the interview in this issue) as well as William S. W. Lim and Lim Chong Keat are key figures in the architectural development of both Singapore and the wider region. The works of Lim Chong Keat were presented by Shirley Surya, curator of Design and Architecture at M+ Museum in Hong Kong, on the basis of the museum's collection (see Shirley Surya's article in this issue). Lim Chong Keat's approach to culture and design were shaped by his international network, which included Buckminster Fuller, and his broad interests that went far beyond the discipline of architecture. The same applies to William S. W. Lim, who has been an important source of reference for curator Ute Meta Bauer, founding director of CCA at Nanyang Technological University in Singapore since 2014, in her internationally oriented and transdisciplinary work (see the interview in this issue).

The discussion at the symposium at NTU CCA, which concluded the event tour in December 2019, once again highlighted the importance of interdisciplinary and regional exchange. Each of the places we visited has its own history and a narrative that stands on its own—a fact that is obscured rather than conveyed by the use of the geographical construct "Southeast Asia." These distinct histories are reflected not least in the curators' very different contributions, and in the diverse spaces where the exhibitions and events took place. In Phnom Penh, many young and culturally curious people gathered in a freshly renovated apartment located on the upper floor of a typical residential building in the Chinese Quarter. The otherwise private location was kindly made available by the owner, an art collector. In Jakarta, the project was present at both Gudskul, co-initiated by ruangrupa, and at Kopi Manyar, a café and cultural meeting place designed by the renowned architect Andra Matin. In Myanmar, the exhibition and accompanying symposium were hosted by the Goethe-Institut in Yangon. In Singapore, there were again two venues: the government-run Urban Redevelopment Authority (URA) for the exhibition, and the NTU CCA for the closing symposium.

In order to connect the cultural and architectural heritage to the here and now, each location, each situation with its specific characteristics, requires targeted and critical consideration. It is also necessary to develop a mutual sense of understanding between these countries that can challenge the dominant Western perspective. This task remains a challenge, because, at least in Grace Samboh's estimation at the closing symposium, the countries are still too busy negotiating their own history to look beyond their national borders. But networks like the mASEANa project, launched in 2015, are doing significant work that is transcending these boundaries.

The exhibition at Haus der Statistik in autumn 2021 brings together the positions of these curators from Southeast Asia in order to compare and contrast them, and to intensify transnational collaboration.

III. Contested Modernities

The title chosen for this issue reflecting on the project *Contested Modernities*, refers to a lecture given by Vuth Lyno at the 2019 inaugural symposium in Berlin, titled "Exhibiting the Contested Modern in Cambodia." In it, he illuminated the competing narratives in the modernist discourse and its promise in Cambodia by looking at several exhibitions held in Phnom Penh between 1955 and 1967 promoting the benefits and achievements of the modern world. Based on the many discussions we have had in the course of our encounters in Germany and Southeast Asia, this term seemed ideal for representing the current state of the discourse on the various (not only) Southeast Asian modernisms in all their diversity.

"Contested" refers to something that is disputed, fought for, or even doubted. In our case, it refers, among other things, to the historical situation—the struggle for independence in many countries in the region and the accompanying process of modernization; the complex dynamics of separation and self-determination yet continued reliance on the former colonial powers (see the contributions by Benjamin Bansal, Michael Falser, and Moritz Henning in this issue); and how this newly gained independence awakened the superpowers' desire for regional influence under the auspices of the Cold War. On the other hand, *contested* also refers to the political upheavals that followed independence—such as the anti-urban and anti-modern attitude of the Khmer Rouge in Cambodia; the military dictatorship in Myanmar (at that time still Burma); and, not least, as reflected here in this issue, the struggle to author one's own architectural history. Of course, *contested* also refers quite specifically to the danger faced by important modernist buildings in many places—due not only to rapid urbanization in many Asian metropolises, but also to reappraisals of local (architectural) history, which often go hand in hand with the political tides.

Finally, *contested* refers to the concept of modernism. On the one hand, its use implies the existence of a unified movement that originated in the West and was then "exported" to other regions as a civilizing project. Despite the positive light in which it is always framed, this common understanding is historically unfounded. The diversity of architectural, political, and social moments in the region that came to be under the umbrella of modernism clearly demonstrate that a revision of this view is urgently needed.

For the exhibition in Berlin, it is also important for us to take a look at Germany's role in the process of modernization in the region. An exploratory review by our team reveals the complex relationship between West Germany (FRG) and East Germany (GDR), as exemplified by their respective policies for "developmental aid" and "socialist solidarity" in faraway Southeast Asia. Although Germany did not have any colonies there, there were various points of contact with the region in the second half of the 20th century. Budding architects from Indonesia studied in the FRG, while students from Myanmar were trained in the GDR. The architectural historian Julius Posener, who emigrated from Germany during the Nazi era, helped to establish the Faculty of Architecture in Kuala Lumpur in Malaysia in the 1950s before returning to Berlin (see Eduard Kögel's article in this issue). While the GDR helped to rebuild cities that had been destroyed during the Vietnam War, the FRG assisted through construction projects in South Vietnam and Cambodia. It is clear that the projects were initiated not only for humanitarian reasons, but also out of geopolitical and economic interests. Earlier in ARCH+ 226, Christina Schwenkel examined the reconstruction of Vinh, a city destroyed by the war, whose reconstruction was supported by the GDR, and the tensions between the rationalist ideas of German architects, the culturally specific wishes of local inhabitants, and the Vietnamese government's plans to modernize its society.

The fact that the Western architects' ideas were not always met with undivided approval is illustrated by a debate between Julius Posener and the Malaysian architect Lim Chong Keat. Excerpts from their written exchange, which was conducted over the course of several articles in architectural magazines, can be found in Eduard Kögel's essay in this issue and are also intended to open up an important perspective in the exhibition, as they exemplify the debate about architectural modernism and the political reality in the transition to independence.

This publication both summarizes and complements *Encounters with Southeast Asian Modernism* and *Contested Modernities* and was produced in close collaboration with the ARCH+ editorial team. Additionally informed by their own critical perspectives, it documents and expands on our own ongoing research process spanning several years and countries. Our approach is based on our ambition to create a shared, international discursive space with the architects, scholars, artists, curators, and activists who have worked in Southeast Asia to preserve and find new uses for modernist architecture in their cities. We see this as a long-term project, in which local urban practices become networked with one another, and narratives about the past, present, and future of modernism are corrected, expanded, or created in the first place.

MANAGING CHANGE THROUGH HISTORIC PRESERVATION
Conserving Asia's modernist architectural heritage

Text: Johannes Widodo

"Today in Macau, at the heart of the Mediterranean of Asia, we affirm Asia as a dynamic source of our identities and recognize the numerous experiences that we share with the rest of the world. Industrialization, urbanization, westernization, colonization, de-colonization, and nation-building—these phenomena have variously defined Asian modernism. Modern Asia has not developed in a vacuum but has evolved through sustained interactions with the West, which has had a constant presence in our collective consciousness."

modern Asian Architecture Network,
Macau Declaration, 2001.

The modern Asian Architecture Network (mAAN) was formed in Macau in 2001 to kickstart a discourse on Asian modernisms. Small "m" and plural "modernisms" speak for an understanding of modern architecture as an ongoing process of production and adaptation of architectural forms constantly evolving in a continuous layering process. One of the main factors triggering this discourse back in 2001 was the realization that we, as Asians, often perceive our own architecture history as Eurocentric. Although relatively little work has been produced in terms of studies, interpretations, and theories from an Asian perspective, in the past 20 years, there has been a growing interest in developing a comprehensive inventory of modern architecture heritage in Asia with the aim of challenging the long-standing dependence on Western textbooks and paradigms, often narrating modernity solely as a European export. In the 1896 classic *A History of Architecture on the Comparative Method*, for example, cowritten by Banister Fletcher Sr. and Jr., Asian architecture was placed under the category of "non-historical style"[01] and in the famous Tree of Architecture, printed as the frontispiece of the first edition, the Fletchers trace the genealogy of modern architecture as a linear evolution stemming from the ancient Greek and Roman styles, while leaving others—namely the Peruvian, Mexican, Egyptian, Assyrian, Indian, Chinese, and Japanese—as truncated branches. The mAAN promotes a more comprehensive, cross-cultural understanding of modernity, one that is based on the idea that references can travel and influence each other in a multitude of directions and can be reproduced across different geographical contexts.

Crucial figures of the European and American modernist movements, such as Bruno Taut and Frank Lloyd Wright, were deeply influenced by their Asian experiences, especially in Japan. Wright traveled to Japan several times before and during the construction of the Tokyo Imperial Hotel, especially between 1917 and 1922. Japanese art and material culture had a huge influence on his work. A passionate collector of Japanese woodblock prints himself, Wright greatly contributed to the popularity of Japanese art in the USA. In his 1912 pamphlet *The Japanese Print: An Interpretation*, he describes Japanese art as "a thoroughly structural art; fundamentally so in any and every medium. … The realization of the primary importance of this element of 'structure' is also at the very beginning of any real knowledge of design."[02] Similarly, Taut wrote countless notes and essays on Japanese culture and architecture, drawing parallels between Japanese simplicity and the modernist discipline.[03] His encounter with the 17th-century Katsura Villa in Kyoto was a revelatory moment in the elaboration of his architectural ideas.[04] In his design for the extension of Villa Hyuga in Atami, completed in 1936, Taut successfully integrated material and spatial sensibilities of both Eastern and Western cultures, setting an eminent example for a multidirectional understanding of modernism.

Today, one of the main challenges faced by scholars attempting to write a history of modernism from an Asian perspective lies in the fact that the conservation of modernist buildings in Asia is itself a challenge. The transition from traditional to modern construction materials in Asia occurred during the late colonial era. Modern materials such as concrete and steel were initially imported from

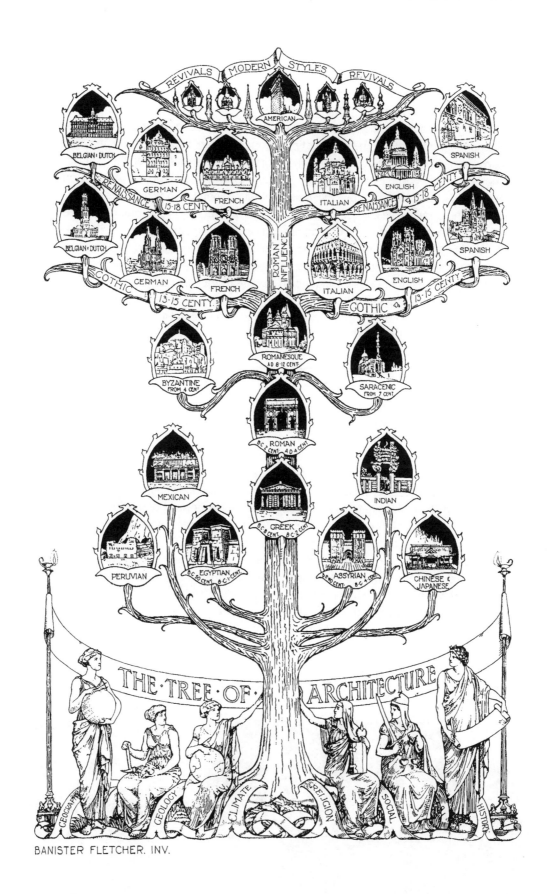

"Tree of Architecture," in Banister Fletcher, *A History of Architecture on the Comparative Method* (1896, Reprint, London B. T. Batsford Ltd., 1954).

Europe, but the local industry developed fast. A cement factory was established by the Portuguese in Ilha Verde, Macau, as early as 1886; a French cement factory opened in Hai Phong, Vietnam, in 1899; the Dutch opened one in Indarung, West Sumatra, in 1910; the British established the Burma Cement Company in 1935; and King Rama VI of Thailand founded his Siam Cement factory in 1913. The introduction of reinforced concrete soon intertwined with the evolution of traditional Asian architecture. The shophouse, or townhouse—which exists in different variations everywhere across Asia—is probably the most common urban mixed-use dwelling and qualifies as the quintessential typology of Asian modernism. Extremely functional in terms of program and spatial configuration, the layouts of 19th- and 20th-century shophouses—essentially two-story units with a 1.5-meter-wide hallway and a back courtyard—were translated by the British Singapore Improvement Trust into modern four-story apartment blocks in the 1930s, laying the foundation for the progressive housing policies later implemented by the postcolonial Housing and Development Board (HDB) (see Ho Puay-Peng's article in this issue).

After the Second World War, as almost all former colonial territories in Asia gained independence, colonial heritage was often destroyed in an attempt to bury the painful memories attached to it. The subsequent rapid economic growth, and the succession of opposing political regimes in many countries in the Southeast, led to the frequent erasing and rewriting of histories. Today, in the dense and rapidly expanding Asian cities where real estate values are soaring, economic interests often outweigh the interests of local conservationist movements. Shophouses, with their fragmented ownership status and central location, are the perfect target for speculative regeneration plans. Without attractive public incentives and a well-designed legal framework, it is not easy to convince private owners to sacrifice their economic benefit for the sake of memory. Furthermore, even if the buildings themselves are saved from demolition, preserving the authenticity and diversity of a neighborhood has proven a much harder task. Singapore's successful preservation of Chinatown stands as a blatant example of how conservationist arguments can easily be deployed at the service of tourism and real estate speculation.

Because, for the most part, the conservation of heritage is seen as hampering progress and economic development, a pragmatic approach of only keeping the facade or the envelope of a building is often pursued as a good alternative. The former Cathay Cinema in Singapore is a notable example: originally part of a 1939 complex designed by Frank Brewer, the Cathay became popular as the first air-conditioned movie theater in Singapore. During Japanese occupation, between 1942 and 1945, the complex was used as the Japanese propaganda office. After the war, it successively hosted the headquarters of the Supreme Allied Commander of Southeast Asia, a hotel, a nightclub, and an office complex. In the early 2000s, the Cathay went up for redevelopment and the complex was almost entirely knocked down, except for the cinema's facade, which is now standing as the extravagant entrance to an anonymous shopping mall. One tangible memory of the cinema was preserved, but at the cost of its architectural integrity.

A more successful approach is that of the widely acclaimed Blue House Cluster in Hong Kong's central district of Wan Chai. The Blue House, one of the oldest still-existing workers' tenement blocks in the city, is a very early example in a multistory building realized in a hybrid brick and reinforced concrete slab-and-beam system with cantilevered balconies. Built in 1922, the building was acquired by the government in the 1970s. Despite it standing at the heart of one of the most competitive property markets in the world, in 2007, the Urban Renewal Authority and the Development Bureau put forward a plan that not only protected the building as historical heritage, but also reactivated it as a publicly run community space. Next to its original commercial activities, including a clinic for traditional medicine, the Blue House today hosts a local museum and a multifunctional space where workshops and public events are held regularly. The project won the UNESCO Asia Pacific Awards for Cultural Heritage Conservation in 2017 and was described as "a triumphant validation for a truly inclusive approach to urban conservation. A broad alliance, spanning from tenants to social workers and preservationists, waged

Left
Cathay Cinema in Singapore, 1954.

Right
Only the facade of the cinema was retained, and serves as the entrance
to The Cathay shopping mall, built in 2009 behind it.

Courtesy Powerhouse Museum of Arts and Sciences, Sydney

© Wikimedia Commons

The renovated Blue House
in Hong Kong, 2019.

a grassroots advocacy campaign to save the last remaining working-class community in the fast-gentrifying enclave of Wan Chai, which was threatened by demolition and wholesale redevelopment. Succeeding against all odds, their impassioned efforts and innovative participatory programs have safeguarded not only the architecture, but also the living history and culture of a neighborhood."[05] Examples like this show that a contextualized and open-ended understanding of modernist heritage can trigger positive change, not just for the sake of the buildings themselves, but for the upholding or critical reevaluation of the social and political structures that underlie the architecture, be it colonialist domination, nation-building, or adhesion to one political model or another.

In October 2020, the announcement by the Urban Redevelopment Authority of Singapore that the Golden Mile Complex (see feature on the Golden Mile Complex in this issue) should be preserved was welcomed with enthusiasm by the many who had campaigned to save the building. This futuristic megastructure, completed in 1973 by Design Partnership, is not only one of the most iconic architectural outputs of its time but also a legacy of the very progressive public-housing policies that are unique to Singapore and which have defined the social and political ambitions of the nation for the past 50 years. The 718 strata-title units[06] will now be sold en bloc and the complex put up for redevelopment with exceptional planning incentives, but on the condition that the original structure is left intact, a decision which was applauded as a pragmatic win-win situation for developers and residents alike. It remains to be seen, however, what the outcome of this public-private conservational effort will be, and if the brutalist look of the Golden Mile Complex will simply be exploited for a clever market operation, or if its renovation will be faithful to the building's original program to provide modern, high-standard affordable housing for the people of Singapore.

As we have seen from these few examples, modernization is a structural process both in an architectural and in a cultural sense. Transplantation, adjustment, adaptation, assimilation, and hybridization are all legitimate paths through which the architecture of a country evolves and comes to mirror the society it represents. Asian modernity is a layered one. It produced many architectures whose physical presence can teach us invaluable lessons for the future. Conserving them is a process of managing change which is absolutely essential, not only for Asian scholars to be able to process and evaluate their history, but also for them to be able to write a new history.

01 Banister Fletcher, *A History of Architecture on the Comparative Method* (Cambridge, MA: Scribner's Sons, 1905), 603–51.
02 Frank Lloyd Wright, *The Japanese Prints: An Interpretation* (Chicago: Ralph Fletcher Seymour Company, 1912), 5–6.
03 Bruno Taut, *Nippon mit Europäischen Augen Gesehen* (Berlin: Gebruder Mann Verlag, 2009), originally published in Japan in 1934; Bruno Taut, "Das Architektonische Weltwunder Japans," in Bruno Taut, *Ich liebe die japanische Kultur* (Berlin: 2003), 92–100; Bruno Taut, *Das japanische Haus und sein Leben: Houses and People of Japan*, ed. Manfred Speidel (Berlin: Gebruder Mann Verlag, 2017), originally published in Japan in 1937.
04 Manfred Speidel, "Bruno Taut and the Katsura Villa," in *Katsura Imperial Villa*, ed. Virginia Ponciroli (Milan: Electa, 2005), 319–29.
05 UNESCO Asia-Pacific Award for Cultural Heritage Conservation, "Project profiles for 2017 UNESCO Heritage Award winners," 2017, accessed July 4, 2021, bangkok.unesco.org/sites/default/files/assets/article/Culture/files/project-profiles-2017-unesco-heritage-award-winners.PDF.
06 The strata title is a special form of ownership of a part of a property (generally a unit in a multilevel building), whereby the building plot remains common property. This form of ownership was introduced in Singapore in May 1967 with the Land Titles (Strata) Act.

Text: Eduard Kögel

"POELZIG'S GRANDCHILDREN"
Julius Posener and CW Voltz in Kuala Lumpur (1956–61)

In the early 1930s, the architectural historian Julius Posener (1904–1996), who studied architecture in Berlin with Hans Poelzig (1869–1936) until 1929, worked for the Paris-based magazine *L'architecture d'aujourd'hui*. From Paris, Posener moved to Palestine in 1935, where he joined the British Army in 1941. Between 1948 and 1956 Posener taught at the Brixton School of Building in London.[01] More or less by chance, he applied for a position advertised by the Colonial Office: an architecture department was to be established at the Technical College in Kuala Lumpur, then capital of the British-controlled Federation of Malaya. To his surprise, he was awarded the job after all the other applicants dropped out. The Technical College had been built between 1951 and 1955 to train future public service engineers in all technical fields. The new architecture course was to be set up in accordance with the stipulations and regulations of the Royal Institute of British Architects (RIBA). In July 1956, Posener left England with his family. Upon arrival in Kuala Lumpur, however, he found that the Technical College was still unsure about the need for an architecture department, although at the time nearly all local architects in Malaya had to be trained in Britain or Australia.

Left
Julius Posener (center left)
and CW Voltz (center right)
with students at the Technical College in Kuala Lumpur.

Right
Postcard of a Malay fishing
village with wooden
houses on stilts by the sea.

Malay Kampongs, Mala...

Courtesy Eduard Kögel

Shortly before leaving, Posener wrote a letter to Le Corbusier, telling him about the challenges: "The task to which I will devote myself seems interesting and necessary. Over the past few years, you have made your own contribution to architecture in tropical climates, a contribution we will study carefully in Malaya."02

In his first year, Posener had only three students; the following year the number increased to 15. It was clear he would need more teaching staff to run a successful training program. However, neither London nor Kuala Lumpur would consider additional funding. So Posener turned to the West German consulate in Kuala Lumpur for help. The Foreign Office in Bonn agreed to fund a position. Posener then wrote to, among others, Max Bill (1908–1994), whom he did not know personally, but he was aware of his activities at the Ulm School of Design. Bill replied, "Dear Mr. Posener, your new colleague is called Karl Voltz."03 Voltz (1924–1998), who abbreviated "Carl Wilhelm" to "CW," had studied architecture at Darmstadt, then gone to work for Alfred Arndt (1898–1976), an architect and a former Bauhaus teacher, before joining up with Max Bill's team at Ulm in 1951. In November 1957, Voltz arrived in Kuala Lumpur, where he would stay until the

spring of 1960. After that, Günter Naleppa, an architect from the planning office in the Wilmersdorf district of Berlin, took over the position, which continued to be financed by the German Foreign Office for another two years.

The planner and architect Vernon Z. Newcombe (1912–2013) was another German-British figure in the Kuala Lumpur network. Newcombe began his studies of architecture and urban planning in 1930, under his original name Werner Zunz, at the Technical University of Darmstadt, where he graduated with distinction in June 1934. However, because of his Jewish heritage, he emigrated to London, where he would later change his name. In London he worked from 1936 to 1939 with Erich Mendelsohn (1887–1953) and Serge Chermayeff (1900–1996), among other prominent figures. Between 1939 and 1952, Newcombe was employed by various companies and local authorities in Britain. This included a period as deputy chief architect and planner for the construction of Stevenage New Town, the first British new town project implemented after the war. In January 1953, he took a position in Kuala Lumpur, where he became the director of the Federal Housing Trust at the National Housing Agency of

Malaya. He remained in this position—where among other things he developed new ideas on housing for the poor—until after independence in July 1958, when his job fell victim to the new government's austerity policies.[04] Posener said of Newcombe's work: "In the city of Kuala Lumpur, Vernon Newcombe built tenement houses for poor Chinese people. What was built was only the shell. Everything else people made collectively—doors and I think even windows, floors, ceilings, and built-in furniture. To me this seems to be an extremely good principle. The people did it with great enthusiasm."[05] Since Posener was always on the lookout for teachers, he hired Newcombe to teach a course in urban planning for the 1957–58 academic year at the Technical College, where Newcombe was able to bring his experience in Malaysian low-cost housing.

Theories of tropical construction

We can presume that Julius Posener came to Kuala Lumpur with no practical experience in construction in tropical contexts.[06] So it is unsurprising that, early on, he corresponded with Le Corbusier and also contacted Otto Koenigsberger (1908–1999) in London, seeking professional support for his own on-site assessments.[07]

Voltz was equally unprepared for building in a tropical context. In February 1958, he wrote to Walter Gropius (1883–1969) in the United States: "What moved me to write to you is the situation that there are no teaching materials here. … What I discovered here is the continental English school [*sic*]. Here in the tropics, people actually build stone boxes as if there were no sun."[08] He asked Gropius for contacts at American universities, details of their curricula, and the contacts of people like Charles Eames (1907–1978), Raphael Soriano (1904–1988), and Richard Neutra (1892–1970). Gropius sent him various addresses of universities and architectural magazines, and enclosed a book on his own ideas on the subject.[09]

In October 1958, Voltz wrote to his family about his work at the Technical College. Shortly beforehand, Norman Lehey (1923–2009) had been brought in from Melbourne to start a discussion about curriculum change. Voltz wrote, "I was absolutely against teaching too much material. It was exactly the opposite of what architecture schools are striving for today: emancipation from books, less

Design-build student project for a timber home in Kepong.

Design-build student project for a timber home in Kepong.

knowledge, but better methodology."[10] In his first semester, Voltz had twelve students—eleven men and one woman. "Unlike the TH [Technical University in Darmstadt], we are going straight into design practice here. Incidentally, this is also Max Bill's view of things. Results are good. We had some excellent work done in the foundation course too, for the first time. ... My hours are spread across the week, so that of 24 hours of college work, only two hours are lectures; the rest is all studio work."[11] In his free time, Voltz designed buildings for private clients, seeking to adapt modernism to the location, local climatic conditions, and the life people lived there.

After returning to Berlin, Posener worked his Kuala Lumpur teaching experience into his reflections on "educating the architect" and the future of design training: "The first part of the course also includes designing for real-world projects. In Malaya, we did this with students as early as their second year. ... That was extremely valuable experience; and since then, I have felt that a city which does not manage somehow to continuously provide its [architecture] school with small commissions to carry out is neglecting its duty to the next generation of architects."[12]

From timber house to housing block

Along with Voltz, Posener taught design at the Technical College, while statics and other technical subjects were taught in the engineering departments. Around the turn of the year 1957–58, an informal meeting was held with Posener, Voltz, and Peter Morley from the city's Department of Public Works. The two architects complained to Morley that students had no practical projects. Just a week later,

Morley asked if students could design and construct houses for the Forest Research Institute in Kepong. Construction would start in March 1958. Voltz wrote to his family, "The building is to be constructed almost entirely from wood, which will mean us coming up with completely new concepts. They are swimming in wood there, and it would be too expensive to build in stone."[13]

The construction site was located in the middle of the rainforest, on a steep slope, not far from Kuala Lumpur. A competition for the design was held among twelve students. As in Poelzig's seminar, they critiqued each other's designs in class.

Norman Lehey helped with blueprints, since neither Volz nor Posener had much knowledge of wood construction. The building was constructed quickly, with students making repeated visits to the site to learn about problems encountered during the building process. The Forest Research Institute also passed on other assignments to the students, such as designing standardized housing, and designing the title page of their journal, which changed every year. Twenty years later, Posener revisited the Kepong site and discovered many of student-designed wooden buildings were still there.

The Straits Times newspaper reported on the first three wooden homes in Kepong, observing that timber was as long-lasting as bricks and concrete, but significantly less expensive.[14] A three-room house made of wood cost around one third less than brick and concrete. This three-room student residence measured 26 × 5.5 meters, with an additional porch, 1.80 meters wide, and cost $30,000. As well as commissioning the student project, Peter Morley built a wooden house in Kepong for $10,000, while Patrick Campbell, a forest engineer, built a basic house there for just $6,000.

The high-rise with twelve
maisonettes is based
on Le Corbusier's Unité
d'Habitation and was
designed by Lai Lok Kun,
a student at the Technical
College in 1957–58.
The first two floors were
kept mainly open, for
increased air circulation.

A BLOCK OF FLATS

GOLF VIEW ROAD KUALA LUMPUR

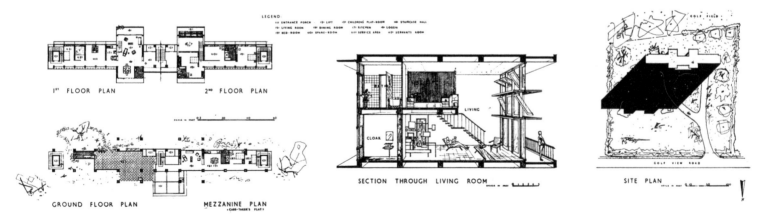

LEGEND:

(1) ENTRANCE PORCH	(2) LIFT	(3) CHILDRENS PLAY-ROOM	(4) STAIRCASE HALL
(5) LIVING ROOM	(6) DINING ROOM	(7) KITCHEN	(8) LOGGIA
(9) BED-ROOM	(10) SPARE-ROOM	(11) SERVICE AREA	(12) SERVANTS ROOM

1ˢᵗ FLOOR PLAN   2ᴺᴰ FLOOR PLAN

GROUND FLOOR PLAN   MEZZANINE PLAN «CARE-TAKER'S FLAT»

SECTION THROUGH LIVING ROOM

SITE PLAN

A BLOCK OF FLATS AT GOLF VIEW ROAD KUALA LUMPUR

LAI LOK KUN
FINAL YEAR 1957-58
TECHNICAL COLLEGE
KUALA LUMPUR

On the one hand, Posener and Voltz's educational philosophy included vernacular wooden stilt-supported structures, which they wanted to use to develop new ideas for local architecture. It was clear, however, that these wooden houses would primarily be used in village and suburban settlements. For this reason, they also worked on developing new idioms of urban architecture, clearly based on Le Corbusier's ideas for the Unité d'Habitation.

In the academic year 1957–58, a student design by Lai Lok Kun won a prize; it proposed a 14-story high-rise, each with twelve maisonette apartments. The entire ground floor was to remain open, and in one half of the building this would extend over two floors, allowing air to circulate below the building. The south facade was fully glazed, and protected from direct sunlight by a loggia and horizontal shading elements. Such a tall, narrow building with two housing units per double floor was obviously aimed at the luxury market.

Malayan architecture

From the start, the criteria and aims of student training preoccupied the new architecture professors. At the time, there was considerable professional debate about what "Malayan architecture" should look like, mostly among foreign architects.[15] Posener also addressed this question. In late 1958 he wrote to Le Corbusier, "Architecture? Well I hope you like *PETA*,[16] our little magazine, which will give you a taste of what is going on here. Of course there is a lack of originality. Even worse, it is lacking in the spirit of the archipelago that this peninsula belongs to. There are some very interesting villages with houses made of wood and bamboo, on pilotis! This is the tradition here, both among Malays and the indigenous people.[17] ... Whereas our so-called modern architects put blocks on the ground and use brick and reinforced concrete. A lot of thorough research has yet to be done; but our school could be a starting point for this kind of research."[18]

At the Technical College, Posener tried to get students interested in traditional timber construction. "When I suggested drawing the houses to the students, the Chinese asked what could possibly interest me about these ridiculous peasant cottages, and the Malays were embarrassed because we wanted to make their 'shame' public. Others said: nowadays we have concrete and steel, thank God. We did not put up with their resistance and they got started on two houses."[19]

After preliminary assessments, the students were tasked with drawing sections and floor plans. This work prompted a rethink among the students, according to Posener. However, he was realistic enough to recognize that these exercises would not lead to an increased use of wood in building. He later wrote, "This was the experience of our timid attempts to open the eyes of the children of this nation to the value of ancient Malaysian wooden structures."[20]

Posener also used public events to advocate for wood as a building material. Above all, he opposed the view that wood was a building material only for the poor. His statement that many "ultra-modern" homes in Malaysia were copied from US magazines certainly did not win him any new friends in this context.[21]

In 1960, Posener even made several half-hour radio broadcasts, aiming to make basic architectural issues known to the people. The program, entitled *Crossfire,* addressed topics like "Architect and Client," "Architecture and the Public," "Architectural Competitions," "Originality," "Timber as a Building Material," and "Training Architects in Malaya." Posener prepared the episodes and discussed the topics with the architect Kington Loo (1930–2003) and the librarian Beda Lim.[22]

The question of national identity in the federation, independent since 1957 and with a very multiethnic population, repeatedly came up for discussion in various contexts. In September 1960, a newspaper article by Posener warned that an architectural style could not be forced. "It may be wise to restrict ourselves to tackling our tasks honestly, thoughtfully and lovingly; and to leave the development of a distinctive Malayan architecture to the future."[23] One month later, on October 5, a public debate was held at the Federation of Malaya Society of Architects, entitled "What Is Malayan Architecture?" In addition to Posener, attendees included architects CHR Bailey, AA Geeraerts, Hisham Albakri, Kington Loo, F. Sullivan, TAL Concannon, and chairman of the debate Raymond Honey. The question was discussed in all its breadth and complexity, although here, too, it was mainly foreigners who spoke.[24] As part of the discussion, Posener suggested people should go and study recent architecture in Brazil, since the climate was similar to Malaya. Geeraerts spoke of a new Indo-Saracen architecture, which could closely match the culture and history of the country, while Kington Loo complained that although there was plenty of wood, architects knew too little about it. These aspects would dominate discussion of architectural forms and perspectives for a long time. More than two decades later, in 1983, the Aga Khan Foundation hosted a series of scholarly events in Kuala Lumpur, on the topic of "Architecture and Identity."[25]

Architectural criticism

Posener's first contract in Kuala Lumpur expired in 1959, but was extended for another two years. When it became clear that he was going to leave, he wrote to Klaus Müller-Rehm (1907–1999) in Berlin, another former Poelzig student, "I am reluctant to leave this school, despite the many difficulties I have had here, which at times made the whole undertaking seem futile. What I have always found gratifying here have been the students, and it is because of them that I am sad to leave."[26] Later, Posener recalled his own teacher and how he made use of his methodology in Southeast Asia: "Poelzig was still the model, and students knew that they were Poelzig's grandchildren."[27] However, Posener feared that his ideas "had been swept away by the tide of international architecture."[28] In May 1961, he left Kuala Lumpur after five years as head of the Department of Architecture at the Technical College, during which time he trained 85 students.

As shown above, Posener repeatedly intervened in contemporary architectural discourse, and his essays sparked quite a few debates. In England, he published two articles on architecture in Malaya. The second of these, from October 1961, was written just after Posener returned to Europe; the piece focuses more on architectural history and has a notably distant tone. In it, Posener mainly addresses local traditions—Malayan timber houses, Chinese shophouses, and colonial architecture.[29] In contrast, his first article was written while he was still in Malaya, and appeared in July 1960, in a special edition of *The Architectural Review*. Although published in London, that particular issue was devoted to contemporary architecture in former British colonies in Asia, and almost every piece was written by architects from Britain, who almost exclusively presented projects by other British architects. Posener's article on contemporary developments in Malaya is illustrated with around ten projects, but there is not one by a local architect. In the main text, he does not criticize the local architects by name, but instead offers a general assessment: "It may seem paradoxical but it is largely true that the local British architect cares more about a tropical architecture—and certainly no less about a

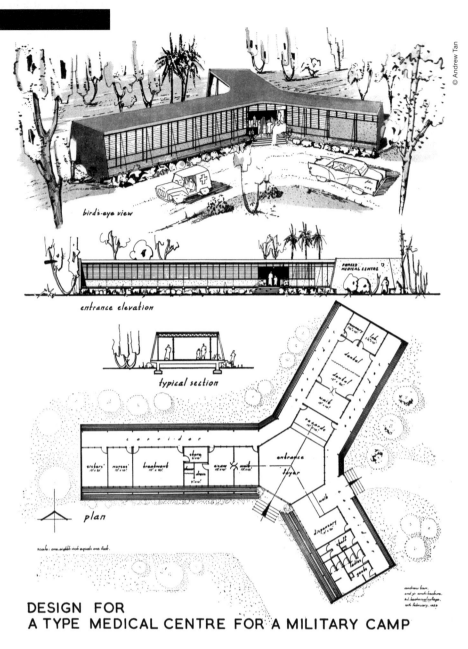

bird's-eye view

entrance elevation

typical section

plan

DESIGN FOR
A TYPE MEDICAL CENTRE FOR A MILITARY CAMP

Design for a military medical
pavilion by Andrew Tan,
a student at the Technical
College in 1958–59.

Malayan one—than his Asian colleague."[30] His overall judgement is quite negative: "Compared with the architecture of those tropical countries which have recently moved into the very focus of the new architecture, recent Malayan buildings can at best be called responsible and at worst frankly amusing."[31]

Posener's piece caught the attention of the young architect Lim Chong Keat, who responded in an article of his own for *Rumah* magazine, addressing the *Architectural Review*'s features on Singapore and Malaya. Lim had studied at Manchester University and at MIT with György Kepes; he also taught at Singapore Polytechnic, where he helped pass on the ideas of the Bauhaus. Entitled "The Malayan Architect on Trial,"[32] Lim's article briefly dismisses a contribution on Singapore by Lincoln Page, before going into more detail on Posener's text, which he obviously took seriously: "Julius Posener, writing on Malaya, is a rather more skillfully barbed reviewer; his barbs are sometimes concealed by a quaint ability to be amused."[33] Lim's essay reminds European readers of what Posener had not told them about, namely that under colonial rule, Malayan and Chinese architects were never entrusted with public buildings, and thus never in a position to prove themselves. Referring to Posener's claim that British architects worked more closely with local traditions than their Asian colleagues, Lim counters with a sarcastic swipe at the colonial education system: "This wonderful and almost professional amateurism is something to cause both admiration and shame to all Malayan nationals. Indeed one would wonder why, together with our guided education, it has not succeeded in kindling enthusiastic emulation or interest."[34] But Lim then addresses his local architects in equally sarcastic tone, since there was, apparently, no architectural criticism in existence in Malaya: "We should be indignant; here is a critic who dares to be critical, a critic who dares to criticize, a foreign critic. ... We should react: we should write strong protests to the *Architectural Review*. ... How would we react, if he were only a local critic?"[35]

Lim did not regard Posener's criticism as an affront. Rather, he saw it as a challenge for Malayan architects and critics. He addresses his colleagues with a long list of questions, aimed at prompting reflection on and support for strong independent traditions of construction and architecture, something foreign architects could not easily emulate. He concludes with an appeal to the "architects of Malaya," that if they continually ask themselves such questions on their work, "to spur themselves onward, then they can indeed afford to banish the *Architectural Review,* with or without Pages and Poseners, to dusty shelves until the subscription expires."[36]

Lim's essay called on local architects to redouble their efforts, so they could stand up better to external critics. Together with colleagues of his own generation, Lim later proved that a local yet universal architecture is possible, completely dispensing with national, ethnic, or historical forms of expression. His work is today seen as exemplary of its time (see Shirley Surya's article in this issue).

From today's perspective, Posener's essays and reviews retain colonial undertones. However, his argument also clearly posits traditional forms of construction as models from which, he feels, contemporary architecture can emerge, adapting gradually, going step-by-step. Posener's voice was a very unusual one in the Asian context. He had a resolute point of view, advocating for a design that would be adapted to local conditions: of its time, but without mimicry. This was extraordinary in a place where open criticism was often accompanied by loss of face. Posener used critical questions as the basis of his teaching, challenging students with historical references and vernacular designs, as well as with elements of the Western avant-garde. His questions went beyond the university, opening onto broader social inquiry. After all, what use is the best architecture if it is not understood? Posener wanted to create space for adaptations from tradition, and urged future architects to develop forms adapted to local needs. Last but not least, his design criticism was also an argument in favor of independent Malayan education.

Posener received Lim Chong Keat's reply to his *Architectural Review* article before he left the country, and he defended his position in an open letter. Without specifically referring to Lim's article, in April 1961, in the next issue of *Rumah,* he wrote, "So I did look at the buildings. I know that some of you have been very angry with me for looking at them so critically, but the point was that I looked for an answer to the question 'Is Melbourne good enough?' I mean, is any training overseas good enough? The proof of the pudding is in the eating. And at the risk of putting my foot into it again, I can only repeat that I found the pudding spiced with plenty of second grade rum, plenty of fruit from the bottom of the tin, and rather thin in pastry, thin in substance, in fact. This, of course, applies to the average. It would be the height of presumption to talk in these terms of the excellent buildings which do exist. Still, there remained a great deal of work to do, HERE."[37]

01 For an overview of Posener's biography, see Julius Posener, *Fast so alt wie das Jahrhundert* (Basel: Birkhäuser, 1993); Julius Posener, *Heimliche Erinnerungen – In Deutschland 1904 bis 1933* (Munich: Siedler 2004). A useful overview can be found in Sylvia Claus and Matthias Schirren, eds., *"Zeittafel," Julius Posener – ein Leben in Briefen: Ausgewählte Korrespondenz 1929–90* (Basel: Birkhäuser, 1999), 265–69.
02 Julius Posener, Letter to Le Corbusier, June 28, 1956, in Claus and Schirren, eds., *Julius Posener – ein Leben in Briefen,* 185.
03 Julius Posener, "Kuala Lumpur," manuscript, Akademie der Künste (AdK), Posener Estate, handwritten copy, pos-01-1792, 489.
04 "Funds Cut – So Housing Trust Heads Have to Leave," *The Straits Times* (August 6, 1958): 7.
05 Posener, "Kuala Lumpur," manuscript (see note 3), 491.
06 There was of course discussion in Britain about building in the tropics, with which Posener was at least partially familiar, including a book by Jane Drew and Maxwell Fry, *Tropical Architecture in the Humid Zone* (London: B. T. Batsford, 1956); and magazine and journal articles, such as George A. Atkinson, "Building in the Tropics," *Royal Institute of British Architects Journal* 57 (1950): 313–19; George A. Atkinson, "British Architects in

the Tropics," *Architectural Association Journal* 69 (1953): 7–21; and Otto Koenigsberger, "The Role of the British Architect in the Tropics," *Architectural Design* 24 (1954): 1–4.
07 Koenigsberger was also a student of Hans Poelzig at the Technische Hochschule Charlottenburg in Berlin, but was later forced to emigrate to India via Egypt, because of his Jewish origins. In 1953 he and others organized a groundbreaking conference on tropical buildings in London. In 1957 he was appointed director of the Department of Development and Tropical Studies at the Architectural Association. See Arthur M. Foyle, ed., *Conference on Tropical Architecture 1953: A Report on the Proceedings of the Conference Held at University College* (London: UC London, 1954).
08 CW Voltz, letter to Walter Gropius, February 6, 1958; Bauhaus Archive Berlin, BHA_GS19_Mp715_02_006r.
09 Walter Gropius, letter to CW Voltz, February 21, 1958, Bauhaus Archive Berlin, BHA_GS19_Mp715_02_007r. The book mentioned was probably a paperback by Gropius, *Architektur – Wege zu einer optischen Kultur* (Frankfurt am Main: Fischer, 1956).
10 CW Voltz, letter from October 5, 1958, in Beate Voltz, *Briefe aus Malaya, November 1957–April 1960* (Munich: Metropolitan, 2011), 218.
11 Ibid., 218.

12 Julius Posener, "Erziehung des Architekten," *Bauen + Wohnen* 2 (1966): 4–12; 10.
13 CW Voltz, letter from January 3, 1958, in Voltz, *Briefe aus Malaya* (see note 10), 60.
14 "Ideal Home in Malayan Wood: Three Houses Built to Prove a Point—Timber is Cheaper, Safe and Lasting," *The Straits Times* (January 14, 1961). Newspaper clipping, Akademie der Künste (AdK), Posener Estate, pos-01-1908.
15 See PWE Campbell, "Timber For Building," *The Straits Times* (January 6, 1956): 13; R.N. Hilto, "The Basic Malay House," *Journal of the Malayan Branch of the Royal Asiatic Society* 3 (1956): 134–55; Peter G. Morley, "Malay Timber Buildings: Towards a Malayan Architecture," *PETA: Journal of the Federation of Malaya Society of Architects* 2 (1955): 2–16; R.A. Hewish, "The Influence of the West: Towards a Malayan Architecture," *PETA: Journal of the Federation of Malaya Society of Architects* 4 (1956): 2–14; Raymond Honey, "An Architecture for Malaya," *PETA: Journal of the Federation of Malaya Society of Architects* 2, (1960): 1–3.
16 *PETA: Journal of the Federation of Malaya Society of Architects* began publication in 1955.
17 The "indigenous people" referred to here are indigenous groups collectively referred to under the name

Orang Asli; Posener visited their villages in the Cameron Highlands.
18 Julius Posener, letter to Le Corbusier, December 27, 1958, in Claus and Schirren, eds., *Julius Posener – ein Leben in Briefen* (see note 1), 186.
19 Posener, "Kuala Lumpur" manuscript (see note 3), 497.
20 Ibid., 499.
21 "Modern Houses Copied from US Magazines," *The Straits Times* (November 28, 1958): 16.
22 See Julius Posener, "Architecture Under Crossfire," *PETA: Journal of the Federation of Malaya Society of Architects* 2 (1960): 4f.
23 Julius Posener, "Architecture: The long search ...", *The Straits Times* (September 3, 1960): 8.
24 See especially "What is Malayan Architecture?" *PETA: The Journal of the Federation of Malaya Society of Architects* 4 (1961): 2–8.
25 See Robert Powell, ed., *Architecture and Identity: Exploring Architecture in Islamic Cultures* 1 (Singapore: Concept Media, 1983).
26 Julius Posener, letter to Klaus Müller-Rehm, December 20, 1960, in Claus and Schirren, eds., *Julius Posener – ein Leben in Briefen* (see note 1), 190f.
27 Posener, "Kuala Lumpur" manuscript (see note 3), 186.
28 Ibid., 184.
29 Julius Posener, "House Tradition in Malaya," *The Architectural Review* 130 (October 1961): 280–83.

30 Julius Posener, "Malaya," *The Architectural Review* 128 (July 1960): 59–65; 60.
31 Ibid., 60.
32 Lim Chong Keat, "The Malayan Architect on Trial," *Rumah: Journal of the Society of Malayan Architects III* (1960): 34–36.
33 Ibid., 35.
34 Ibid., 35.
35 Ibid., 36.
36 Ibid., 36.
37 Julius Posener, "A Letter from Julius Posener: Views on Architectural Education," *Rumah: Journal Singapore Institute of Architects IV* (1961): 13–16.

DEVELOPMENT AID AND SOCIALIST SOLIDARITY
West German and East German engagement in Southeast Asia

Text: Eduard Kögel

Many states that gained political independence from the late 1940s on nonetheless remained culturally and economically dependent on their former colonial powers. Much of the time, industries and educational systems were lopsidedly oriented towards the colonial power, making independent economic activity barely possible. This was also the case for many countries in Southeast Asia. The countries covered in this issue achieved independence between 1948 (Burma, today Myanmar) and 1965 (Singapore). The French colony of Indochina was dissolved by 1954, releasing both Laos (1949) and Cambodia (1953) into complete independence. Meanwhile, the Vietnamese struggle for independence gradually developed into a violent war, in which the Soviet Union supported the north of the country and the United States the south. Part of British-ruled areas in what is now Malaysia achieved independence as the Federation of Malaya in 1957, then in 1963 merged with the crown colonies of North Borneo, Sarawak, and Singapore to form the new Federation of Malaysia. However, Singapore was excluded from the federation in 1965 and went on to establish itself as an independent city-state. Indonesia gained independence from the Netherlands in 1949. Alongside Yugoslavia, Egypt, and India, the country played an important role in the Non-Aligned Movement during the Cold War. In 1955, for example, Indonesia organized and hosted the Bandung Conference, where newly independent non-aligned countries in Africa and Asia sought to establish their own political, economic, and cultural position between the two superpowers. Nevertheless, structures that had been established by the former colonial powers often persisted, while new actors among the Western industrialized nations and from the Eastern Bloc tried to gain access through frameworks like the Colombo Plan and the Commonwealth, providing aid either in the name of development or of socialist solidarity; both of which came loaded with economic and ideological self-interest. This was also true of West Germany (FRG) and East Germany (GDR), which were both active in the countries of Southeast Asia, albeit with different premises.

The two German states were constantly competing, their relations marked by ongoing efforts to set themselves apart from one another. Against this backdrop of East-West confrontation, the FRG adopted the Hallstein Doctrine in 1955, which sought to prevent third countries from granting diplomatic recognition to the GDR by imposing West German sanctions on those that did so.[01] Until 1969, the government in Bonn used this foreign policy doctrine primarily to exert influence over newly independent states in Africa and Asia. The political division of the world, and respective affiliation to opposing blocs, defined the context for the two German states' engagement in Southeast Asia. Buzzwords like *exports*, *development aid*, *military aid*, *socialist solidarity*, and *humanitarian assistance* could fit with a range of political positions, from economic self-interest to ideological window-dressing.

Projects undertaken in Myanmar, Singapore, Indonesia, Cambodia, Vietnam, and other countries included in this overview were designed in roughly equal parts by East and West German architects. They show the engagement of the two German states with the region, even if ultimately only a small number of architecturally relevant projects were built on either side.

Myanmar

As early as the 1950s, Burmese politicians ignored the Hallstein Doctrine, cooperating with both German states, and not only in civilian affairs. In 1955, the first Burmese trade delegation visited the Leipzig Trade Fair, where they agreed to make barter deals: GDR engineers would build a cement factory in Thayetmyo on the Irrawaddy River, 400 kilometers north of the capital Rangoon, in exchange for the delivery of 50,000 tons of rice. By 1962, the factory had been completed by the East German cement manufacturing works VEB Zementanlagenbau Dessau, capable of providing enough concrete for the entire national demand. The GDR also supplied extraction and refining plants for rice bran oil to Rangoon, Pegu, and Moulmein. In the early 1960s, the Dresden Hygiene Museum equipped a similar museum in the Burmese capital. However, the relationship between Burma and both Germanies was always complex. When the Thayetmyo cement factory was due for servicing in 1984, the FRG provided the necessary loan for Burma to do so.

In 1965, the GDR sold weapons to the Burmese military junta, even though the West German company Fritz Werner had already been operating with a Burmese subsidiary since 1953. The company was de facto nationalized in the mid-1960s, and thereafter was 90 percent owned by the West German state. It was active in a large number of civil and military projects in Burma until 1988, lending support to the dictatorship of General Ne Win, both directly and indirectly, including through military aid and weapons production facilities. This support for the Burmese government, which also included architectural activities, has never been dealt with historically. Following the most recent military coup in Myanmar, in February 2021, attention was refocused on Germany's highly problematic arms export practices, which did not sit well with the country's widely perceived responsibility toward the democratically elected government.

Cambodia

During the 1960s, the FRG promised the Cambodian government to donate an auditorium to Phnom Penh university. But since the planning contract was unexpectedly awarded to a French studio, a decision was made to redirect the funding, with Georg Lippsmeier commissioned to design a train station for Sihanoukville. With its striking roof and a bright entrance hall, Lippsmeier's design combined aesthetic and functional excellence with climate-friendly construction. In 1969, the architect summarized his building experiences in Asia and Africa in a groundbreaking book, *Tropenbau. Building in the Tropics*. A project for a new slaughterhouse in Phnom Penh, whose plans were drawn up with German help, was canceled by the FRG after Cambodia recognized the GDR as a state in 1969.

Vietnam

In the name of socialist solidarity and "fraternal aid," the GDR backed North Vietnam during the Vietnam War and later also supported the united Socialist Republic of Vietnam with infrastructure and industrial projects. This commitment, among other things, included a concrete slab factory in Dao Tu (1977), producing materials for residential construction; a glass factory in Haiphong (1959–63); and the largest and most important project, the Quang Trung residential area (1974–80) in Vinh, a city that had been completely destroyed by the US Air Force.

West Germany had been on the South Vietnamese side during the war, providing humanitarian aid for the duration of the conflict. The country sent the hospital ship *Helgoland*, used to treat civilian victims at the port of Da Nang between 1967 and 1971. Georg Lippsmeier was also active in Vietnam. To replace the hospital ship, he designed a single-story hospital building on behalf of the German Red Cross and the Malteser Hilfsdienst. A youth residential facility near Saigon (now Ho Chi Minh City) was to offer 450 war-disabled youths a new home. The psychologist Walter Molt developed an innovative therapeutic concept, while architects Klaus Jessel and Alois Gerlach planned the buildings. However, liberal West German ideas aimed at reintegrating young people into society did not go well with the rigid ideas put forward by the South Vietnamese authorities, who soon turned the facility into a prison. The Federal Republic withdrew from the project, while the East German press denounced the "concentration camp–like facilities," calling West German financial support for the youth center a "war subsidy."

A completely different project, partly financed by donations, partly by the West German government, was also launched near Saigon in 1967. Prefabricated wooden buildings by the Austrian architect Willi F. Ramersdorfer were manufactured in the Austrian province of Vorarlberg for the charity SOS Children's Villages (SOS-Kinderdorf), then shipped to Vietnam from Bremerhaven and assembled on site. Hermann Gmeiner, the inventor of children's villages, came up with the slogan: "A ship to Saigon, with a village on board." The weekly newspaper *Die Zeit* reported that the 41 prefabricated buildings would be home to around 600 children, headlined "The Sensation of Goodness." But the children's village only lasted until the end of the war, finally closing in 1976.

Singapore

In the 1970s, West German companies began to relocate production to Southeast Asia for economic reasons. In 1970, for example, Rollei, the Braunschweig-based camera manufacturer, moved its production of 35mm cameras and other photographic equipment to Singapore, where costs were low and the political situation was considered stable. Professor Walter Henn, then a lecturer in architecture at the Technical University of Braunschweig, received the commission to design the new plant. Henn used Lippsmeier's book *Tropenbau. Building in the Tropics* to familiarize himself with rational construction for this climate; his design, featuring long cantilevered galleries attached to the façade, followed suggestions made in Lippsmeier's book.

Indonesia

Economic interests also underlay East Germany's decision to export a sugar factory to Yogyakarta in Indonesia. The facility was opened by President Sukarno in June 1958, an event which, according to the official East German newspaper *Neues Deutschland*, attracted half a million spectators. The newspaper however did not report what the crowd saw, which was the system failing to work as planned. The state planning commission interpreted the failure politically, since the plant, built for an "anti-imperialist state," had great propaganda value as an example of GDR export performance. The political plan provided for "penetrating capitalist markets" with exports. However, in practice, the failed factory caused "material damage" and a "considerable loss of prestige" to East German industry. Production finally began in the spring of 1959. The difficulties were not discussed in the East German press. Secret reports from the CIA suggested that, after protests from the client, the GDR was prepared to pay between half a million and one million dollars to compensate for loss of production.

These East and West German projects in Southeast Asia, briefly presented here and on the accompanying map, are only the tip of the iceberg. There has as yet been no systematic recording or archiving of German activities in the region during the Cold War. Failed projects and difficulties with planning and implementation were also largely hidden from the German public. German ideas, both from East and West, were not always compatible with local ways of living. Moreover, these projects sometimes competed directly with companies from former colonial powers, who continued to have advantageous business networks in the region. The architectural legacy of German-German involvement in Southeast Asia needs further research; this will offer a retrospective understanding of the political, social, and cultural self-image of German participants, as well as colonial and postcolonial attitudes. These attitudes highlight some of the more problematic ideas underlying concepts of socialist solidarity, and of development aid in support of progress and civilization.

I learned of many of the East German projects through Andreas Butter, who, along with Christoph Bernhardt and Monika Motylinska, has researched GDR architectural exports at the Leibniz Institute for Research on Society and Space in Erkner. The list of West German projects in Myanmar is mainly based on the study by Hans-Bernd Zöllner,

Unverstandene Partnerschaft in der "Einen Welt" – Eine Studie zu den deutsch-birmanischen Beziehungen am Beispiel der Firma Fritz Werner in Birma (Hamburg: EMW, 1993).

01 The doctrine was named after Walter Hallstein, a prominent state secretary in the West German Foreign Office in the 1950s.

WEST GERMAN BUILDINGS AND PROJECTS

* Realization unknown
** Not realized

Abbreviations:
GTZ = German Technical Cooperation Agency.
UIA = International Union of Architects.

SINGAPORE
Rollei photographic equipment factory, Walter Henn, 1971–73.

LAOS
Vientiane
Lao-German Vocational Secondary School, Georg Lippsmeier, 1964.

MALAYSIA (MALAYA)
Cameron Highlands
Water power station, Hochtief-Holzmann, 1958–62.

THAILAND
Bangkok
Thai-German Technical School, 1960.
German Pavilion, Georg Lippsmeier, 1966.

VIETNAM
Ho Chi Minh City (Saigon)
Bus garage, 1965.**
Go Vap social center, 1965–68.
Bay Hien social center, 1965–68.
Khanh Hoi social center, 1965–68.
Bien Hoa social center, 1965–68.
Binh Duong social center, 1965–68.
Tan Hao refugee village, 1966–68.
Nam Hai refugee village, 1966–68.
Hans Böckler kindergarten, 1967.
Nam Hai social center, 1967.
Binh Thuan social center, 1967.
Training center for social professions, 1967–68.
Tan Hao model social center, 1967–70.
Thu Duc youth rehabilitation center, Klaus Jessel, Alois Gerlach, 1967–70.
Go Vap SOS Children's Village, Willi F. Ramersdorfer, 1967–69.
Vocational school, until 1973.
Training center for cement panel production, 1973.

Slaughterhouse, 1973.
An Hoa Nong San industrial complex, near Ho Chi Minh City, 1973.

Da Lat
Da Lat SOS Children's Village, 1969.

Da Nang
Hospital, Georg Lippsmeier, 1967–72.

Hue
University hospital and medical school, Georg Lippsmeier.*
Social center, 1965–68.
Home economics and handicraft school, 1966.

Quy Nhon
Social center + five apartment buildings, 1966.

Haiphong
Children's hospital, 1970–79.

Vinh Linh
Pavilion hospital, 1967.

My Tho
Social center, 1965–68.

Quang Ngai
Social center, 1965–68.

Location unclear
Mobile field hospital, 1967.

CAMBODIA
Sihanoukville
Sihanoukville train station, Georg Lippsmeier, 1966–68.

Battambang
Trade school, 1960s.

Phnom Penh
Slaughterhouse, Lu Ban Hap, City of Hamburg, 1960s.**

Province Kampong Speu
Prek Thnot Dam project, 1960s.**

MYANMAR (BURMA)
Sinde
Electric motor and pump factory, Fritz Werner Co., 1965.
Industrial Training Center, technical cooperation, 1969.
Pump and machine factory, technical cooperation, 1969.
Industrial Training Center, technical cooperation (GTZ), 1987.

Pyay (Prome) near Sinde
Weapons factory, technical cooperation.

Yangon (Rangoon)
Central laboratory, Fritz Werner Co., 1956.
Quay, technical cooperation, 1958.
Rice mill, technical cooperation, 1959.
Bicycle factory and extension, Fritz Werner Co., 1960–77.
Razor blade factory, Fritz Werner Co., 1963.
Cutlery factory, Fritz Werner Co., 1963.
Navigation channel expansion, Rangoon port, technical cooperation, 1968.
Household glass production, Fritz Werner Co., 1980.
Printing plant for school books and training materials, technical cooperation (GTZ), 1983.
Weapons factory, Fritz Werner Co.
Danyingone Brickworks, consulting by Fritz Werner Co.

Thanlyin (Syriam)
Thermos flask production, Fritz Werner Co., 1981.
Industrial Training Center, technical cooperation (GTZ), 1983.
Glass bottle factory, technical cooperation.

Nyaung Chi Dauk
Brass rolling mill with wire drawing mill, Fritz Werner Co., technical cooperation, 1969.
Machine tool factory, Fritz Werner Co., 1976.
PVC copper cable factory, Fritz Werner Co., 1980.
Glass bottle production (oxygen/nitrogen), Fritz Werner Co., 1981.

Hmawbi
Ballpoint pen factory, Fritz Werner Co., 1981.
Brickworks, consulting by Fritz Werner Co.; technical cooperation.

Heinda, Dawei District
Tin mine, consulting by Fritz Werner Co.

Zeyawaddi
Alcohol factory, Fritz Werner Co., 1962.

Paleik near Mandalay
Textile factory, technical cooperation, consulting by Fritz Werner Co., 1973.

Malun
Injection pump factory, technical cooperation, Fritz Werner Co., 1983.

Thaton
Tire factory, Fritz Werner Co., 1984.

Pathein (Bassein)
Bottle factory, technical cooperation.

Htonbo
Civil explosives plant, technical cooperation, Fritz Werner Co., 1987.

Location unclear
Munitions plant with the War Office, Fritz Werner Co., 1956.
Cement plant, Kayah state, technical cooperation, 1960.
Trade school, Shan State, technical cooperation, 1962.
Fertilizer plant, technical cooperation, 1968
Meteorological observatories, technical cooperation, 1968.
Fertilizer plant, Kyun Chaung, technical cooperation, consulting by Fritz Werner Co., 1973.
Training workshop for Burmese railway, technical cooperation (GTZ), 1976.
Corrugated board production, Fritz Werner Co., 1981 or 1982.
Experimental and training sawmill, technical cooperation Powder plant, Fritz Werner Co.

EAST GERMAN BUILDINGS AND PROJECTS

* Realization unknown
** Not realized

INDONESIA
Yogyakarta
Madukismo sugar factory, Padokan near Yogyakarta, VEB Ipro Berlin, VEB Ipro Magdeburg, VEB Mafa Sangerhausen, VVB Chemie- und Klimaanlagen, VEB Thälmannwerk, Magdeburg, 1956–59.

Location unclear
Rice mill, 1968–69.

MYANMAR (BURMA)
Yangon (Rangoon)
Export sample show, Roland Korn, 1957.
Rice bran oil extraction plant, 1963.
Hygiene Museum, furnishings, 1966.
Sugar factory, IPRO Rostock.

Thayetmyo
Cement plant, VEB Zementanlagenbau Dessau, 1960–63.

Pegu
Rice bran oil extraction plant, 1963.

Moulmein
Rice bran oil extraction plant, 1963.

CAMBODIA
Phnom Penh
Trade fair hall for foreign trade.

PHILIPPINES
Manila
Printing and binding plant, 1980.*
UIA competition, housing, 1983.*

VIETNAM
Hanoi
Tien Bo printing plant, 1956–58.
Co Loa film studio, near Hanoi, 1959.
Hospital for tropical diseases, 1968–71.
Cultural center, 1970.**
Telecommunications building, 1971–75.
Institute for forensic technology and medicine, 1968–78.
Nam Dang housing estate, UIA competition, students: Folke Dietzsch, Jürgen Arnold, Ingo Gräfenhahn, HAB Weimar, 1984.**

Ba Vi orthopedic clinic, before 1990.
Textile factory, before 1990.
Hospital and polyclinic for Ministry of State Security.

Dao Tu
Concrete slab factory, IPRO Dessau, 1979.

Thai Nguyen
Gia Sang steel bar and wire rod mill, VEB Schwermaschinen-kombinat Ernst Thälmann Magdeburg, 1971–75.

Haiphong
Glassworks, VEB Ipro Dresden I (Brigade 5), 1959–63.

Buon Me Thuot
Coffee processing plant, 1980s.
Rubber processing plant, 1990.
Dray Linh hydroelectric power station, before 1990.

Vinh
Quang Trung housing estate, Karlheinz Schlesier, Hans-Ulrich Mönnig, Madeleine Grotewohl, et al., 1973–1980.
Spinning mill from 1976 (1974–80).
Sewing factory
Thong Nhat joinery, modernization.
Oxygen plant.
Cau Duoc cement plant, modernization.
Brickyard 22.12, modernization.
Hung stoneware pipe factory, modernization.
Concrete plant.
Song Lam sand and gravel extraction plant.
Repair workshop.
Cua Tien building materials warehouse.
Quy Hop marble quarry.
Hung Dong lime kiln
Waterworks, modernization.
Provincial administration building, renovation.
Quang Trung transformer station.
Guest House 2, extension.
Vinh Tan wastewater treatment plant.
Viet-Duc Pioneer House.
Quang Trung trade center.
Market hall.
Tent pavilion.
Cinema 1.9., modernization.
Vinh train station, renovation.

Cement factory, Thayetmyo,
1960–63.
© Landesarchiv Sachsen-Anhalt

Student design for Nam
Dang residential
quarter, Hanoi 1984.
From: *Tropenbaubriefe* 1/1985
(HAB Weimar) Designers: Jürgen
Arnold, Folke Dietzsch, Ingo Gräfenhahn
Ingo Gräfenhahn

Quang Trung housing estate,
Vinh 1973–80.
© Bestand Karl-Heinz Schlesier

Madukismo sugar factory, Padokan,
near Yogyakarta, 1956–59.
From: *Handbuch der Deutschen
Demokratischen Republik*, Berlin 1964

Concrete slab factory,
Dao Tu, 1979.
© Bestand Karl-Heinz Schlesier

Georg Lippsmeier:
Da Nang hospital, 1967–72.
From: *Deutsche Bauzeitung* 7, 1972

Georg Lippsmeier: Sihanoukville train station, 1966–68.
From: *Baumeister* 10, 1969

Klaus Jessel and Alois Gerlach:
Thu Duc youths rehabilitation
center, Ho Chi Minh City 1967–70.
From: *Baumeister* 10, 1969

Willy F. Ramersdorfer: Go Vap
SOS Children's Village,
Ho Chi Minh City 1967–69
© vorarlberg museum, Elmar Bertsch

Walter Henn: Rollei photo-
graphic equipment factory,
Singapore, 1971–73.
From: *Baumeister* 12, 1971

BODIA កម្ពុជា CAMBODIA

CAMBODIA កម្ពុជា CAM

DIA កម្ពុជា CAMBODIA

កម្ពុជា CAMBODIA កម្ពុជា

CAMBODIA កម្ពុជា CAMB

CAMBODIA កម្ពុជា CA

IBODIA កម្ពុជា CAMBO

កម្ពុជា CAMBODIA ក

កម្ពុជា CAMBODIA កម្ពុជា

BODIA កម្ពុជា CAMBODIA

AMBODIA កម្ពុជា CAMB

Cambodia was placed under French colonial rule in 1863, later becoming part of French Indochina along with what is now Vietnam and Laos. In 1953, the country gained independence from France and was heavily modernized under the leadership of head of state Prince Norodom Sihanouk and the Sangkum Reastr Niyum ("People's Socialist Community"), his party-like organization.

The architectural style of New Cambodia, hailed as "New Khmer Architecture," was a merging of Western modernism with Khmer traditions. In addition, developments in music, dance, literature, and film renewed Cambodian cultural self-understanding and created the myth of a coming Golden Age, which would be connected to the splendor of the historical kingdom of Angkor. Architecture as a discipline did not become established in Cambodia until 1967. In the first few years after independence, architects and planners from abroad—mainly from France—were active in Cambodia, sometimes bringing financial support from their countries of origin. Only gradually did Cambodian architects who had trained abroad return home, sometimes taking on important positions in ministries and in public administration.

The phase of renewal that was implemented under the slogan "Buddhist Socialism" ended in 1970 with the removal of head of state Prince Sihanouk. Cambodia proceeded to sink into chaos. The Vietnam War raged on its borders and within the country itself, while the emerging civil war drove the rural population into the arms of the Khmer Rouge, which invaded the capital Phnom Penh in 1975, taking power on April 17 of that year. The brutal violence of the Khmer Rouge movement was directed in particular against ideas of modernity, progress, and urbanity. Within a few days, the majority of the urban population was deported to the countryside and forced to do rural labor. Between 1.7 and 2.2 million Cambodians died of starvation or were deliberately murdered by the Khmer Rouge.

In 1979, Vietnamese troops ended the Khmer Rouge regime, remaining in the country for ten years. In 1991, a peace agreement was signed under the supervision of the UN, followed by the rebuilding of state structures. This interim period ended in 1993 with the establishment of a new constitution and the restoration of the monarchy. Today, Cambodia is one of the fastest growing economies in the world. This has been accompanied by the rapid capitalization of nature, public space, and common goods. SB/MH/CH/EK

Between 1950 and 1970, Cambodia's leading architect, Vann Molyvann, designed a variety of government buildings, educational institutions, and industrial and residential complexes across the country for the Sihanouk regime— including the National Sports Complex and the Institute of Foreign Languages, pictured here. Vann Molyvann himself repeatedly cited the historic temple complex of Angkor Wat as a source of great inspiration for his work (see Michael Falser's article in this issue). The historical model and the modernist sports complex indeed reveal structural similarities, which Giovanna Silva compellingly juxtaposes in her book *17 April 1975: A Cambodian Journey*, accompanied by a text by Peter Fröberg Idling.

JOURNEY THROUGH CAMBODIA
Photo essay: Giovanna Silva

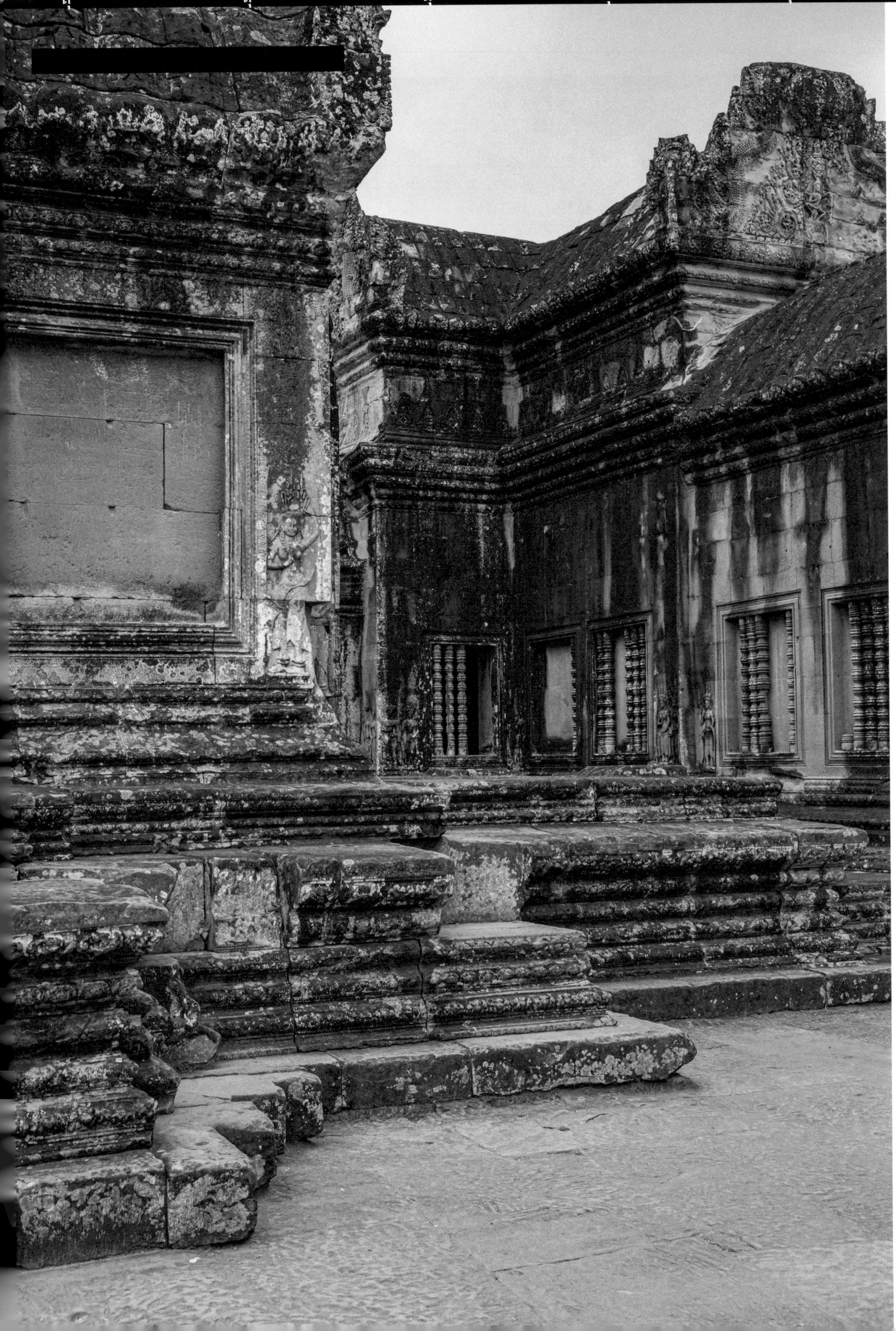

À L'ÉCOLE DES MAÎTRES ANGKORIENS?
Nouvelle Architecture Khmère, Vann Molyvann, and the postcolonial myth of Angkor (Wat)

© École française d'Extrême-Orient, Paris

Text: Michael Falser

Angkor Wat, photograph by
the French colonial air
force of Indochina, 1936.

"Upon my return to Cambodia in 1956, it was profoundly moving for me to rediscover our monuments of the past and see them in an entirely new light. The easiest decision might have been to content myself with the excellent [French] Beaux-Arts masters and to follow in their path. But this choice would not have aligned with the national course that my country had taken to affirm its Khmer identity. So it was entirely natural for me to eagerly learn from the teachings of the Angkorian masters [*que je me suis mis à l'école des maîtres angkoriens*]. ... Everyone knew that we had to return to the sources and profound motivations that had initially created this country. ... Of course that does not mean to simply reproduce the artistic creations of the Angkorian past, but to draw inspiration from them, and to translate and adapt them to the new realities. In doing so, being able to draw on the rules and construction methods of architectural modernism, especially from France, was invaluable. [It was about] a synthesis. ... Just as we Khmer had already appropriated the [Hindu] traditions of ancient India and brought them to a new zenith of our own in the 12th century, so now, with the regaining of national independence in 1953, it was a matter of a fresh attempt. We have borrowed much from the Occident, but we must khmerize [*khmériser*] this loan, so we do not fail again. We need to integrate it into our civilization in a very real way."

Vann Molyvann
in *À l'école des maîtres angkoriens*, 1969[01]

When Vann Molyvann (1926–2017) expressed these thoughts in a 1969 interview for the art journal *Nokor Khmer,* published in Phnom Penh in French, he was already a widely acclaimed architect and had even been made Minister of Education of Cambodia by his great patron, the king and head of state Norodom Sihanouk.[02] But his country, a young nation-state that had only been able to free itself from 90 years of French colonial rule in 1953, was already on the brink of the greatest catastrophe in its modern history. One year later, in 1970, a bloody civil war broke out in the newly proclaimed Khmer Republic. In 1975, the Maoist-nationalist Khmer Rouge guerrilla group established its autogenocidal regime of terror under Chinese patronage. From 1979 to 1989, the country was occupied by the Socialist Republic of Vietnam, this time with Soviet support. Cambodia finally regained independence in the early 1990s, under a UN protection mandate—coinciding with the end of the Cold War.

Which past for which future?
The cultural and political backdrop

Today, Vann Molyvann is rightly celebrated by architectural history as the main protagonist of Cambodian postcolonial modernism.[03] One problem with any closely biographical retelling about so-called star architects is that the larger overall context, in which the "individual genius" was able to develop their full creative power in the first place, is often underestimated. In this case, the context is particularly relevant, since Vann Molyvann's unusually extensive oeuvre was not only created in an extremely short period of time—barely 15 years between 1956 and 1970—but also in a country as small as Cambodia, which had just begun to liberate itself from its colonial legacy. For this reason, it seems important to begin with a very special cultural-political coincidence, whose parameters were decisive in the formation of one of the most important works of architectural modernism in Asia.

In Norodom Sihanouk, Vann Molyvann and his circle of colleagues could rely on a charismatic visionary and increasingly autocratic state leader as well as an unconditional promoter of building culture and proponent of identity politics—who, however, ultimately drove his country financially and politically into ruin and, after just 14 years of leadership, into the clutches of its internal and external enemies. With his megalomaniacal projects, Sihanouk, as the builder of a newly decolonized country, had a certain kinship with rulers of other countries in similar situations, such as Sukarno (Indonesia) or Gamal Abdel Nasser (Egypt). But in Sihanouk's case there was another aspect, which was particularly well suited for political instrumentalization: he himself was genealogically descended from the kings of the Khmer Empire, at the center of which the world-renowned temple site of Angkor Wat was built in the 12th century. This ancestry, which was systematically deciphered by colonial French epigraphists, particularly in the 1920s and 1930s, additionally endowed Sihanouk with a kind of authentic sense of mission. As critical historians have noted, he was able to "extol the virtues of the Angkorian age as a guide for modern actions [and elevate] the Angkorian ideal" to the new standards of modern life in Cambodia.[04] His proclaimed agenda of reviving Angkor's architectural tradition found an ideal mouthpiece in his person as a quasi-reincarnated "son of the builders of Angkor."[05] In postcolonial Cambodia, all this promoted the process of a kind of (re-)"invention of tradition," in which invoking an allegedly glorious past served to legitimize the vision of a glorious future.[06]

With the independence of Cambodia, which Sihanouk started to secure in 1941 and which was finally achieved in 1953, Asia's smallest newborn nation-state had to take on a cultural heritage of superlatives almost overnight: that of the approximately 200-square-kilometer Archaeological Park of Angkor, which was designated as such by the French colonial power in the 1920s,[07] and which boasts the largest stone religious building in the world, Angkor Wat. In this context, the physically and politically inherited "Angkor complex" was not to be understood solely in terms of its planning and architectural dimensions. It was also a psychological complex, which for Cambodia was associated with a sense of historical superiority and contemporary inferiority.[08] The emotionally highly charged topos or myth of Angkor was thus rhetorically invoked by Sihanouk as a yardstick for the national rebirth of cultural grandeur. At the same time, its stylistic qualities, the amount of buildings, and not least the gigantic scale of the legacies from the Angkor period also served Molyvann as a reference in envisioning and justifying his own new building projects. In detail it was almost irrelevant that the persistant politically and architecturally staged recourse to "Angkor" (with its core period from the 10th to 13th centuries) was applied to a temporally much broader spectrum of pre-, classical-, and even post-Angkorian architecture, reaching from the 7th to even the 19th centuries.[09]

It is only by considering these cultural and political dimensions in the following examination of architectural case studies that we can do justice to Vann Molyvann's buildings and their place in architectural history within the extended radius of "contested modernism" in the postcolonial architecture of Southeast Asia.

LE CAMBODGE
A L'EXPOSITION UNIVERSELLE DE BRUXELLES 1958

EXPOSITION COLONIALE INTERNATIONALE — PARIS 1931

21 TEMPLE D'ANGKOR-VAT

Blanche, Arch.

Courtesy Michael Falser

Left
Postcard from the 1931
International Colonial
Exhibition in Paris, depicting
a 1:1 reproduction of the
central structure of the
Angkor Wat temple complex.

Below
Postcard of Palais du
Cambodge at the Marseille
Colonial Exhibition, 1906.

Above
Pavillon du Cambodge at
the 1958 Brussels World's
Fair.
Cover of a brochure by the
Commissariat général du Cambodge:
*Le Cambodge à l'Exposition universelle
de Bruxelles 1958, Paris 1958.*

26. Marseille. – Exposition Coloniale 1906
Le Palais du Cambodge

© Archives municipale de Marseille

Episode 1:
Multiple strategies (1955–61)
Internationalist, archaeological, vernacular

Classical architectural and art history(-ies) neatly separate their objects of study according to periods and styles. Both are only possible to a very limited extent for the case studies chosen here. This is because the architects, due to the time pressure and variety of tasks they faced with their building projects for the nascent nation-state, by no means resorted to uniform procedures. Rather, they used multiple, parallel, or even overlapping strategies. In doing so, they looked to three main sources of reference, which gradually merged to form a characteristic style of Cambodian postcolonial modernism: a) the architectural language of international modernism, b) the archae-ologically based representation of Angkorian architecture, and c) traditional wooden Buddhist pagodas and vernacular homes.

The influence of the first source was evident in, among other things, the planning for the Exposition Internationale de Phnom Penh in 1955, for which various national themed and international country pavilions were arranged along a central axis with a view of the Buddhist structure Wat Phnom (lit. "hill pagoda"), which had been erected on an artificial hill. The formal, stylistic, and programmatic references to international modernism were likely no coincidence, as the chief architect Seng Suntheng had just returned from studying at the École Nationale Supérieure des Arts Décoratifs in Paris. Both in Europe and now also in Asia, the legendary Exposition internationale des Arts décoratifs et industriels modernes in Paris in 1925, to which Le Corbusier had contributed his famous Pavillon de l'Esprit nouveau, set the standard for world exhibitions in the 20th century.

© Michael Falser 2010

Above
Pre-Angkorian-style stupa for Princess Kantha Bopha at the Royal Palace of Phnom Penh, designed and built by Tan Veut, 1952.

Below
Small-scale replica of an early Angkorian temple tower, used here as a foun-tain at the new Chamkar Mon State Compound of Norodom Sihanouk (second from left), during a visit by a South Vietnamese delega-tion in 1969.

AUJOURD'HUI

HIER

Above
"Today" and "Yesterday"—juxtaposition of classical French colonial architecture (Phnom Penh post office headquarters, bottom) with the new architecture of the emerging International Style (National Bank of Cambodia, 1956, above), in the journal *Cambodge d'aujourd'hui* 6 (June 1958).

Below
Vann Molyvann's temporary timber pavilion for the 2,500th anniversary of Buddha (left); and the Royal School of Medicine by Leroy & Mondet. From: *Cambodge d'aujourd'hui* 6 (June 1958).

Regarding the second strategy, it is interesting to see that Cambodia's first international country pavilion after gaining independence—for the 1958 Brussels World's Fair—was intended as an archaeologically "faithful reproduction of Prasat Preah Damrei, a jewel of 10th-century Khmer art" and was built by French architects.[10] This project remained in the tradition of the French world and colonial exhibitions from 1878 to 1937, where, with ever more precise archaeological precision, Angkorian architecture served as a mere shell for representative pavilions of the French protectorate, Le Cambodge. The highpoint of this approach was the Palais du Cambodge at the colonial exhibition of 1906 in Marseille and the gigantic 1:1 reproduction of the main building at Angkor Wat for the Exposition coloniale internationale in Paris in 1931. These Western representations of Angkorian eras, one might speculate, were effective as reverse translations in Cambodia as well. This was the case, for example, when Tan Veut, an architect from Battambang, was commissioned by Sihanouk to design various tombs, called *stupas,* at the Royal Palace of Phnom Penh according to much older models. Tan based the stupa for Sihanouk's deceased daughter Kantha Bopha (1952) on the pre-Angkorian style of Banteay Srei from the 10th century, while the stupa for Sihanouk's father King Suramarit (1960) was designed in the style of the post-Angkorian capital of Udong (17th–19th century). Sihanouk not only used precolonial cultural references variably in terms of their pre-, classical- or post-Angkorian styles, but also adapted them in scale to the size of the architecture and urban spaces representing the new state. The presidential palace at the Chamkar Mon Compound, planned and executed by Vann Molyvann, for example, is furnished with myriad scaled-down decorative elements *à la Angkorienne*, a miniature landscape meant for the eyes of Sihanouk's many state guests.

Çi-dessous: L'Internat et la Faculté Royale de Médecine (Architectes Leroy-Mondet) de lignes sobres, un peu austères. A gauche, une construction en bois de style traditionnel construite pour les Fêtes du 2.500ème anniversaire de l'ère bouddhique.

Chaktomuk Conference
Hall by Vann Molyvann,
1961.

Aerial view of the Chaktomuk
Conference Hall, showing
its fan-shaped reinforced
concrete roof structure
with traditional *pyatthat* and
generously glazed facade
facing the river.

An article in the popular magazine *Cambodge d'aujourd'hui* features a polemical juxtaposition of the French colonial column-and-stucco style of Phnom Penh's central post office building with the emerging International Style, illustrated by the new National Bank of Cambodia building from 1956.[11] In contrast, Vann Molyvann—in the sense of a third strategy—installed one of the first buildings he designed after his return to Cambodia, a temporary wooden hall for the 2,500th anniversary of Buddha, in front of the rationalist architecture of the Royal School of Medicine of Phnom Penh by the French architectural firm Leroy & Mondet. A few years later, he interpreted historical vernacular monastic architecture in a much more mature way, with his Chaktomuk Conference Hall, which was inaugurated in November 1961 for the Sixth Conference of the World Fellowship of Buddhists and co-financed by the United States government. The conference hall held a prominent spot on the capital's newly developed waterfront, at the confluence of the Mekong and Bassac rivers. For this project, Molyvann reinterpreted the wooden pagoda style from the nearby Royal Palace, resulting in a fan-shaped hall, featuring a folding roof, external reinforced concrete framework, and a glass facade offering a view of the water. He crowned the structure with a traditional *pyatthat* tiered roof. This building was certainly one of Vann Molyvann's first great masterpieces, marking his emancipation from both the French-colonial dogma of an archaeologically true-to-style mimicry of Angkorian building tradition and the "universalist" formal language of the International Style.

39

Left
Vann Molyvann (left)
and Tan Veut at
the construction site,
probably ca. 1960.

Above
Aerial view of the
Independence
Monument,
Phnom Penh.

40

Episode 2:
The Independence Monument (1962)
An ambivalent hybrid

It was along this extended waterfront area that the most daring urban and social planning project of the old and new capital of Cambodia was developed in parallel over a period of eight years (1960–68): the Bassac river front. Covering an area of about 80 hectares, it included a host of new public facilities, such as a theater, a school, a museum, state government buildings, and large residential buildings. The complex was designed and implemented by an international planning team, including Vann Molyvann, Gérald Hanning and Robert Hansberger (both French), the Russian Vladimir Bodiansky, and Cambodian architect Lu Ban Hap. Perpendicular to the so-called White Building, an urban block in the style of global post-war modernism, the capital's central axis runs along Norodom Boulevard. At the central junction of Norodom and Sihanouk Boulevards rises the Independence Monument, which, together with its surrounding public areas and the large Naga [snake] Fountain, soon developed into a popular, photogenic meeting place for the population. Assessments of this unique building are still ambivalent today due to its stylistic hybridity. It was only inaugurated on November 9, 1962, nine years after political independence in 1953. The lengthy construction process was likely due to issues with the statics and structural design, as the subsoil was extremely unstable and required costly civil engineering work. Early blueprints from January 1957 identify Du Ngoc Anh from Saigon and Ing Kieth as road engineers appointed by the Cambodian government, while Vann Molyvann was named alongside Seng Suntheng and U Som Ol (the latter as architect of the Royal Palace) as co-initiators of the project. However, it was only in 2011—during my visit to Tan Veut's descendants in Battambang—that I was first able to find floor plans and elevation plans for the monument, which identify the designer of the stupas at the Royal Palace as the actual author of the monument.

Similar to the stylized replicas of Angkorian architecture erected as temporary pavilions at the world and colonial exhibitions in Marseille and Paris, the Independence Monument in Phnom Penh was based on a modern, internal supporting frame clad with a decorative stone surface.[12] While the architectural embellishments of the expo pavilions were made of light gypsum elements that were colored after application, the monument in Phnom Penh used prefabricated concrete panels made from red marble aggregate, which were modeled on "kbach [decorative patterns] from Banteay Srei Temple" north of Angkor from the 10th century.[13] Parallels have also been drawn between the monument and the crowning tower structure of Cambodia's first hilltop temple of Bakong, also from the 10th century, located southeast of Angkor. The irony of this attempt at a recourse to early Angkorian masterpieces for a postcolonial independence monument lies in the fact that both the Banteay Srei and Bakong temples—as well as all the other buildings and facilities at the Angkor Archaeological Park,

Left
Color photographs of the Independence Monument (left) and the Naga Fountain (right), ca. 1962.

institutionalized between 1925 and 1931—had their basic structures restored by French colonial archaeologists and architects in the 1930s. Only then did they attract the attention of the new Cambodian architectural elite. It is noteworthy that the Francophile state leader Norodom Sihanouk continued to maintain the École française d'Extrême-Orient, a scientific institution established in 1898 to explore all of French Indochina, throughout the entire period of Cambodian independence (1953–70), tasking it with the restoration and preservation of the temples of "his" ancestors.

But the connection to France was even more fundamental, especially for the Independence Monument, because Vann Molyvann based the entire composition in Phnom Penh on the one in Paris. As in Paris, the stepped structure with its square base is situated at the center of a roundabout with streets radiating from it.[14] In the following years, the "God King" head of state Norodom Sihanouk staged the annual national holiday with ever greater pomp against the backdrop of this symbolically charged structure. This occured for the last time in 1969, when Sihanouk—already seeming strangely absent in the presence of the Buddhist monks—lit the central flame to commemorate the heroes of independence. A few months later, he was deposed by his own military in a coup d'état.

Episode 3:
National Sports Complex
Imbued with the spirit of Angkor (Wat)?

If there was one project for postcolonial Cambodia that represented a kind of "Angkorian challenge"[15] in terms of ambition, logistics, and scope, it was the National Sports Complex. The complex was originally planned for the Southeast Asian Peninsular Games, which were eventually canceled, and was inaugurated on November 12, 1964, to mark the 11th anniversary of Cambodian independence. The entire ensemble was designed by Vann Molyvann, in accordance with Olympic standards, but was again implemented by a planning team of several people.[16]

In order to understand the architect's personal motivation and the project's cultural and political importance, there is perhaps no more relevant primary source than the 14-page article "La nouvelle architecture khmère: le complexe sportif national," in the premier issue of the journal *Nokor Khmer* in 1969, which was assembled around a interview with Vann Molyvann (excerpted at the beginning of this text).[17] The creative appropriation of Angkorian architecture, which Molyvann addressed in very general terms in the interview, was applied concretely by the architect to this project. For example, he described the National Sports Complex as his most important work, in which he took his cue from the great Angkorian ensembles:

> "I think the most characteristic project of the Cambodian architectural renaissance is indeed the National Sports Complex. It is inspired by the greatest traditional principles and is in no way inferior to the great Angkorian ensembles in its ambition and scale. Nevertheless, it was executed with the latest construction techniques. ... We have every reason to be highly optimistic about the future. Our head of state, Samdech Norodom Sihanouk, personally supports artistic creation. ... The kings of Angkor and their architects built for their people and for their country ... and today's Cambodian monarchy has no other ambition than to restore some of that past greatness to our land."[18]

41

Photographs comparing the purported first leveling of the marshy area of the National Sports Complex by Cambodian oxcarts with the impressive reinforced concrete elements of the complex, reproduced in the internationally renowned *Cahiers du Centre scientifique et technique du bâtiments* 73 (April 1965).

Neither before nor since has any publication drawn such an explicit, direct connection between the Angkorian built legacy and the New Khmer Architecture of the independent Cambodian nation-state. Vann Molyvann had photographs of the complex placed directly next to those of Angkorian buildings on the journal's eight double pages, and even compared a schematic topographic section with that of the absolute masterpiece of classical architecture in Cambodia, namely Angkor Wat itself. In doing so, he was also able to establish connections between architectural elements of the old and new structures and show that the latter's symbolic rhythm of negative and positive volumes (water basins vs. towering buildings) was directly derived from the Golden Age.

The National Sports Complex was also reviewed by professional journals in the former colonial power of France, first in *Cahiers du centre scientifique et technique du bâtiments* (April 1965). In that article, architects Vladimir Bodiansky and Gérald Hanning, members of the sports complex's planning group, had their say on no fewer than twelve pages. In addition to touting the advantages of climate-adapted, cost-effective, and above all rapid construction in just under two years, as well as the great cultural and political relevance of the project for the young Cambodian nation-state, Hanning expanded on Molyvann's myth-making nexus linking to the golden age of Angkor. He wrote of an "amphibian country" which, in a "world-building act [*acte de démiurge*], divided land and water from one another, and—in tireless earthworks by the Cambodian peasantry—had created the masterful monuments of Angkor."[19] In order to relate this myth to the current construction activities, photographs of the alleged first leveling of the marshy stadium area by Cambodian oxcarts were juxtaposed with the impressive, steeply rising, and widely projecting reinforced concrete elements of the sports facility.

That this understanding of modernity—between mythical prehistory, traditional past, and a high-tech present or future—was not only a suitable storyline for small, recently independent states and (as they were later called) "developing or newly industrialized countries," such as Cambodia, was proven by the special issue on "Sport and

Leisure" by the renowned French journal *Architecture d'aujourd'hui* in 1964. It featured a report by Vann and Bodiansky on their project, while another article illustrated the buildings for the 1964 Tokyo Olympics and similarly essentialized Kenzo Tange's "new constructions" of reinforced concrete as being derived directly from the "traditional Japanese architecture" of wooden pagoda construction.[20]

Of course, Sihanouk's PR machinery also picked up on this theme. Included in a 1964 publication by the Cambodian Ministry of Information, *Dans la grande tradition angkorienne: Le complexe sportif national,* issued for the inauguration of the sports complex, was an article titled "More Than an Inauguration: An Apotheosis!" which stated, "Cambodia has always had its sanctuaries. Now it has another pedestal that takes it even higher: between the creators of Angkor Wat and those who made the *Sangkum* [lit. Community of the Common People] of the 20th century, the same soul is reincarnated, the soul of the builders of empires."[21] In his opening speech, Sihanouk then placed Vann Molyvann himself in a line with the master builders of Angkor: "My countrymen ... in this very moment you are all making possible the definitive rebirth of our homeland in all the grandeur of the Angkorian epoch! ... The creator of this building complex is our minister and architect Vann Molyvann, who has proven to us that the blood of the builders of Angkor today is by no means tainted!"[22]

This direct connection, between Angkor Wat and Vann Molyvann's new megaproject as the high points of Cambodian culture, was not only staged through rhetoric and visual propaganda, but also performatively at both locations. In the winter of 1966, when the GANEFO Games[23] were held in Phnom Penh, the quasi-Olympic flame was lit—as Sihanouk's newspaper *Kambuja* recounted in a 16-page photo story—in the innermost sanctuary of Angkor Wat by an Apsara dancer.[24] The flame was then handed over to an athlete who escorted it along the temple's long entrance corridor through the Angkor Archaeological Park to the National Stadium in Phnom Penh, some 300 kilometers away, where thousands of spectators were gathered to show their appreciation for Cambodia's main temple on signs held aloft at the opening, in French.

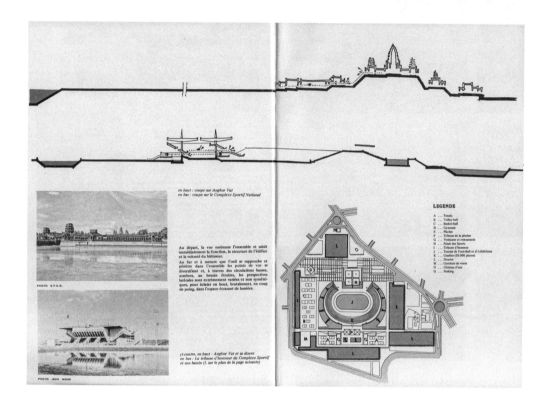

Above
Torch relay for the Games of the New Emerging Forces (GANEFO), from Angkor Wat to Phnom Penh. The athletes run along the central axis of the temple complex, accompanied by a Cambodian military honor guard.

Left
Juxtaposition of Angkor Wat and Vann Molyvann's National Stadium, in the Cambodian cultural journal *Nokor Khmer* 1 (1969).

A movie ending?

But Norodom Sihanouk, as a self-dramatizing god-king and "enlightened dictator,"[25] was even more than a perfect initiator of the neo-Angkorian Renaissance, which he realized in the medium of an architectural program whose quality was virtually unsurpassed throughout postcolonial Asia. As an active filmmaker, he also used the medium he was familiar with to create an appropriate illusory world.[26] In 1969, one year before the coup d'état directed against him, Sihanouk directed his last major film, with the title *Crépuscule,* meaning "twilight" in English (nomen est omen?). The film was produced by Société Nationale de Cinématographie du Cambodge (Khemara Pictures), which was under his control. No other film by Sihanouk features such compelling architectural sequences that symbolically interweave a projected grandeur of the past with the real utopia of a

postcolonial reborn nation-state. Sihanouk himself performed the leading role in this tragic love story. As Prince Adit, a retired Royal Khmer Army general suffering from malaria, he meets a beautiful Indian widow, named Maharani Maya, who is played by Sihanouk's real wife, Monique. After their rendezvous in the small town of Siem Reap and elegant rides in a convertible through the nearby Angkor Archaeological Park, the two protagonists settle down at the moat of Angkor Wat, where Prince Adit begins to talk about the Indian influence on Khmer culture. He opens and recites from the book *Angkor: Hommes et Pierres*, published in 1956 and written by the French art historian and archaeologist, Bernard Philippe Groslier. In that book, the French chief architect of Angkor Park and close friend of Sihanouk, who remained in office beyond the colonial-postcolonial

43

Top left to bottom right:
1 Main perspective, towards the central shrine of Angkor Wat.
2, 3 Prince Adit (played by Norodom Sihanouk) reads to the widow Maharani Maya (played by Sihanouk's wife Monique) from Bernard Philippe Groslier's 1965 book, *Angkor: Hommes et Pierres*.
4 Visit to the Bayon temple.
5 View of the Independence Monument in Phnom Penh.
6 Chaktomuk Conference Hall.
7 State Palace.
8 White Building.
9 National Sports Complex.
10 Documentary scene, depicting the stadium's opening ceremony.
11 Dance sequence.
12 Young Cambodian couple.
13 Prince Adit and Maharani Maya.
14 Maharani Maya at a funeral service.
15 Prince Adit alone on the beach at sunset (French: *crépuscule*).

Scenes from the film *Crépuscule*, directed by Norodom Sihanouk, 1969.

threshold of 1953 until 1970, reflects on the civilizational feats of emancipation and genius of the Khmer and their Angkorian architects. In the next film sequence, Adit and Maya (Sihanouk and Monique) are in a nearby Buddhist monastery, standing in front of a sculpture of the great 13th-century Angkorian king, Jayavarman VII, who—like Sihanouk himself, as a 20th-century king and statesman—tragically found his way into Cambodia's historiography as a visionary yet megalomaniacal and increasingly autocratic builder. Then Maya leaves the prince and travels to Phnom Penh for diplomatic celebrations of Cambodian independence. What follows in the film is a clever montage, combining preexisting "real" documentary footage showing the cultural achievements of the new nation-state with fictional elements. These include the latest architectural projects: the Independence Monument, Chaktomuk Conference Hall, the Presidential Palace at the Chamkar Mon Compound, the White Building, and the National

Stadium with its striking open-air grandstands, where the public itself puts on an Angkor show. The film then switches to a "real communist utopia of Cambodia" in which scenes of ongoing rural traditions, such as dancing and singing, overlap with those of cosmopolitan city life. In a final farewell scene to an ultimately impossible liaison, Maya returns to India while the ailing Adit is left behind, leaning on his walking stick, gazing into the sunset and facing his imminent end.

Indeed, in 1969, the same year that *Crépuscule* was released in the cinemas, Sihanouk lit the (now defunct) eternal flame to Cambodia's birth as a nation-state for the last time as head of state. No building could have provided a more symbolic setting for this than the Independence Monument.

In the following 20 years of Cambodia's national—social as well as cultural—catastrophe during the civil war (1970–75), under Khmer Rouge rule (1975–79), during the subsequent occupation by Vietnam

(1979–89), and even to this day, Cambodia's postcolonial modernism and its "historical" reference buildings from the Khmer Golden Age remain in a precarious situation. As UNESCO World Heritage Sites, many of the monuments from the 7th to 15th centuries have been excessively restored and are suffering from the destructive effects of global overtourism. Many of the architectural masterpieces by Vann Molyvann and his colleagues—despite their patriotic references to a creatively appropriated myth of Angkor—were later demolished on the directive of Hun Sen, Cambodia's prime minister and extremely repressive head of state since 1985. Other buildings are threatened by the rampant building boom, especially by Chinese and Korean high-rise investment projects.

The good news is that, while the National Stadium from 1964 defies its fate in the face of banal perimeter block development, the Independence Monument from 1962 still stands tall and, illuminated every evening, is circled by the capital's rebellious youth on their noisy motorcycles.

This article is mainly based on two texts by Michael Falser: "Performing Grandeur: Re-Enacting Angkor. Cambodia's Independence 1953–70," in Michael Falser, ed., Angkor Wat: A Transcultural History of Heritage *(Berlin: De Gruyter, 2020), vol. 2, Angkor in Cambodia: From Jungle Find to Global Icon, 153–234; and "Cultural Heritage as Performance: Re-Enacting Angkorian Grandeur in Postcolonial Cambodia (1953–70)," in Ruth Craggs and Claire Wintle, eds.,* Cultures of Decolonization: Transnational Productions and Practices, 1945–70 *(Manchester: Manchester University Press, 2016), 126–55.*

01 Vann Molyvann, "À l'école des maîtres angkoriens," *Nokor Khmer* 1 (1969): 36. The text was translated from the French by Michael Falser.

02 The same issue included a short biography of Vann Molyvann: Born 1926 in Ream/Cambodia, school in Phnom Penh, French scholarship to study architecture at École Supérieure des Beaux-Arts in Paris and state D.P.L.G. diploma, 1956 return to Cambodia, Director of Urbanism and Housing and State Secretary for Public Transport and Telecommunications 1962, Rector of the Royal University of Fine Arts in Phnom Penh 1965, and Minister of Education and Fine Arts since 1967. But the story went further: Vann left Cambodia in 1971, worked as a lecturer at École Polytechnique Fédérale de Lausanne until 1979, and until 1993 was an advisor to the United Nations Centre for Human Settlements, among other activities. After his

second return to Cambodia in 1991, he was appointed by the reinstated King Norodom Sihanouk as Minister of State for Culture, Urban Planning, and Construction (1993–98) and Director of the Apsara Authority in Siem Reap/Angkor (1995–2001). After that, he was successively dismissed from his roles by Hun Sen, the head of state who still rules dictatorially. Vann then lived in Cambodia, with the protective honorary title of "private secretary" to King Sihanouk, until his death in 2017. In 2010, the author was able to interview him, together with his second wife, Trudy, at the villa that Vann designed for himself in Phnom Penh.

03 This neologism deliberately refers to the already established concept of so-called "postwar modernism," but also alludes here to the specific achievement of gradually overcoming the French colonial architecture that had shaped Cambodia for so long.

04 Milton E. Osborne, "History and Kingship in Contemporary Cambodia," *Journal of Southeast Asian History* 1 (1966): 1. See also Milton E. Osborne, *Sihanouk: Prince of Light, Prince of Darkness* (St. Leonards: Allen and Unwin, 1994).

05 Jean Lacouture, "Norodom Sihanouk ou le prince d'effervescence," in Jean Lacouture, *Quatre hommes et leurs peuples: Sur-pouvoir et sous-développement* (Paris: Éditions du Seuil, 1969), 189–219; 211.

06 This process has also been studied with regard to nation-state fantasies of the European nation-building process. See Eric Hobsbawm and Terence Ranger, eds., *The Invention of Tradition* (Cambridge: Cambridge University Press, 1983).

07 The idea of an Angkor Archaeological Park was concocted by the French colonial power in the 1920s. It was accompanied by the

legal and administrative demarcation of the park and contributed to an increasing decontextualization of Angkorian temples from a site of lived social practices and (trans)regional Buddhist pilgrimage to a stylized heritage site of dead colonial archaeology. See Michael Falser, "From Colonial Map to Visitor's Parcours: Tourist Guides and the Spatiotemporal Making of the Archaeological Park of Angkor," in Michael Falser and Monica Juneja, eds., *"Archaeologizing" Heritage? Transcultural Entanglements between Local Social Practices and Global Virtual Realities* (Heidelberg: Springer 2013), 81–106; 82.

08 The idea of the *complexe d'Angkor* was first mentioned in 1981 by the Vietnamese author Nguyen Khac Vien in his article "Problème de la convalescence," in Nguyen Khac Vien and Françoise Corrèze, eds., *Kampuchéa 1981: Témoignages.* Special supplement to *Doan Ket.* Also published in English in 1981 under the title *Kampuchea 1981, Eyewitness Reports* (Paris: Union générale des vietnamiens en France, 1981), 3–18; 11. The term "temple complex" (where "complex" refers at once to the physical constellation of Angkor and to a group of associated ideas or impressions) was introduced by Penny Edwards in *Cambodge: The Cultivation of a Nation, 1860–1945* (Honolulu: University of Hawai'i Press, 2007), 242.

09 The references to the pre-Angkorian period (ca. 7th to 10th century) mainly concern the temple areas around Roluos, located southeast of the (chronologically later) Angkor (with the temple mount of Bakong) and the small temple group of Banteay Srei, located northeast of Angkor. The classical Angkorian phase (10th–15th century) refers mainly to the main temple of Angkor Wat (commissioned by the Hindu king Suryavarman II ca. 1120–50 AD) and the temple city of Angkor Thom (12th–15th century, with the main Buddhist king, Jayavarman VII, c. 1200). The post-Angkorian period begins with the fall of Angkor in the 15th century and was accompanied by the relocation of the kings to southern Udong (17th–19th century) before the French expanded the capital Phnom Penh with the establishment of the French protectorate Le Cambodge in 1863. However, the Angkor area did not come into French control from Siam (now Thailand) until 1907, and the Angkor Archaeological Park was not institutionalized

as a protected area until 1925–31.

10 "Le Cambodge à l'Exposition universelle et internationale de Bruxelles 1958," *Cambodge d'aujourd'hui* 2 (February 1958): 6.

11 "Nouvelles construction, nouvelles styles," *Cambodge d'aujourd'hui* 6 (June 1958): 7–13.

12 For more information on plaster cast replicas in world and colonial exhibitions, see Michael Falser, "Krishna and the Plaster Cast: Translating the Cambodian Temple of Angkor Wat in the French Colonial Period," *Transcultural Studies* 2, no. 2 (2011): 6–50, accessed July 26, 2021, doi. org/10.11588/ts.2011.2.9083. See also Michael Falser, *Angkor Wat: A Transcultural History of Heritage,* vol. 1, *Angkor in France: From Plaster Casts to Exhibition Pavilions* (Berlin: De Gruyter, 2020).

13 Vann Molyvann explicitly emphasized this in an interview with the author. See also Ingrid Muan, Ly Daravuth, and Preap Chan Mara, "A Conversation with Vann Molyvann," in Ly Daravuth and Ingrid Muan, eds., *Cultures of Independence: An Introduction to Cambodian Arts and Culture in the 1950s and 1960s* (Phnom Penh: Reyum, 2001), 3–23; 22.

14 Vann Molyvann confirmed this in the 2010 interview with the author in Phnom Penh.

15 Helen Grant Ross and Darryl Leon Collins, *Building Cambodia: New Khmer Architecture 1953–1970* (Bangkok: The Key Publisher, 2006), 208. See also Roger Nelson, "Locating the Domestic in Vann Molyvann's National Sports Complex," *ABE Journal* 11 (2017), accessed July 26, 2021, https://doi.org/10.4000/abe.11019.

16 The group included Um Samuth (former student at the École nationale supérieure des Arts appliqués in Paris, and then employee in Vann's Public Works department), Gérald Hanning, the Parisian architects Claude Duchemin and Jean-Claude Morin, again Vladimir Bodiansky (see above), and the Société Française d'Entreprise de Dragage et de Travaux Publics.

17 Norodom Sihanouk himself was responsible for the journal as "director," while his long-time private secretary, Charles Meyer, served as "editor-in-chief," and, as for the many other state-controlled journals of Cambodian independence, contributed his own pictures. Charles Meyer left behind a rich picture archive, which is now in Paris. Many thanks to his son, Frédéric Meyer, for providing

the photographic material.

18 "La Nouvelle Architecture Khmère: Entretien avec Vann Molyvann," *Nokor Khmer* 1 (1969): 34–47; 37.

19 "Équipe du complexe olympique de Phnom-Penh: Forum de la ville de Phnom-Penh, Cambodge. Complexe olympique du Sud-Est asiatique," *Cahiers du centre scientifique et technique du bâtiments* 73 (April 1965): 1–12; 1.

20 Vann Molyvann and Vladimir Bodiansky, "Complexe olympique du Phnom-Penh, Cambodge," Architecture d'aujourd'hui 116 (1964), 30–33. See also "Jeux olympiques de Tokyo 1964 et les constructions sportives," *Architecture d'aujourd'hui* 116 (1964): 5–19; 16.

21 Ministère de l'Information, *Dans la grande tradition angkorienne: Le complexe sportif national* (Phnom Penh, 1964), 8.

22 " ... que le sang des bâtisseurs d'Angkor n'avait point dégénéré." Ministère de l'Information, *Les progrès du Cambodge 1954–64* (Phnom Penh, 1964), 11.

23 GANEFO stands for Games of the New Emerging Forces, which were set up by Indonesia as a counter to the Olympic Games. They were first held in Jakarta in 1963. A second GANEFO Games in Cairo scheduled for 1967 was canceled. The last iteration of the games were held as the Asian GANEFO in Phnom Penh in 1966. – Eds.

24 These figures adorn the wall surfaces of Angkor Wat by the hundreds and were already "brought back to life" for "authentic" dance performances during the French colonial period. See Michael Falser, "From a Colonial Reinvention to a Postcolonial Heritage and Global Commodity: Performing and Re-Enacting Angkor Wat and the 'Royal Khmer Ballet,'" *International Journal of Heritage Studies* 7–8 (2014): 702–23.

25 See Osborne 1966 (see note 4) and Lacouture 1969 (see note 5); see also Helen Grant Ross, "The Civilizing Vision of an Enlightened Dictator: Norodom Sihanouk and the Cambodian Post-Independence Experiment (1953–70)," in Michael Falser, ed., *Cultural Heritage as Civilizing Mission: From Decay to Recovery* (Heidelberg: Springer, 2015), 149–78.

26 See *Norodom Sihanouk, Roi cinéaste,* written by Frédéric Mitterrand, directed by Jean-Baptiste Martin (64 min., France 2), 1997.

© Kim Hak

Images: Courtesy Vann Molyvann Project

THE VANN MOLYVANN PROJECT

Above
*A historical photo, a model,
and an architectural sketch
of one of Vann Molyvann's
100 Houses, in an exhibition
organized by the Vann
Molyvann Project at the
French Cultural Center,
Phnom Penh, 2010.*

Right
*Presentation of Vann
Molyvann's National
Stadium in Phnom Penh
(1964). Exhibition view,
Taipei Biennial 2016.*

Text: Pen Sereypagna

After Cambodia's independence in 1953, under the leadership of prince Norodom Sihanouk, the country sought to transform its image from that of a small colonial state with an agrarian economy to that of a modern independent nation. An extensive building campaign was central to this effort. The buildings of this era have come to be known as New Khmer Architecture. Vann Molyvann was a pioneer of this movement and his work was crucial for the development of an Asian modernism. His engagement reached far beyond the architectural profession, encompassing questions of human habitat, local tradition, and culture. Astonishing both in terms of scale and their unique architectural language, buildings such as the National Sports Complex, the Chaktomuk Conference Hall, and the Institute of Foreign Languages, in Phnom Penh, still stand as a testament to Molyvann's invaluable contribution to the crafting of a new Cambodian national identity. But these were not the architect's only projects: lesser known than his majestic buildings in Phnom Penh is the 100 Houses project, for which he proposed an alternative to traditional Khmer wooden homes to improve the living standards of the largely rural Cambodian population. Molyvann's design, which attributed great value to the climatic and cultural specificities of the tropical context, combines vernacular architecture with modern materials and techniques that Molyvann learned about while studying in Paris. After the Khmer Rouge regime seized power in 1975, Cambodian scholars were often targeted as political dissidents. Molyvann fled the country, finding refuge in Switzerland with his family. After the civil war, many of Vann Molyvann's buildings fell into decay, while countless documents, drawings, and historical records simply vanished during the years of the Khmer Rouge regime. Today, only a few of the original drawings exist, partly scattered across different collections in Japan and France, and partly held by Molyvann's family in Switzerland.

In recent years, the rapid urban development of Phnom Penh put many modern buildings under threat of demolition. In response to this, the Vann Molyvann Project was established in 2009 as a collaboration between the Royal University of Fine Arts and Norton University, both in Phnom Penh, and the Yale School of Architecture at Yale University in the United States. The goal was to document Molyvann's buildings and produce a new archive of his work. This often meant filling the gaps in the historical records by carrying out new surveys, redrawing the buildings' floor plans, and recording interviews with the protagonists of the post-independence era. Through various exhibitions and publications, the Vann Molyvann Project has offered widespread visibility to New Khmer Architecture, fostering a global conversation about the importance of preserving modernist heritage in Asia and inspiring a new generation of Cambodian architects and scholars.

© Kim Hak

Wooden models of Vann Molyvann's Teacher Training College (1972, now Institute of Foreign Languages). Exhibition view, French Cultural Center, Phnom Penh, 2010.

"I WANTED TO MARRY CAMBODIA WITH THE OCCIDENTAL WORLD"

Lu Ban Hap in conversation with Moritz Henning

Lu Ban Hap, who turned 90 this year, was among the most important architects and urban planners in Cambodia in the 1960s. He studied in Paris from 1949 to 1959, graduating from the École Spéciale d'Architecture. On his return to Cambodia, he became only the second trained architect from Cambodia, after Vann Molyvann. Having come back to Phnom Penh—at that point still the capital of the independent, neutral kingdom of Cambodia—he was immediately asked to develop the new Service Municipal de l'Urbanisme et de l'Habitat (Municipal Department of Urban Planning and Housing). His department, which had twelve staff, was responsible for almost every area of planning and construction in Cambodia's booming capital city, from designating new construction areas to planning and maintaining public buildings and gardens, issuing building permits, coordinating road construction, street lighting, and waste disposal, as well as organizing the public water and electricity supply. There was a complete lack of expertise in Cambodia for some of the tasks that Lu faced, and he regularly traveled overseas in search of expert knowledge.

Being a civil servant was not enough for Lu. Together with his wife Armelle, he set up his own architecture studio; founded a construction company; became a pool technology company franchisee for Indonesia, Thailand, Laos, Cambodia, and Vietnam; and operated a gas station. When the Khmer Rouge invaded Phnom Penh on April 17, 1975, Lu was driven out of the city like millions of others, and forced to work in a rural labor camp. After three months, he managed to escape to Paris, where his wife and children had already fled in 1970. He still lives in the French capital today.

Courtesy Stefan Willimann

Hotel Cambodiana was built in the late 1960s by order of Prince Norodom Sihanouk and designed by Lu Ban Hap together with Chhim Sun Fong. Its planned opening in April 1970 did not take place due to the military coup against Sihanouk. Under the subsequent state leader Lon Nol it became a military barracks, then served as refugee housing. During the Khmer Rouge regime it stood mainly empty, and was used partly as a warehouse. The hotel was finally opened after some modifications in 1990.

MORITZ HENNING:

After studying in Paris, you played a key role in Phnom Penh's urban development and architecture in the 1960s. How did that happen?

LU BAN HAP:

In 1949, I was one of a dozen Cambodian students who were sent to Paris to study. It happened through a competition, which awarded the top student in every subject a scholarship to France—at the time, Cambodia was still a French protectorate.[01] I wanted to become a mechanical engineer, so I studied for about three years at the École Nationale Supérieure d'Arts et Métiers. But then I met Vann Molyvann. At the time there were no architects in Cambodia; he told me this was our chance and managed to convince me to change my course of study.

MH: Did you have any role models? How did you find professional orientation?

LBH: When I was younger, like a lot of other people, I adored Le Corbusier and soaked up everything he did. His Cité Radieuse in Marseille was very good for its time, but it would not work today. People don't want to do everything in the same building nowadays, they can't be squeezed together like that.

MH: Did your studies in France and the influence of people like Le Corbusier have an impact on your later work?

LBH: My training was aligned with what was going on in the West. At Hotel Cambodiana, which I designed in the 1960s, the ornamentation and the roof are done in Khmer style, but the interiors are European. I couldn't design them like Cambodian spaces because in the Cambodian tradition there is no separation of living room and dining room, as there is in France. In

Cambodia everything happened in a single room, and in the evening people just pulled a curtain across to make a separate room. I always designed Western-style plans while at the same time taking Cambodian styles into account, because I wanted to marry Cambodia with the Occidental world, so to speak.

MH: Did you go straight back to Cambodia after you graduated?

LBH: I actually wanted to go to Brasília; I had friends who were already working there. But at an embassy reception in Paris, Prince Norodom Sihanouk told me not to go to Brazil, saying that Phnom Penh needed an architect.

MH: How did you get to know Prince Sihanouk?

LBH: At the time, my mentor, Penn Nouth, was Cambodia's ambassador to France. He had been Cambodia's first prime minister after independence in 1953 and led several governments under Sihanouk. He was unmarried at the time, so my wife took care of his household. Prince Sihanouk often stayed at the embassy with his family when he was in France, and we moved in temporarily; in this way we became close. One time Sihanouk came to France for medical treatment and needed someone to come and keep him company in the hospital. My mentor arranged for me to sleep in the same room as the prince, and we ended up talking the whole time. That's how I became very close to Sihanouk. But every time they asked me which ministry I wanted to take over, I told them: I am a technician by profession, not a minister!

MH: How was the experience of returning to Cambodia? The country had changed enormously in the meantime.

LBH: When I came back, the

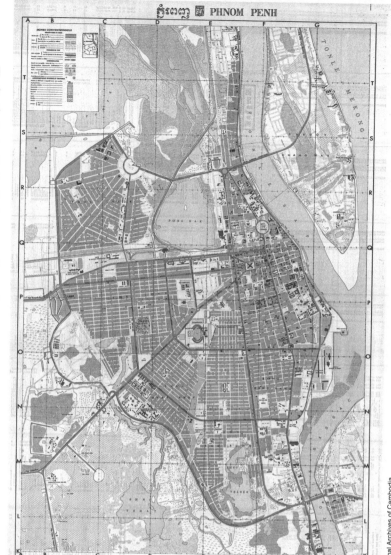

City map of Phnom Penh, 1966. The more open arrangement of buildings at the Bassac riverfront (O,G), the Olympic Stadium (O,E), and the university campus (Q,C) is clearly visible.

French had already left. In fact, they had gone in 1953, leaving the country to the Soviets. There were no cadres and no leadership in Cambodia, because everything in French Indochina had been run from Hanoi. So we had to set up everything from scratch. We established the Service Municipal de l'Urbanisme et de l'Habitat (Municipal Department of Urban Planning and Housing) within the city administration. That was good for me, because it meant I had something like a carte blanche. I could do anything I wanted, and I immediately got whatever I asked for. When Sihanouk needed something, he would tell me to organize it. First, we would discuss the project together, then I would carry it out. He listened to my advice. Whenever I didn't know how to solve something, I asked the government to let me visit similar projects elsewhere in the world. For example, when Sihanouk wanted to build a free port in Cambodia, I went on a special trip to Hamburg to study the facilities there.

I was the first person to begin working on a plan for Phnom Penh; nobody in the French administration had really thought about it. Once, Lee Kuan Yew, the prime minister of Singapore, visited Phnom Penh and asked how I managed to keep the city so neat. The "Pearl of Asia" is what they called Phnom Penh back then, although that was perhaps a bit of an exaggeration.

MH: So you set up and managed the city's planning department, but also ran your own architecture office at the same time?

LBH: Exactly. From 7 a.m. to 1 p.m., I was at the Service Municipal, and in the afternoon I worked in my own office. I was a civil servant and an architect with a private studio at the same time. The draftsmen from the civil service also worked for me in the afternoons. In the studio behind my house, we had six desks for people to work at, as well as working space for my wife Armelle, who helped with the office work.

Cambodian clients who approached me about a project usually had no idea about how they wanted their houses designed, so they left everything up to me. Unlike the Europeans, there was never a concept behind their buildings. They were big, but not comfortable. Since I had studied in Europe, I could fulfil wishes for Western standards like bathrooms, toilets, and all the other comforts. That was one reason why ambassadors in Cambodia turned to me.[02]

ARMELLE LU: In the evening, when it got a bit cooler, we often received clients at our home, in the living room. The women did the planning 80 percent of the time, because they managed the money. The husbands went out to work and left the finances to them. In that respect, it was a matriarchy.

LBH: At that time, we were working with almost no competition, which made it very easy for us. Molyvann and I were the first Cambodian architects. There were a few French people as well, but they only did private projects, and also Leroy & Mondet, who had studied at the same university as I had in Paris.[03] After I went back to Phnom Penh we were like brothers! I often met with them—they always brought me their plans to get my approval. Another important architect at the time was Jamshed Phirosza Petigura.[04]

MH: You built mostly in a modern, rather Western style.

LBH: Yes, most of it was modern, European.

MH: Was that the kind of architecture Prince Sihanouk wanted?

LBH: Sihanouk loved the West! He liked everything modern. But he also liked it when I designed Hotel Cambodiana in the Khmer style. Sihanouk did not insist that things be done in a modernist style, but he did like it. It was up to us to make suggestions. Since we had studied in France, it was clear that we would follow Western developments.

MH: How did Cambodians feel about that?

LBH: Ordinary people liked the combination of modernity and tradition. For example, I was often asked to raise the structure and leave the ground floor free, as is usually done in Cambodian houses. I often put parking spaces underneath, for cars, bicycles, and motorcycles. People liked that very much.

MH: The new universities, theaters, and schools were also built in a modern, international style. How did people respond to that?

LBH: I think it was simply taken as it came. Nobody protested, not even the professors.

Lu Ban Hap with Chhim Sun Fong: Chenla Cinéma d'État Phnom Penh. The state cinema opened in 1969 for the 2nd Phnom Penh International Film Festival.

© Adolf Scherl Collection, Bophana Audiovisual Resource Center, Phnom Penh

Lu Ban Hap built a weekend home for his family in the coastal town of Kep, which also served as a show house for the prefabrication system he developed.
© Lu Ban Hap Archive

In the 1960s, Lu Ban Hap built around 30 low-cost residential buildings in Ta Khmau, south of Phnom Penh, consisting almost exclusively of prefabricated building components.
Courtesy Moritz Henning

MH: They might have thought it wasn't Cambodian enough.
LBH: It never occurred to people to protest against the style when the government was paying for these schools and universities.

MH: Maybe because it was the 1960s, when people were still happy with the state?
LBH: No, I don't think so. The Khmer—with that I mean the people of Cambodia—never had the idea of protesting.

MH: You said you often used to go on study trips abroad, to find examples of possible solutions there. How often were you in West Germany?
LBH: I went there four or five times. It was very easy for me at the time, because I was good friends with Gerd Berendonck, who served as German ambassador to Cambodia between 1964 and 1969. He wanted to help us build a slaughterhouse, so he sent me to Hamburg for a month to study the system there. I had the support of several West German specialists in developing my design. West Germany was going to give us 80 million riels for the slaughterhouse.[05] But it never happened. East Germany was pushing so hard for diplomatic recognition from Cambodia that West Germany ended the collaboration.[06]

Once Sihanouk recognized East Germany, an ambassador was immediately sent to Phnom Penh to find a good location for its embassy.[07] I also gave them a site to set up an exhibition hall to present East German products. That's where they exhibited those little cars, Trabants, they were very beautiful.

MH: You also conducted experiments with prefabrication—how did that come about?
LBH: I designed my very first house for a friend of mine who came to me with a budget of only 100,000 riel. I thought about what might be feasible with that budget and that maybe other people might also be interested. Together with my staff, I developed a system with everything prefabricated except the walls and windows. That was in 1962. We produced the struts, the ceilings, and the beams, all in our workshop. It was the first prefabrication done in Cambodia. I had learned about the basic idea on a trip to the Soviet Union. At first, I experimented with it at my own house in Kep; after that I used it on a larger scale. I built a lot of prefabricated homes in Phnom Penh, but also five or six in Kep, about 30 in Ta Khmau, and even two in Chamkarmon for Sihanouk's daughters.[08] We developed four types in all.

During this time, I set up a construction company in parallel with my architecture office. That way we could offer not only to make the plans for the client, but also to carry out the construction. What began in that small house grew into a proper company. I had trucks, tractors, construction machines. … I came up with the designs, my uncle was in charge of construction management, and my wife took care of the bookkeeping and administration. We used the same system to build all the schools in Phnom Penh.

MH: You planned the schools through your own architectural office?

LBH: The Service Municipal commissioned me to do it. The city didn't have much money at the time, so the governor asked me to make an inexpensive proposal. For that kind of building, the tendering documents suggested costs of 1.8 million riels, but I offered a budget of 1 million maximum. I was able to offer it so cheaply because I planned everything very strictly and was able to use prefabricated materials. I started building schools at the end of 1963 and did one every year until 1968, as outlined in the budget.

MH: One of your most famous buildings is the White Building in Phnom Penh, which you designed with Vladimir Bodiansky. How did that collaboration come about?

LBH: The SEAP Games were supposed to be held in Cambodia in 1963 and Sihanouk needed a building to house the athletes.[09] At the time, Bodiansky was an advisor to the Department of Construction at the Ministry of Public Works and Telecommunications.[10] The building had to be finished in a hurry, but back then I was still the only architect in my department, so in order to get it finished on time, I asked to cooperate with the Public Works Ministry. Bodiansky showed us a building he had once wanted to build in North Africa, and we just adapted the existing design, making it a bit bigger and taller. At that point, the stadium wasn't finished either.[11] Molyvann was in charge of that, while I was given the athletes' buildings.

MH: So you took parts of Bodiansky's plan and modified them?

LBH: Exactly, we didn't have time to completely redevelop the project. I still remember the original building quite well. It was too compact and the air couldn't circulate, so we re-comparted the floor plan better. There is a staircase at each crossing point, and also we redesigned the facade a bit. That was all; it was meant to be inexpensive.

The Service Municipal took over the management of the White Building. First, we rented out the apartments for a year, then we sold them off individually for about 35,000 riels per unit. People who did not have much money could pay it off in installments. It wasn't about making a profit, I just wanted to cover the costs that the city paid for. But the new owners were subject to our rules, so after they bought them, the color of the windows couldn't be changed and the walls couldn't be painted.

MH: Was the White Building an important project for you personally? Do you like the building?

LBH: No. We didn't have much time to plan or build it, and it wasn't my own project. My favorite projects are my own home, Hotel Cambodiana, Chenla Cinema, and the universities.[12] I like the White Building as a symbol, but do I love it? No. But if it were ever torn down, I would still be sad.

This article was compiled from conversations between Moritz Henning, Lu Ban Hap, and Armelle Lu in Chatenay-Malabry between 2014 and 2018. The interviews were originally held in French, then translated by the author into German, and translated for this issue into English.

The first project Lu Ban Hap realized with his firm was his own home, in 1963. The studio was located in a low structure behind the house, while the garden featured the city's very first private swimming pool.

© Lu Ban Hap Archive

The masterplan for the Bassac riverfront was implemented from 1962 to 1968 by Vann Molyvann and Lu Ban Hap. They were assisted by a team of international architects, including UN consultants Vladimir Bodiansky, Gerald Hanning, and Robert Hansberger. The complex included Lu Ban Hap's Municipal Apartments (known as the White Building, center right), as well as Vann Molyvann's Olympic Village Apartments (known as the Gray Building, center) and Molyvann's Preah Suramarit National Theater (center left).

01   Cambodia was under French colonial rule from 1863 to 1953.

02   Lu Ban Hap designed homes for the American and Singaporean ambassadors and other high-ranking figures.

03   Little is known today about the French architects Leroy & Mondet. After the French left Indochina, they stayed on in Cambodia, designing important buildings including the main auditorium of the Université Royale de Phnom Penh (1968).

04   Jamshed Phirosza Petigura was born to Indian and Chinese parents in the Chinese city of Fuzhou. He died in Phnom Penh in 1970. Petigura studied and qualified in France, and worked in Saigon before coming to Cambodia. In Phnom Penh, he was involved in planning apartments for the National Bank of Cambodia, as well as designing Hotel Monorom and the Paradise Hotel.

05   Cambodia was heavily dependent on foreign aid at that time. In the early 1960s, 43% of the national budget was met with foreign funding, of which around 57% came from the United States, 23% from the People's Republic of China, and 17% from France. In 1966, West Germany pledged 20 million Deutschmarks to extend the railway from Phnom Penh to Sihanoukville and build a slaughterhouse. See *Akten zur auswärtigen Politik der Bundesrepublik Deutschland 1969*, vol. 1 (Munich: Institut für Zeitgeschichte, 2000), 651.

06   Cambodia granted full recognition to East Germany on May 8, 1969. In accordance with the Hallstein Doctrine, which stated that no country except the USSR could have full diplomatic relations with both German states simultaneously, West Germany withdrew its ambassador from Phnom Penh and ended its embassy's participation in projects. Economic and technical aid could be used only to fulfill contracts already in existence; no new agreements could be made.

07   The post-unification German embassy is located in the building constructed by East Germany.

08   The government quarter of Phnom Penh, to the south of the city center, which contains the seat of the Senate and affiliated institutions.

09   The Southeast Asian Peninsular Games were meant to take place in Cambodia in 1963, but were canceled due to the domestic political situation.

10   The Ministry of Public Works and Telecommunications was led at the time by Vann Molyvann.

11   The National Sports Complex, better known as the Olympic Stadium, was planned by Vann Molyvann with Vladimir Bodiansky and others, and completed in 1964.

12   During the 1960s, Lu Ban Hap designed the Royal University of Takeo-Kampot and the Royal University of Kompong Cham, both in a more traditional style.

THE WHITE BUILDING AT FRONT DU BASSAC
A symbol of Cambodia's complex relationship to architectural modernism

Upon gaining independence from French Indochina in 1953, Phnom Penh became the dominant urban area in Cambodia, from where the country's political and economic fortunes were controlled. The increase in the city's importance was accompanied by a rapid increase in its population, which went from around 270,000 in 1955 to 464,000 some ten years later.[01]

"Appartements à bon marché pour moyens salariés": Postcard published by the Direction des Services de l'Information with the Gray Building by Vann Molyvann (left), the apartment complex for National Bank employees by Henri Chatel and Jamshed Petigura (back), and the White Building by Lu Ban Hap and Vladimir Bodiansky (right).

Courtesy Moritz Henning

Text: Moritz Henning

Motorcade in front
of the Bassac river front,
mid-1960s.

Courtesy Moritz Henning

By 1961, the housing shortage became so acute that Norodom Sihanouk, the Cambodian head of state, called on builders and architects to "begin the construction of low-cost apartment buildings, that can be rented or sold to average or small-income families."[02] However, these aspirations were only partially reflected in the budget for municipal construction measures in the first Five-Year Plan (1960–64), in which only 25 percent was earmarked for urban development, with over 62 percent of that allocated to administrative buildings.[03]

Some of these buildings, including ministries, administrative units, and university facilities, were built on an axis of development running east-west along Russian Federation Boulevard, while others were constructed running north-south along the banks of the Tonle Sap and Bassac rivers.[04] By 1961, among other things, the river bank area below the Royal Palace had been cleaned up. The building of the Chaktomuk Conference Hall, by Vann Molyvann, would give the district its first new architectural structure. Plans also existed for further development toward the south in the early 1960s.[05]

But it was the Southeast Asian Peninsular Games (SEAP Games), scheduled for 1963 which actually got construction under way.[06] As it would today, the staging of an international sporting event played an important role in a nation as new as Cambodia. The planned Games were both a driver of urban development and a platform for self-presentation in a new political context.[07] The Games provided an opportunity to develop the riverside zone below Sihanouk Boulevard into the "new urban center of Phnom Penh for its function as the capital,"[08] to be given the name Front du Bassac.[09] At the same time, the plan for the new development also aimed to solve the housing problem. Because the necessary sports infrastructure had yet to be built for the SEAP Games, an extensive building program was launched. The main venue was the National Sports Complex, better known as Olympic Stadium, built on the southwestern outskirts of the city on the site of a former horse racing track. As an expression of national sovereignty, the stadium was financed exclusively through a separately levied tax on certain consumer products.[10] In architectural

and cultural terms, the new stadium exemplified the renaissance of the glorious Angkorian Khmer heritage, invoked by Norodom Sihanouk and state architect Vann Molyvann. In addition, a water sports center and two residential buildings for athletes were built on the banks of the Bassac, the latter being two of the most interesting residential buildings of the era: the Olympic Village Apartments, known as the Gray Building because of its gray-clad facade; and the Municipal Apartments, called the White Building because of its white paint. The new wave of construction also included Vann Molyvann's Preah Suramarit National Theater,[11] an exhibition hall,[12] as well as another apartment complex for employees of the National Bank.[13] However, a number of his other planned projects remained unbuilt.

The new riverside cultural and residential area enriched the urban fabric in important ways, while at the same time looking forward to a postcolonial reorganization of the city.[14] The political, social, and cultural center of Phnom Penh shifted away from the city's historical origins, with important buildings such as the National Sports Complex and the Independence Monument[15] built along the new Preah Sihanouk Boulevard, and a new seat of government developed in the district of Chamkarmon, further south. The colonial city had developed around fixed points: the Buddhist temple of Wat Phnom, and the Royal Palace.

The new city district extended over 24 hectares, the development of which was a challenge for the new nation. In the early 1960s, there were just two trained Cambodian architects in the country, Vann Molyvann and Lu Ban Hap.[16] Planning institutions were still in their early stages. At the same time, Cambodian development could only be advanced with the help of foreign donors,[17] who sought to maintain their existing influence in the country, or to obtain new influence. In 1960, development aid amounted to 43 percent of the national budget. The United States was the most important donor nation until a serious split occurred between the two countries in 1963.[18] In addition to the Americans, China, France, the Soviet Union, West Germany (FRG), and later East Germany (GDR), all had a presence in

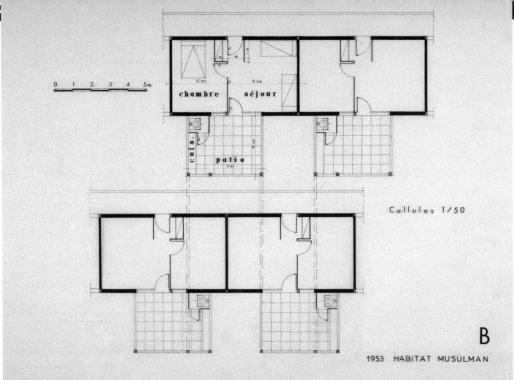

Above
Habitat Musulman floor plan typology for the Nid d'abeille (honeycomb) apartment building in Casablanca, designed by Georges Candilis, Shadrach Woods, Vladimir Bodiansky, and Henri Piot, completed in 1953.

Below
Nid d'abeille apartment building in the Carrières Centrales housing development, Casablanca, 1953.

Cambodia.[19] Like many other newly independent African and Southeast Asian countries, Cambodia became a "Concrete Battleground," with architecture becoming an instrument of power politics (see Benjamin Bansal's article in this issue).

Against this backdrop, it is unsurprising that an international team was put together to manage the task of developing the new district. The team was meant to offer support for the main planner, Vann Molyvann—who at this time was also head of Urban Development and Housing in the Building Ministry, responsible for all public construction projects in the country—and for Lu Ban Hap, head of the newly established Department of Urban Planning and Housing of the Municipality of Phnom Penh.

A key figure in this team was Vladimir Bodiansky, a Ukrainian-born engineer who had been in Cambodia as a United Nations advisor since the early 1960s. Bodiansky had worked on several large-scale housing projects in France in the 1930s and 1940s, including collaborating with Marcel Lods and Le Corbusier. With Le Corbusier he worked on the Unité d'Habitation in Marseille, for the realization of which the two had set up Atelier des Bâtisseurs (ATBAT). Along with Georges Candilis and Shadrach Woods, Bodiansky later founded ATBAT-Afrique, which in the early 1950s carried out projects in Algeria and Morocco, then French colonies. Gérald Hanning—who already knew Bodiansky from Le Corbusier's studio—was also working for the UN in Cambodia in the early 1960s. Upon returning from La Réunion, where he went after his work with Le Corbusier, Hanning had been appointed chief urban planner of Algiers in the 1950s, and moved to Cambodia in 1959. Furthermore, Robert Hansberger, Roger Aujaume, and Guy Lemarchands were also involved in the planning of the Bassac river front. Realized under the leadership of Vladimir Bodiansky,[20] the design of the new river front followed models that contrasted sharply with the preexisting urban structure. The traditional shop-house typology, which continued to develop in the 1950s,[21] generally followed the blocks' structure laid out under French colonial rule. Instead, Bodiansky and his colleagues oriented themselves towards European models of postwar urban planning and towards the experimental projects realized by ATBAT in North Africa—a choice that was meant to symbolize the transformation of Cambodia from a protectorate into a modern independent nation.

During his training at the École Spéciale d'Architecture in Paris, Lu Ban Hap also adopted common postwar urban planning models.[22] So did Vann Molyvann, who trained at the École Nationale Supérieure des Beaux-Arts in Paris and was very familiar with the ideas of European modernism. Le Corbusier's Ville Radieuse was a model of particular importance to him.[23] The new buildings on the Bassac river front not only marked a radical shift from the structures of the colonial city, but also from the commercial pressures that had led to such high density within Phnom Penh's tightly parceled inner city. The new district was to be one of the few in which Vann Molyvann and Lu Ban Hap could implement their ideals of an open, airy, green city.[24] The Bassac project was unique in Phnom Penh in several respects. Apartments were arranged in multistory row buildings on an east-west orientation, which was rather unusual in the region. Moreover, large areas of valuable building land were turned into parks for general public use. The traditional Khmer city—a rather loosely organized system of *wats* (temples), houses, and waterways, with no planned urban structure[25]—gave way to a new district, rigidly planned in functional, aesthetic, and social terms.[26] This was more than just a visual transformation. It had very real effects: the area by the Bassac River previously had "real slums,"[27] whose residents were now relocated to Stung Meanchey, several kilometers away.

Even if not all the building plans were ultimately realized, Cambodia's cultural, societal, and social ambitions were reflected in the plans for the new city district. The carefully designed and curated ideal city included buildings for art, culture, and politics, as well as a range of modern residential typologies, all placed within an open, spacious urban landscape. The plans were aggressively marketed to the public. Images appeared in the magazines *Cambodge d'aujourd'hui* and *Kambuja*, published by Sihanouk, on postcards distributed by the Ministry of Tourism, and at trade fairs abroad. The new district was also a showpiece display location for parades bringing visiting dignitaries from the airport to the Royal Palace.

Given the importance attached to the new district, the origins of the White Building—one of the most discussed buildings of Khmer Modernism—are all the more astonishing. Lu Ban Hap's Department of Urban Planning and Housing was supposed to build it to house athletes at the SEAP Games, but the department itself was still in its infancy. For this reason, Vladimir Bodiansky was called upon to work with Lu in coming up with a pragmatic solution within a very short time. As a template, they used a building Bodiansky had originally designed for North Africa, slightly changing it to reduce construction costs and making it better suited to a more tropical climate.

For Lu, also responsible for the administration of the city's real estate, it was essential that the building be used after the Games as well. Since the city did not want to be the permanent landlord of the building, it was decided to sell the apartments at a later date, using a financial model based on installment payments, with the total purchase price only meant to cover actual construction costs. Thus the "Appartements à bon marché pour moyens salariés"[28] were created, for a target market of administrative and low-income officials. This

group had grown significantly in recent years partly because Cambodia needed to set up its own postcolonial administration, but even more because of Sihanouk's deliberate pursuit of clientelism and preferential treatment for middle-class functionaries.[29]

The building itself was just as unusual by Cambodian standards as the new urban district in which it was located. Until then, the familiar forms of development in Phnom Penh had been the traditional wooden houses and bamboo huts of the poor, alongside free-standing villas and the shophouse format, with business premises on the ground floor and narrow stairwells leading to living spaces stacked above. However, the 468 apartments of the White Building were positioned in a single long row, arranged on both sides of a corridor extending the length of every floor. This was a *rue intérieure*, directly reminiscent of Le Corbusier's Unité d'Habitation in Marseille. The 325-meter-long building was divided by open stairwells, which improved lighting and air circulation, while also allowing passage from the street to the city park behind. In addition, the building was raised along its whole length, placed on pilotis and thin wall panels.

According to the original specifications, the apartments were to be small, with simple floor plans, containing an adjacent living room and bedroom, connected by a door. The kitchen and toilet were in front of the living area, accessible via a small balcony. With some exceptions, where a second bedroom was added, the floor plan was repeated across all floors of the building. The two planners were aware of the novel character of their design: "I felt that Cambodians were not used to living like that," Vann Molyvann later reflected.[30] Lu Ban Hap was also skeptical about the new living arrangements offered by the building.[31]

Although the building was put forward as a great alternative to the existing city and its residential structures, it also contained references

Apartment floor plan for the White Building.

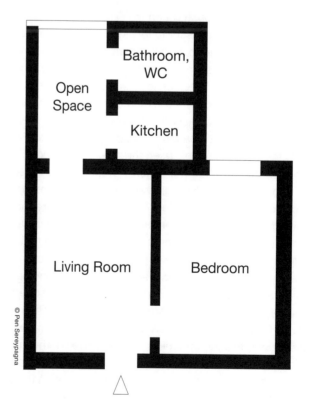

© Pen Sereypagna

to Cambodian tradition: the apartments were divided into two rooms, as in traditional Khmer wooden homes, and the living room and bathroom were located at the back of the house. The fact that the building was suspended on pilotis also reflected traditional Cambodian structures, which kept the ground floor to be used as a storage area, a parking space, or a location for community activities.[32]

Unfortunately, Lu Ban Hap no longer recalls which of Bodiansky's buildings was the model for the White Building. However, if we examine the Nid d'abeille, built in Casablanca in 1952, there are obvious similarities in structure, facade, and floor plan. Although ATBAT-Afrique's basis for planning that building was entirely different—the experimental structure of the Nid d'abeille was intended as a stacked version of Moroccan courtyard houses—the floor plans of the Casablanca building also consisted of two interconnected living rooms with a front exit. Both the kitchen and bathroom of each unit were installed on a suspended, high-walled patio, while access to the apartments was along a breezeway rather than through a central corridor.

During the development of the Nid d'abeille, Bodiansky, Candilis, and Woods conducted studies to see how the building could be adapted to different ethnic communities. Specific house types for European, Muslim, or Jewish residents were designed on the basis of a uniform structure.[33] The floor plans, facades, and balconies were all designed to be "culturally specific" within the overall design, according to the needs and habits the European planners ascribed to particular groups of residents. The *Habitat Musulman* typology built in Casablanca was based on extensive studies of the everyday habits of the local population. The studies focused in particular on bidonvilles (informal settlements beyond the planned city), the living environment of many Moroccans in rural areas, new industrial centers, and the outskirts of the growing metropolises. With the Nid d'abeille, the planners combined an analysis of local architectural traditions with barracks-type housing construction.[34]

There clearly was an assumption that the structure of the Nid d'abeille could be adapted to a Cambodian population with only minor modifications. Nothing is known about whether these architectural strategies were further reflected on for a Cambodian context, comparable to the discussions on planning in Morocco that began with the CIAM Congress in 1953. We may assume, however, that time pressure and Cambodia's lack of participation in critical architectural discourse[35] meant that the planners simply used their next-best model. There is a certain irony in the fact that the flagship project of the recently independent, Buddhist Cambodia originated in the "desert of modernity"[36]—the French North African colonies used as a testing ground for postwar planning in France. The model of modern, inexpensive housing for low-income Cambodian government officials was in fact based on the living conditions of residents of Moroccan bidonvilles.

In the end, the SEAP Games were canceled and the apartments were temporarily rented until they went on sale. But despite favorable conditions, sales of the new apartments were slow. The units were too small for Cambodian families, and living next to other residents on a single floor was still too unfamiliar. In the end, all of the apartments were sold, but their new residents immediately attempted to adapt them to how they wanted them to be, despite this being forbidden by the building's administration. Ultimately, the architectural experiment was not repeated in the city, remaining the only attempt in Phnom

Penh to build this type of apartment building and create this kind of publicly organized housing project.

In 1975, Phnom Penh's development was abruptly interrupted by the Khmer Rouge takeover. Pol Pot's soldiers expelled or murdered almost the entire population of the city, or sent them to rural areas for forced labor. The reign of terror ended in 1979 with the Vietnamese invasion, by which time survivors were roaming the cities and countryside in search of relatives. The cadastral system had been destroyed. Taking over existing housing was often the only way to find somewhere to live. Given the situation, the government decided to turn the White Building into a new home for artists: a living space for painters, dancers, and musicians, located close to Vann Molyvann's iconic Preah Suramarit National Theater. They did this in order to help revive the Cambodian art world, which had been almost completely destroyed by the Khmer Rouge.

Over the years, the population of the building diversified, as almost 500 families made the White Building their own, including drastic redesigns and extensions. The monostructures of residential use were broken up, with facilities on the ground floor expanded, including large and small shops, workshops, and food stalls. The upper floors also had new uses added. The formally restrictive rules imposed in the 1960s by the city government on the gleaming white idyll of Sihanouk's civil servant apartments gave way to informal, creative practices of appropriation, which challenged the functional principles of the modernist city on which the Front du Bassac was based. Instead, the building was adapted to the needs of its residents, who were often poor. Lu Ban Hap questioned the transferability of Le Corbusier's Unité model, which combined almost all everyday functions in a single building. But in time, residents increasingly transformed the White Building into a structure where they could explore new functional possibilities for themselves, and that resembled Corbusier's Unité more than its builders could probably have imagined. The tragedy is that this process was ultimately made possible by the political and legal vacuum left behind by the Khmer Rouge reign of terror.

Beginning in the early 2000s, real estate speculation drove up prices for inner-city plots to European levels. For the Bassac riverside neighborhood, this meant a profound process of transformation. On July 11, 2017, the Department of Land Management announced that the White Building would be demolished and replaced with a new 21-story construction, to be built by a Japanese developer at a cost of $70 million. Most residents accepted the compensation on offer, and moved out. Just a few weeks later, another icon of Phnom Penh modernism simply disappeared.

01 Vann Molyvann, *Modern Khmer Cities* (Phnom Penh: Reyum, 2003), 167.
02 Quoted in Helen Grant Ross and Darryl Collins, *Building Cambodia: New Khmer Architecture 1953–1970* (Bangkok: Key Publications, 2006), 16.
03 Thomas Kolnberger, *Zwischen Planung und Spontaner Ordnung: Stadtentwicklung von Phnom Penh 1860 bis 2020* (Vienna: Institut für Geographie und

Regionalforschung, 2014), 288.
04 In the 1950s, this development was made possible, among other ways, by funds from the United States, which enabled the purchase of the dredgers which gradually turned alluvial land into land for building. Kolnberger, *Zwischen Planung und Spontaner Ordnung* (see note 3), 289.
05 Ingrid Muan et al., "A Conversation with Vann Molyvann," in *Cultures of

Independence: An Introduction to Cambodian Arts and Culture in the 1950s and 1960s*, eds. Ly Daravuth and Ingrid Muan (Phnom Penh: Reyum, 2001), 6.
06 The Southeast Asian Peninsular Games were founded in 1958 by Burma (now Myanmar), Cambodia, Laos, Malaya (now Malaysia), Thailand, and Vietnam. The Games were originally scheduled for Phnom Penh, but were eventually canceled. The

White Building, exterior
view in the 1960s.

National Sports Complex was not completed until the end of 1964.

07   See for example: "Sports and Modern Urbanism," mASEANa project 2017 modern living in Southeast Asia (2017): 22–35, http://www.maseana.iis.u-tokyo.ac.jp/assets/maseana-2017_web.pdf.

08   "Nouveau centre urbain de Phnom Penh pour sa fonction de capitale," inscription on a scale model of the Front du Bassac. Ross and Collins, *Building Cambodia* (see note 2), 16.

09   Muan et al., "A Conversation with Vann Molyvann," (see note 5), 6.

10   Roger Nelson, "Locating the Domestic in Vann Molyvann's National Sports Complex," *ABE* 11 (Oct 5, 2017), accessed Dec 9, 2020, http://journals.openedition.org/abe/3615; https://doi.org/10.4000/abe.3615.

11   The building was completed in 1968 and demolished in 2007.

12   The Sangkum Reastr Niyum Exhibition Hall was designed by Vann Molyvann and opened in 1962. It was intended to present the achievements of Norodom Sihanouk's political organization of the same name.

13   The building was designed by Henri Chatel and Jamshed Petigura. It was completed around 1963 and is located on the present-day grounds of the Russian Embassy.

14   See "Bassac Riverfront Project," The Vann Molyvann Project, accessed Jan 17, 2021, http://www.vannmoly-vannproject.org/archive#/new-page-2/.

15   The monument was designed by Vann Molyvann and inaugurated in 1962.

16   Phnom Penh only got its own architecture faculty in 1967, at the Royal University of Fine Arts. Foreign-trained architects gradually returned to Cambodia.
B. Mam Sophana came back from the United States in 1965; Chhim Sun Fong returned from studying in Australia in 1967.

17   This includes the Khmer–Soviet Friendship Hospital and the Chaktomuk Conference Hall, as well as university buildings, factories, the railway to Sihanoukville, and a variety of road building projects, to name just a few examples.

18   Kolnberger, *Zwischen Planung und Spontaner Ordnung* (see note 3), 273f.

19   West German projects in Cambodia included the construction of a trade school

in Battambang, the railway line and Sihanoukville station, and plans for a slaughterhouse in Phnom Penh, which was never built.

20   Ross and Collins, *Building Cambodia* (see note 2), 16.

21   See for example: Yam Sokly and Seo Ryeung Ju, "Transformation of Shophouses in Phnom Penh, Cambodia: In the Aspect of Spatial Organization," *Family and Environment Research* 54, no. 1 (2016): 13–26, accessed Jul 28, 2021, https://www.koreas-cience.or.kr/article/JAKO201608450941397.pdf; or Wakita Yoshihisa and Shiraishi Hideo, "Spatial Recomposition of Shophouses in Phnom Penh, Cambodia," *Journal of Asian Architecture and Building Engineering* 9 (May 2010): 207–14, https://www.research-gate.net/publication/239416191_Spatial_Recomposition_of_Shophouses_in_Phnom_Penh_Cambodia.

22   See the interview with Lu Ban Hap in this issue.

23   Muan et al., "A Conversation with Vann Molyvann" (see note 5), 11.

24   Further examples include the university campus on Russian Federation Boulevard between the city center and the airport, as well as the National Sports Complex and the

adjoining sports accommodations. Apart from these examples, there were few outlets for architectural ambitions on a scale beyond existing urban plots.

25   Ross and Collins, *Building Cambodia* (see note 2), 131.

26   For example, the larger apartments of the Gray Building faced the river bank, while the smaller, cheaper apartments in the White Building took a back seat.

27   Vann Molyvann, quoted in Muan et al., "A Conversation With Vann Molyvann" (see note 5), 9.

28   In promotional material and publications, the project was advertised with the slogan "Affordable housing for average incomes."

29   Kolnberger, *Zwischen Planung und Spontaner Ordnung* (see note 3), 274–90.

30   Muan et al., "A Conversation with Vann Molyvann" (see note 5), 11.

31   In various conversations with the author, Lu Ban Hap stressed that Cambodians do tend to be open to innovations regarding housing typologies, but only to a very limited extent.

32   Pen Sereypagna, "New Khmer Architecture: Modern Movement in Cambodia

between 1953 and 1970," *docomomo* 57 (Feb 2017): 12–19.

33   For a detailed description of the Carrières Centrales and the Nid d'abeille, see Marion von Osten, "The Patio Grid," ARCH+ Can Design Change Society? Projekt Bauhaus, English edition (2019): 96–103.

34   Ibid, 135.

35   For example, in different discussions with the author, the two Cambodian architects Lu Ban Hap and Mam Sophana explained that there were no architectural journals in the country at that time, nor did the architects exchange information with each other.

36   The term is borrowed from *In the Desert of Modernity*, an exhibition curated by Tom Avermaete, Serhat Karakayali, and Marion von Osten, held at Haus der Kulturen der Welt, Berlin 2008. The exhibition addressed the relationship between colonialism and European modernism.

The White Building in 2016, shortly before its residents were
forced out and demolition work began.

GENEALOGY OF BASSAC

**Section cut through apartment units inside
the White Building, 2015.**

Section cut through the
staircase of the
White Building, 2015.

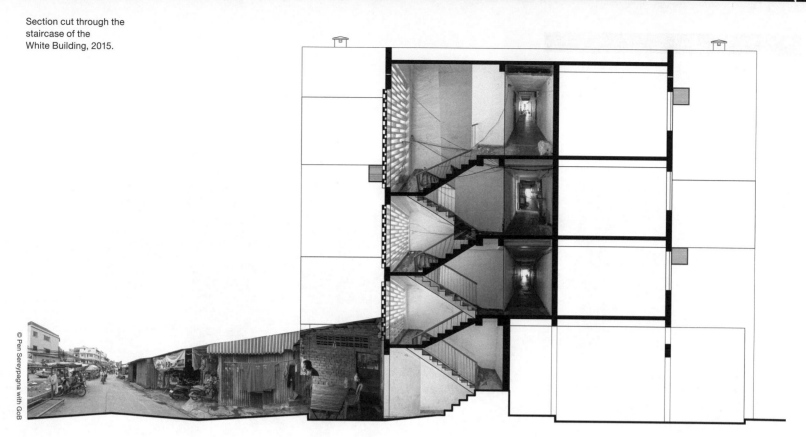

© Pen Sereypagna with GoB

Text: Pen Sereypagna
with Genealogy of Bassac

The collage drawings displayed here are the outcome of *Genealogy of Bassac*—a project started in 2014, realized in partnership with the School of Constructed Environment at Parsons School of Design, hosted by Sa Sa Art Projects, and partly funded by Khmer Architecture Tours. *Genealogy of Bassac* mapped the Bassac Riverfront complex, in central Phnom Penh, as a community-based participatory exercise. The mapping exercise took place within, and was informed by, the artistic residential community of the iconic White Building, designed by Lu Ban Hap in 1963, and demolished in 2017 (see Moritz Henning's article in this issue). Key objectives of the project were to find new ways of visualizing ruptures in urban form that have occurred in the area over different historical eras; to record the past and present of the Bassac Riverfront; and to start a new dialogue that could serve as the basis for developing ideas for the future of the city.

The collage drawings were created by overlaying hundreds of photographs on top of 2D architectural drawings. The photographs were taken between 2014 and 2015 by participating students, whereas the 2D drawings are the outcome of surveys carried out by the Vann Molyvann Project in 2009 (see feature on the Vann Molyvann Project in this issue). The resulting images illustrate both the physical and social transformations that have occurred inside the building and constitute a visual database for artists, architects, urbanists, as well as for the local community, to understand urban change through the story of the White Building.

A book of Genealogy of Bassac was published by Terreform. See: Brian McGrath and Pen Sereypagna, *Genealogy of Bassac* (US: Terreform, Inc., 2021).

West elevation of the White Building, layering photographic built-out spaces on top of 2D drawings.

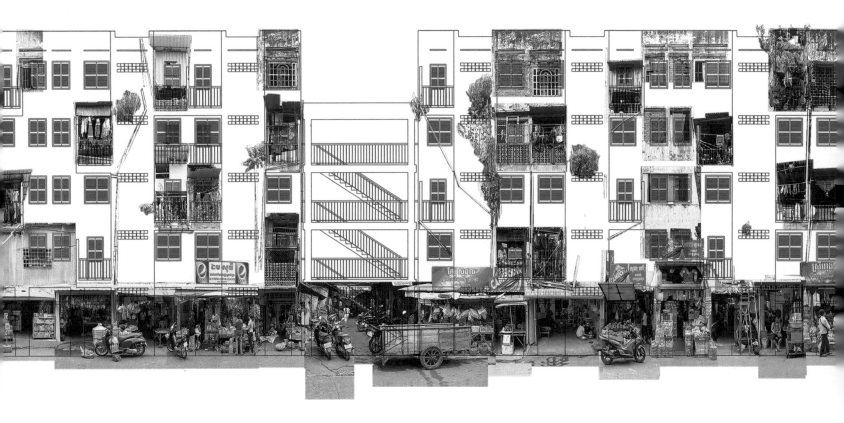

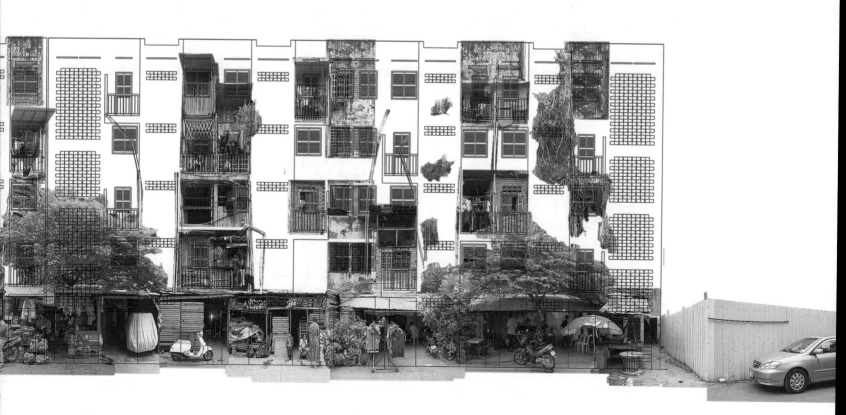

Text: Hun Sokagna (Roung Kon Project)

Vann Molyvann's iconic
Capitol Cinema from 1964
was demolished in 2018.

© Stéphane Janin 1992

KEEPING THE MEMORY OF PHNOM PENH'S CINEMAS ALIVE

Much has been written about Cambodia's lost and rediscovered love affair with films. During the golden age of the Cambodian film industry in the 1950s and 1960s, before the establishment of the authoritarian Khmer Rouge regime in 1975, about 300 films were produced in the country. But little attention has been given to Cambodia's cinemas.

Cine Phnom Penh, which has
since been demolished.

Royal Cinéma,
built during
the colonial period.

Above
Ciné Lux, built in 1938 to
plans by French architect
Roger Colne, is one of
the few remaining modernist
movie theaters in Phnom
Penh. In 2017, operations
ceased, and the nature of its
future use remains uncertain.

Right
Bracheachun Cinema,
Phnom Penh.
© Stéphane Janin 1992

Many old cinemas built during that era have since disappeared, or are currently threatened with demolition. Information about these buildings and the architects who designed them is scarce, because after political dissidents were either killed or fled the country—including movies directors and artists—the Khmer Rouge destroyed public records, archives, and books, truncating the memory of a country that until this day is struggling to deal with its recent past. The first cinemas in Phnom Penh were built by the French in the colonial style of the time. The Brignon was the country's first cinema, inaugurated by the French administration in 1909 and located on the Preah Sisowath Quay overlooking the Tonle Sap River. Prior to independence, going to the cinema was a prerogative of the colonialist class and of the Cambodian élite. It was only from 1953 that films became a form of mass entertainment, and, together with people's growing thirst for films, the number of cinemas in Phnom Penh grew exponentially. Under the patronage of appointed king Norodom Sihanouk—who was himself a film director and producer—French film productions gave way to Cambodia's own groundbreaking industry, which flourished in the 1960s and early 1970s. Many films produced during this time, such as the popular Ly Bun Yim's *12 Sisters* (1968) and Tea Lim Koun's *The Snake King's Wife* (1970), received widespread international recognition, especially in Southeast Asia. Modern cinemas were erected throughout Phnom Penh, designed in the so-called New Khmer style, an architecture that combined international modernism with elements of the Khmer vernacular. These pioneering movie theaters were places where Cambodia's past, present, and future aspirations converged.

Following the brief but violent period of Khmer Rouge rule (1975–79), during the long years of the Vietnamese occupation and the transition leading up to the establishment of the constitutional monarchy in 1993, many cinemas continued to operate, albeit with an offer that consisted mainly of imports from Vietnam and the Soviet Union. Popular productions like those from Hong Kong were banned in Cambodia. The films of socialist realism, with their monotone depiction of the working classes, bored audiences over time and stifled Cambodian cinematographic culture.

Today, Phnom Penh and other Cambodian cities are experiencing rapid and uncontrolled urban expansion, in which many historically and culturally significant buildings must give way to new developments. This is especially true for modernist architecture, whose cultural importance is often difficult to read from within the framework of Cambodia's complex political history. Over the past decade, a number of preservationist movements and groups have formed, including the Roung Kon Project, whose scope is to promote and record the legacy of Phnom Penh's old cinemas by means of architectural drawings, interviews, photographs, and maps. Their goal is to convince the owners of these buildings to renovate them and preserve them as cultural institutions, rather than selling them—which, in most cases, equates to a demolition sentence.

Today's fast-growing Cambodian middle class has attracted regional and international cinema operators to Phnom Penh. With young generations preferring to visit the newly built cineplexes, watching films in an old-fashioned movie theater has lost its appeal. A few of the old theaters have found new use, such as the Hemakcheat Cinema, which has been occupied since the early 2000s by people in need of shelter upon return from their forced relocation to the countryside by the Khmer Rouge. However, most of the cinemas built during the years of colonial rule and shortly after independence have closed down. In 2017, Ciné Lux theater on Preah Norodom Boulevard was the last independently run cinema to close its doors, leaving the former Chenla Cinéma d'Etat—designed by Lu Ban Hap and built for the 1969 edition of the Phnom Penh International Festival—as the only living record of the city's vibrant cinema(tographic) history.

The Hemakcheat Cinema, built in the 1950s, has long ceased functioning as a movie theater. Since the 1980s it has been a shelter, inhabited by people who were deported to the countryside by the Khmer Rouge and then became homeless on their return to the city.

© Philip Jablon 2008

In the late 1960s and early 1970s, Mam Sophana was one of the main protagonists of New Khmer Architecture. Having studied in the USA, his style differed remarkably from that of other Cambodian architects of his time, many of whom studied in France shortly before or immediately after independence. During the Cambodian Civil War, before the Khmer Rouge seized power in 1975, Mam Sophana fled to Singapore, where he worked as an architect until his return to Cambodia in 1992. Today Mam continues to practice in Phnom Penh and is a consultant for the Cambodian government.

© Moritz Henning

"ARCHITECTURE IS ABOUT EVERYTHING AND NOTHING"

Mam Sophana:
Vocational school for
employees of Électricité du
Cambodge (now National
Technical Training Institute),
Phnom Penh, ca. 1969.

Mam Sophana in conversation with Moritz Henning

MORITZ HENNING: You were born and grew up in Cambodia, and studied architecture in the United States, instead of France as many others did. What was behind this decision?

MAM SOPHANA: I was around 20 years old when I finished secondary school in the early 1950s, when Cambodia was still a French colony. Almost all of my friends went to France to study, but I wanted to go to the USA. Once I was in the American Library, flipping through the pages of some magazines, and I saw photographs of beautiful mountains, water, and clean places. This attracted me. I liked America. It was not only the architecture but also American society; the way it fosters independence. They offer jobs. While I was there, I had many jobs to finance my studies: I washed dishes, was a babysitter, and I cut the neighbors' lawns. That made me feel independent.

MH: What was the most important thing you learned in the USA?

MS: In America I learned two main things: I learned how to design a building and I learned how to be free and independent. To be happy often means giving up responsibility, but if you find the right balance between work and play, you are free and can do everything. When I arrived in the USA in the 1950s, I discovered what I call the "culture of no fence." It frightened me at first. Back then, in a small town like Oxford, Ohio, where I studied, there were no fences between the houses. This was new to me, but soon I, too, learned how to live a life with "no fence."

MH: And what did you learn at the American university?

MS: The most important thing I

learned was teamwork. Creating architecture is teamwork. You have to sit down and discuss a project a million times: "Why is it good? Why is it not good?" You have to ask yourself these questions until you find the solution. As a young architect, I wanted to do everything by myself, but then I learned that life doesn't work like that. The things of life are all interrelated. In America I learned to be a part of society. Architecture is not just about designing a building; architecture is about everything and nothing. Once we had to go to the laboratory and dissect a mouse. It made me very nervous. "I study architecture," I said, "why should I cut a mouse?" Later I realized that, even if you are an architect, it's good to know about biology. At some point, they asked me to study psychology and I said, "I want to learn how to design a building, not psychology!" Their answer was, "Don't be so stubborn, just do it." It was terribly frustrating, but 20 years later I realized that it had been helpful to learn some psychology. In college I learned that, as an architect, you have to go outside, discover things, draw them, paint them, look at magazines, and so on. To understand architecture you have to ask yourself many questions: "Where is this building? In what country? Is it in Asia? Is it in America? What kind of government was in place when it was built? What kind of society?" This is why we talk about architecture, because there are so many things that are connected to it. Now you are probably thinking, "Oh god, this man is too old! I ask him something and he answers a completely different question."

MH: Not at all, it's all very interesting, please continue.

MS: You see, to be an architect,

you have to create your own identity. When you see a good building, you cannot just copy it. That's not how architecture works. You can be inspired by Le Corbusier and Frank Lloyd Wright, but you cannot simply copy their work. To be inspired means to learn from someone or something. That's how I learned to create my own identity. For example, a lot of my architecture is curved. I hate angles. Angles are easy to draw, but curves—curves have feeling. When you draw a curve, you feel it in your fingers. But you need to sketch it by hand; you can't feel it with the computer. Designing a building with curves also means that you have to design the process, not only the building. I used

to make the molds for the concrete by myself; I didn't ask the workers to make them. I took the time and I did it myself.

MH: You went back to Cambodia in 1965. At that point Cambodia was independent, a parliamentary monarchy headed by prince Norodom Sihanouk. What was it like to be a young architect back then?

MS: When I came back to Cambodia I had only one pair of pants, one shirt, and no dollars. I rented a small studio, just for myself. Who was the architect? Me. Who was the engineer? I was the engineer. Who cleaned the office? Still me. Who spoke with the contractor and supervised

Main facade with expressive columns.
From: Helen Grant Ross and Darryl Collins, *Building Cambodia: New Khmer Architecture 1953–1970* (Bangkok: The Key Publisher Company Limited, 2006).

73

Above left
Villa of Samdech Son Sann, the former Cambodian prime minister (1967–68) and later president of the National Assembly, Phnom Penh, ca. 1970.

Above right
Workers' housing for an oil company, Kompong Som (now Sihanoukville), 1972.

Left
Villa for a banker, Phnom Penh, ca. 1969.

Right
Villa for a banker, Phnom Penh, ca. 1969.

Villa for a customs officer, Phnom Penh, ca. 1972.

Left
Villa of former Cambodian
Deputy Prime Minister Sok An.

Below
Round House, Phnom Penh,
ca. 1971.

ROUND HOUSE
phnom penh 1971

the works? It was me again. I did everything by myself. I didn't even have a car, I had to take a cyclo. People used to tell me, "Young man, you are nice and respectable, but a cyclo is for poor people." I didn't care.

MH: How did you get your first clients?

MS: The most important thing that a father can give his children is not property, but a good name. My father was a very nice, good-hearted man. When I came back from America I went to Samdech Son Sann,[01] who was then head of Bank Khmer, the national bank of Cambodia. When he saw me, the first thing he said to me was, "Sophana, you are very young. What kind of work are you doing?"

I replied, "I studied architecture in America." He said, "Architecture? Nice. So, you design houses? Very good! And who are your parents?" "My father is Mam Soth." "Oh, Mam Soth! Mam Soth is a good man!" And so he called his secretary and he said, "Secretary, will you please take Sophana with you and find him some work? Right now, please." And so the secretary asked me to design his home. I did everything myself. I calculated the loads and built the foundations all alone. That was 1967; the house is still standing.

MH: There weren't many Cambodian architects at the time. People must have looked at you and thought, "Look, that's the young architect who came back from America." Was it like that? Did people want you to design American-style homes?

MS: No. Back then, the clients didn't ask for anything in particular. They just said: "Go ahead, do what you want! We heard about you, we trust you!" There were only about seven or eight architects in Cambodia at that time. Vann Molyvann and Lu Ban Hap were the most famous ones. They both studied in France. They came back before me and mainly worked for the government.

MH: It looks to me as if Frank Lloyd Wright had a strong influence on your work. With others, like Vann Molyvann, you can see the influence of the French, of

Le Corbusier. But your design approach is closer to that of Frank Lloyd Wright, am I right?

MS: Yes, I was certainly influenced by Wright. In America I learned how to balance proportions. Proportions are very important when you design a building.

MH: Was there any dialogue among Cambodian architects about the new architecture? Did you ever discuss your ideas with Vann Molyvann, Lu Ban Hap, and the others? Or was everyone working separately?

MS: Very little; there was no time. We all had different styles. There was not much to say, just a lot of work. We were so few, maybe ten in total. We were not even enough to make an association. There was one who came back from Australia, one from Czechoslovakia, one from America, but most of the others had studied in France. Everyone was working on their own projects.

MH: Before people like you came back from their studies abroad there were only French architects in Cambodia. But after independence, with Norodom Sihanouk, everything changed. It must have felt like building a whole new country, right?

MS: It felt exactly like that. But architecture has changed tremendously since then, mostly because two things happened. Number one: between 1975 and 1979, Pol Pot killed most of the architects. Educated people were not liked by the Khmer Rouge. Number two: most of those who were not killed fled the country, including me. I am lucky to be here now, but I am struggling. Not in terms of money, but I am struggling to understand why I am here alone. Before, people came to me, they trusted me, they paid me well, and I designed beautiful houses

Today, many new high-rises are shooting up in Phnom Penh.

© South China Morning Post

for them. Why isn't it like that anymore?

MH: After 1970, when Lon Nol established the short-lived Khmer Republic, but before the Khmer Rouge seized power in 1975, you were still in Phnom Penh, while many others had already left the country. Can you tell us about this time? What was it like, working during the time of Lon Nol?

MS: I built a lot of houses during that time; there was nothing to stop me then. It was mostly private homes, but I also helped build a professional training school for the employees of Électricité du Cambodge. This was until 1974, when the Khmer Rouge started launching their rockets. I was just working as an architect; I was not in a military group; I was not a politician; I was just working like an ox and playing basketball in my free time. I couldn't have been happier. I made money, not much, but enough money to have a good life.

MH: When Lon Nol took power, it was quite a radical shift in the political system. Did this influence your work as an architect?

MS: No, this shift did not influence my work because the Khmer Republic was so short-lived. Space and culture did not change much in just a few years. Cambodia was still Cambodia.

MH: In 1974, when the Khmer Rouge was about to seize power, you moved to Singapore. In 1992, you came back, opened a new office, and went into politics. What made you decide to come back?

MS: I was in Singapore for 17 years. I worked for a company as a senior architect, and learned how they work in Singapore. But as soon as Cambodia opened its doors I came back to serve my country. That's why. When I came

back, the prime minister told me, "You have the right to open a private office because your salary is not enough."

MH: There has been a big change in style since your return from Singapore. The buildings look quite different.

MS: Since I came back to Cambodia, I have two different shoulders: one as a politician and one as an architect. It's a big challenge, because you don't forget that people know very well that you have two shoulders.

MH: How has Phnom Penh changed in recent years? My impression is that a lot of the old buildings are being demolished to make space for new ones. Can you tell us more about the latest urban developments in Phnom Penh?

MS: That's a very easy question. Change is a must, because everywhere you look the population is growing. This means that the country needs income. The country needs foreigners to invest here and to create jobs. Job creation and finding investors is very important—the country needs this to survive. Preserving the old buildings is only possible in places like Angkor Wat, or for colonial architecture, like they did in Singapore. But we all know that, sooner or later, this place where we are now, in the center of Phnom Penh, will no longer be a residential area but a commercial area, like in Kuala Lumpur, Singapore, or Bangkok. A home is where a family can have peace, quiet, and fresh air. This area used to be full of homes built by the French—there were small roads and small houses. Today we still have the same small roads, but the buildings are tall. Do you get the picture? It means that there is money here now! Take Boeung Keng Kang for

example: it started out in the 1960s as a residential district. But in 20 years, it will be a shopping district. And what will happen to the people? They will buy a house in the suburbs, like everywhere else.

MH: Are you saying that, basically, economic development in Phnom Penh is more important than preserving the old buildings?

MS: Well, what I am saying is that we love culture, and we love preserving the old buildings, but there is a conflict here. You cannot look at your lover and say, "Oh darling, I love you, but we don't have money, what shall we do?" "Oh dear, I don't know, just lock the door and let's go to sleep." And then you go to sleep and you die…hungry!

This conversation took place on January 29, February 3, and February 23, 2016, at Mam Sophana's office, in Phnom Penh.

01   Samdech Son Sann was a Cambodian politician and anti-communist resistance leader who served as the 22nd Prime Minister of Cambodia from 1967 to 1968 and as the President of the National Assembly in 1993.

NEW KHMER ARCHITECTURE

While studying architecture in Phnom Penh, where he gained his degree in 2012, Poum Measbandol began collecting old photos of Cambodian modernist buildings and sharing his finds with his friends on social media. There was still little research on Cambodian modernism done in the country, and this architectural legacy was gradually being destroyed. Witnessing this over the years motivated Poum Measbandol to engage with the topic more intensively and to record it in the form of computer drawings.

In his graphic series *New Khmer Architecture*, Poum Measbandol highlights characteristic elements of buildings designed by Vann Molyvann, Lu Ban Hap, Mam Sophana, Ung Krapum Phkar, Henri Chatel, Leroy & Mondet, Georg Lippsmeier, and others. The result is a great homage to the pioneers of Cambodian modernism, whose legacy is slowly but surely threatening to disappear.

Graphic essay: Poum Measbandol

Higher Technical Institute of Khmer-Soviet Friendship (now Institute of Technology of Cambodia), Phnom Penh, 1964. Design by unknown architects from the USSR.

Mam Sophana: Vocational school for employees of Électricité du Cambodge
(now National Technical Training Institute), Phnom Penh, ca. 1969.

**Leroy & Mondet: Auditorium at Sangkum Reastr
Niyum University, Phnom Penh, 1967.**

Ung Krapum Phkar: Royal University of Battambang,
Phnom Penh, 1968.

Georg Lippsmeier:
Sihanoukville
train station, 1969.

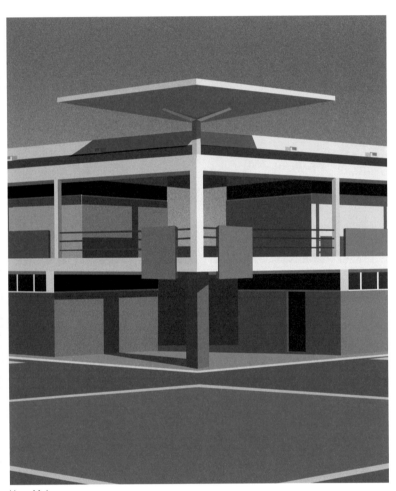

Vann Molyvann:
Water Sports Center,
Phnom Penh, 1964.

**Vann Molyvann: Preah Suramarit National
Theater, Phnom Penh, 1968.**

**Lu Ban Hap and Chhim Sun Fong:
Hotel Cambodiana, 1970/1990.**

Gordienko & Erchov: Hospital of Khmer-Soviet Friendship, Phnom Penh, 1960.

IDONESIA *Indonesia*

esia INDONESIA *Indo*

Indonesia INDONESIA

ONESIA *Indonesia* IN

Indonesia INDONESIA

ESIA *Indonesia* INDO

Indonesia INDONESI

sia INDONESIA *Indo*

Indonesia is the largest island nation in the world. With around 270 million inhabitants, the country has the fourth largest population globally, made up of over 30 ethnic groups. In terms of religion, about 87 percent of people profess Islam, with the rest divided between Christianity, Hinduism, Buddhism, Confucianism, and various animist religions. The capital of the Republic of Indonesia is Jakarta, located on the northwest coast of the island of Java. Over ten million people live in the city, which is the largest in Southeast Asia and the second largest urban agglomeration in the world, with a metropolitan region of around 30 million inhabitants.

At the beginning of the 16th century, the Portuguese arrived in the region with colonialist ambitions. In the following century, the Dutch East India Company took over large parts of today's Indonesia, which the Dutch state administered as a colony from 1799 until the middle of the 20th century. In 1942, during the Second World War, the Japanese army occupied the Dutch East Indies (now Indonesia). Two days after the Japanese surrendered, on August 15, 1945, Sukarno—the future first president of Indonesia—and his vice president, Mohammad Hatta, proclaimed independence from the Netherlands. This was followed by a war of independence, which eventually brought sovereignty to Indonesia in 1949, after the Dutch government had come under pressure from the international community. In 1963, Indonesia occupied the last Dutch colony of West Papua (in Indonesian referred to as Irian Jaya), against the declared will of the region's population, who would have preferred to become independent.

In the mid-1950s, President Sukarno called for a new architecture to reaffirm the country's independence and continue the construction of the nation. "Build Jakarta as beautiful as possible, build it as spectacularly as possible, so that this city, which has become the center of the struggle of the Indonesian people, will be an inspiration and a beacon for all of struggling humanity, and for all emerging forces." In contrast to the architectural styles of the colonial period, Sukarno's concept of "guided democracy" found expression in a radically modern, international style, in terms of both architecture and urban development.

After a military coup, General Suharto took power in 1965, ruling as dictator until 1998. Suharto's takeover went hand in hand with the mass murder of opposition members (1965–66), and ten years later with the occupation of the Portuguese colony of Timor-Leste (which became independent in 2002). Suharto's "New Order" brought Western-oriented economic policies, coupled with the idea of reinventing Indonesian tradition and culture to strengthen national identity.

Several important Indonesian architects studied in West Germany in the 1950s and '60s. Soejoedi Wirjoatmodjo and Han Awal graduated from the Technical University in West Berlin, returning to Jakarta in 1960, where they would design important buildings. Yusuf Bilyarta Mangunwijaya (also known as Romo Mangun) studied at RWTH Aachen University, moving back to Yogyakarta in 1966. He worked as an architect, writer, priest, and sociopolitical activist, and was awarded the Aga Khan Award in 1992 for his slum renovations along the Code River in Yogyakarta. Today, Indonesia is a presidential republic—the president is head of state as well as head of government, and also commander-in-chief of the armed forces. Joko Widodo has held the office of president since 2014. SB/MH/CH/EK

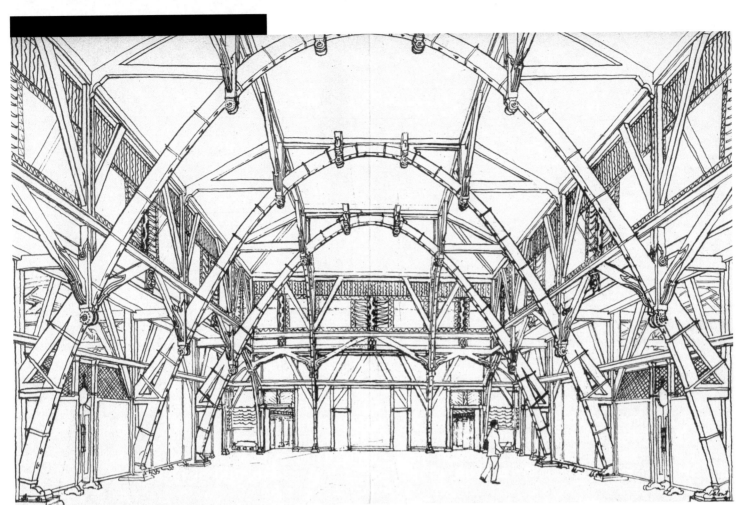

Text: Setiadi Sopandi

Perspective drawing of the
main hall of the West Building of
the Technical College (today:
Bandung Institute of Technology)
by Henri Maclaine Pont, 1919.

IMAGINATION AND NATIONAL IDENTITY
A brief history of modern architecture in Indonesia

Construction of the wooden
arches for the main hall
of the Technical College.

When I first set foot in architecture school in 1993, as a student, I was told to be "contextual" in anything I did. My professors however were unclear about what being contextual in Indonesia really meant.

Exterior view of the West Building of the Technical College, opened in 1920.

I was told that buildings should perform in the hot and humid tropical climate and that they should speak for the local culture, but the two things were hardly distinguished. The first architectural texts that I read in Indonesian were the papers compiled in the book *Menuju Arsitektur Indonesia* (Towards Indonesian Architecture), presented at the national congress of the Indonesian Institute of Architects in 1982.[01] The book was an attempt to formulate the foundational principles of a truly Indonesian architectural style. Heavily injected with moral and religious values, more than half of the papers focused on the importance of learning from traditional building cultures and customs. They often referred to vernacular buildings from villages located on remote islands or famous archaeological sites, but rather then analyzing their technological elements or typological advancements, they simply told stories about the semantic value of these architectures. I studied in Bandung, a city hosting a large number of early 20th-century modernist buildings from the colonial era. Nevertheless, I only learned about these buildings from illegal copies of a 1990 Dutch catalog titled *Architectuur & Stedebouw In Indonesie, 1870–1970* (Architecture & Urbanism in Indonesia, 1870–1970), by the Dutch researcher Huib Akihary.[02] I did not understand most of the text because it was in Dutch, but I could get an idea of the main architectural features of these buildings. Among them were streamlined cubist villas with flat roofs, as well as buildings inspired by vernacular forms. For the first time, I understood that there is a tendency among Indonesian architects to read almost every architectural phenomenon as a dichotomy of two opposing categories. At one end are the buildings that fall into the semantic category of modern, colonial, international, Western, and global, while at the other end are the buildings that qualify as traditional, vernacular, local, and Eastern. The former are often built with materials such as steel, glass, and reinforced concrete; they are white-washed, clean-looking, and flat-roofed. The latter feature elements built with organic materials and are romantic, charming, and rigorously pitched-roofed. A brief journey through the architectural history of modern Indonesia, from colonial times until today, will help adjust the focus on this dichotomy.

Dutch architects and engineers like Hendrik Petrus Berlage, Henri Maclaine Pont, and Thomas Karsten were deeply fascinated by "indigenous" architecture in the Dutch East Indies. Maclaine Pont, inspired by the works of Gottfried Semper and Viollet-le-Duc, did extensive research on Indonesian architectural and structural systems. In his writings, Maclaine Pont talks about an "Indies Gothic" style,[03] which he implemented himself in one his best-known works: the hall of the Technische Hogeschool (Technical University) in Bandung, whose roof structure is supported by very sophisticated hand-crafted laminated wood arches. In his view, the great advancements of Javanese architecture lay in the versatility of spatial layouts and in the subtle-yet-advanced tectonics. Thomas Karsten was one of the key founding members of the Java Instituut, a scientific-cultural institute established in 1919 to promote the preservation and revitalization of Javanese culture. In the 1930s, on behalf of the Java Instituut, he designed the Sobokartti, a modern theater dedicated to developing and modernizing Javanese performing arts. The building features a traditional *joglo,* a two-tiered roof type with a gap between the tiers allowing light and natural airflow through the space. The audience is distributed over balconies on three sides, facing the performance ground in the middle, much like in a Western auditorium. Despite their being unquestionably modern architects, both Karsten and Maclaine Pont believed the *pendopo*—the traditional Javanese portico structure—to be of highly refined technical and artistic value, and they were fascinated by the symbolism it embodied in the Hindu-Buddhist tradition.

Charles Prosper Wolff Schoemaker, on the other hand, was one of the most severe critics of such romantic views on Javanese vernacular architecture. He scorned the fascination with Javanese traditional typologies, calling its proponents "Pendopo maniacs."[04] Schoemaker was a pioneering figure of Dutch colonial modernist style in Indonesia and his critical position towards vernacular architecture also stemmed from his personal frustration with the European obsession for the exotic, which at the time materialized in ethically

Left
Postcard depicting the
Dutch Pavilion by Pieter
Adriaan Jacobus
Moojen at the Paris Colonial
Exposition, 1931.

Below
1:1 reproduction of a traditional Minangkabau
house from West Sumatra at
the International Colonial
and Export Exhibition
(Internationale Koloniale en
Uitvoerhandel
Tentoonstelling) in
Amsterdam, 1883.

EXPOSITION COLONIALE INTERNATIONALE — PARIS 1931

324 PAVILLON DES PAYS-BAS — FAÇADE PRINCIPALE

Moojen et Zweedijk, Archs.

Photo: Pieter Oosterhuis

and aesthetically questionable colonial expositions, such as the grand International Colonial and Export Exhibition of Amsterdam (1883) and the Colonial Exposition of Paris (1931). The former included a display of hundreds of models of vernacular Asian buildings from all throughout the colonies, as well as a 1:1 reproduction of a "native settlement" with real people performing ordinary tasks with their domestic animals. At the latter exposition in Paris, a Dutch pavilion, designed by Pieter Adriaan Jacobus Moojen, consisted of a pastiche of various architectural elements from all over the Dutch East Indies presented as a mere object of curiosity, rather than for their intrinsic architectural quality.

A pestilence outbreak in the 1920s starting from a few Eastern Javanese towns marked a sharp shift in the colonialist approach towards vernacular Indonesian architecture. Following the outbreak, the colonial government launched a massive campaign for the "rationalization of the native settlements" in several Javanese cities, indicating as the culprit the rats nesting in unsanitary and unruly houses built of bamboo and other organic materials. The sanitation projects that followed contributed to the dichotomy between the vernacular and the modern, widening the formal and technological gap between the settlements of the ruled and those of the rulers. To this day, this opposition

unified Indonesian state and many intellectuals used their influence to advocate for the nation's integrity. The renowned poet Sutan Takdir Alisjahbana, for example, promoted Bahasa Indonesia (a standardized variety of Malay) as a modern lingua franca for the multilingual archipelago, arguing that it was inevitable that "countless old Indonesian words have been pushed into the background or been eliminated" because the concepts and the circumstances that surrounded them no longer corresponded to "substantial reality."[05] Sukarno himself—the leader of the nationalist independence movement and first president of Indonesia—was trained as a civil engineer and practiced as an architect under Schoemaker. Sukarno was well aware of the power of architecture to inspire the soul of a young nation and so he commissioned Friedrich Silaban, his favorite architect, to design the monumental public buildings of the 1950s and 1960s which were to become the symbols of the new Indonesian state. Silaban won three consecutive competitions in the mid-1950s with his designs for the National Monument—ultimately not realized because deemed too expensive—the Bank of Indonesia headquarters, and the National Mosque, all located in the former Koningsplein, the Dutch Royal Square that after independence was renamed Medan Merdeka (Independence Square). In his designs, Silaban shunned regional and ethnic expressions and

Bubonic plague awareness exhibition at a night market in Klaten, Central Java, 1926–29.

Courtesy Nationaal Museum van Wereldculturen, Amsterdam

has not been solved and we are still debating Indonesian architectural styles within the framework of this colonialist opposition.

Fast forward to the early independence years, after 1945, when the Indonesian elites started to look suspiciously at regional cultural expressions in the archipelago. The Indonesian political system in the 1950s and 1960s was fragile, and concerns about complete territorial disintegration were very valid. Local cultural expressions were often seen as defiant of the elite's nationalist aspirations towards a solidly

opted for a clean, modernist architectural language, which he found more suitable as an expression of national identity in the newly independent Indonesian state. The bank and the mosque are dressed in a modernist fashion without any reference to regional building tradition. At the same time, Silaban claimed it was important for Indonesian architects to examine the "soul" of tropical architecture and to express it in their designs.[06] His designs are not out of context, on the contrary, from a typological and technological perspective they feature

Friedrich Silaban:
Bank Indonesia,
Jakarta, 1958–63.

elements that are suited to the Indonesian context, such as porticos, galleries, layered brise-soleils, and carefully calculated structural elements, whose depth offers shelter from extreme tropical weather conditions.

The fourth Asian Games, hosted by Indonesia in 1962, offered a second opportunity for Sukarno to celebrate modern architecture as an instrument of nation-building, albeit often under the economic influence of foreign powers. The games triggered the development of large infrastructures in Jakarta and the construction of the vast Gelora Bung Karno sports complex, which was built halfway between Jakarta and the satellite town of Kebajoran Baroe, merging the two into one metropolitan area along Thamrin-Sudirman Road. The original complex comprised six iconic buildings: the monumental main stadium, which could host up to 150,000 spectators, as well as the sports palace, the athletics stadium, the tennis stadium, and the aquatic center. The Gelora Bung Karno complex—partly funded by a loan from the USSR—was designed by a team of engineers and architects under

the supervision of the Soviet all-unions association Technoexport, an agency of the Soviet Ministry of Foreign Trade in charge of providing industrial and technical assistance to commercial partners of the USSR. Similarly, the iconic Hotel Indonesia, which was originally built to host the athletes during the games, was funded by the Japanese war reparations scheme and designed by the American-Danish architect Abel Sorensen. President Sukarno's fiery speeches amplified the patriotic and nationalist scope of these projects, whose architecture came to embody values of anti-colonialism, progress, and internationalism, bringing Indonesia on equal footing with "first world countries." In 1963, a year after the Asian Games, the sports complex hosted the first Games of the New Emerging Forces (GANEFO), an event initiated by Sukarno as a diplomatic strategy to establish Indonesia's position on the global stage and promote solidarity between emerging economic powers, mostly newly independent socialist nations. The games were conceived as a kind of anti-Olympics, to counter the economic and cultural hegemony of former imperialist

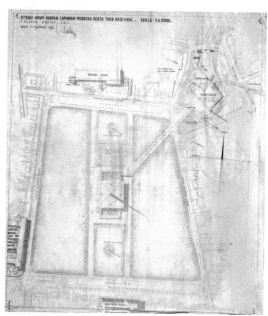

Site plan of Merdeka Square
in Jakarta, planned by
Friedrich Silaban. With Istiqlal
Mosque at the top right,
National Monument in the
middle, and Bank Indonesia
(lower left, not visible), 1961.

Above
Preliminary design by
Friedrich Silaban for
the Monumen Nasional
(National Monument)
in Jakarta, 1961.

Below
Friedrich Silaban:
Istiqlal Mosque, Jakarta,
1961–78.

From: "GANEFO Opens New Era in World Sports," in *Chinese Sports Delegation in Djakarta* (Beijing: People's Sports Press, 1964).

Above
The main stadium of the
Gelora Bung Karno Sports
Complex, built in 1962 for
the Asian Games in Jakarta.

Left
Historic postcard of Hotel
Indonesia, designed
by American-Danish
architect Abel Sorensen in
1962.

nations. The second edition was going to take place in Cairo but fell through. The Games only took place a second time, in 1966, in a more modest Asia-only edition, in Phnom Penh.

Despite this failure, Sukarno's diplomatic and architectural efforts continued: in 1964, he called a competition for a new congress hall to be realized behind the stadium. This was meant to host the Conference of the New Emerging Forces (CONEFO), a rival organization to the UN envisioned by Sukarno himself. A sleek modernist shell-dome design by the young architect Soejoedi Wirjoatmodjo was selected. But the idea of CONEFO was abandoned in 1965, following an attempted coup and subsequent uprisings that shook the country's entire political system, leading to the deposition of Sukarno in 1966 and to the establishment of the "New Order"—the authoritarian, anti-communist government of General Suharto that lasted for 30 years. Nevertheless, construction works were continued and the building, which now hosts the main parliament assembly of the Indonesian State, was completed in 1968.

In the mid-1970s, the Suharto regime defined Indonesian culture as "a creation, effort, and intent of the Indonesian people derived from the integration of the finest of old and original cultures,"[07] but instead of celebrating all the wide-ranging cultures that are present across the archipelago, Suharto very carefully selected only the most politically and economically influential ethnic groups as the representatives of each administrative area, absorbing local minorities into the dominant groups. During the oil-boom of the 1970s, when Indonesia embarked on a massive campaign to promote international tourism, vernacular architectural traditions became an important factor in attracting visitors fascinated by ancient temples and traditional villages. Resort hotels started to appear across the country, offering the experience of living inside vernacular buildings. This tendency went amplifying over the years with the rise of cheap international travel, especially after the Asian financial crisis of the late 1990s. The financial crisis also marked the end of Suharto and the beginning of a series of decentralization policies that granted more and more power to provincial and municipal governments. The 34 provincial administrations began an ongoing style war, each one competing to express their individual regional identities through the design of local public, administrative, and religious buildings. In this new political and cultural context, the diametrical opposition between the categories of Western, modern, international, and technological versus Eastern, traditional, regional, and vernacular is recurrently deployed at will to serve the economic and political interests of the powerful, rather than for pursuing a unified national Indonesian architectural identity.

In the 1990s, a generalized lack of pedagogical coherence and the recurrence of arbitrary dogmatic values within the architecture curriculum were the cause of much discontent among students and young architects. Young Indonesian architects felt the need to free themselves from the straightjacket idea of a national or regional style. In 1995, an old guard of academics known as Lembaga Sejarah Arsitektur Indonesia (Institute of Indonesian Architectural History) responded with a symposium on "how to place Indonesian young architects in the history of modern Indonesian architecture."[08] One of the main topics was how to convince young architects to be accountable for upholding values of national identity in their work. I attended the event as a third-year student. It was then that I realized that the Indonesian architectural discourse was not about "context" as I had understood it until then—the physical, environmental, and social surroundings of a building. It was about something that was largely imaginary, something that was more often a cultural construct rather than an objective condition.

This is by no means a uniquely Indonesian problem; on the contrary, architectural discourse has always been used as a tool to define national identities, both in Asia and elsewhere. The drawing of territorial lines often follows the trails of building traditions, of delicate proportion systems, craftsmanship, ornaments, styles, and the like; but within this narrative the complexity of architecture is reduced to a mere representational function. Identities, differences, symbols, and meanings, like audio feedback, produce echoes and noises that are in fact of no relevance to the practice. But as we develop an obsession with categorizing almost everything into either "modern" or "traditional," the topics of social, environmental, and technological progress seem to have gone lost in contemporary Indonesian architectural discourse.

01 Eko Budihardjo ed., *Menuju Arsitektur Indonesia* (Bandung: Alumni, 1993).

02 Huib Akihary, *Architectuur & Stedebouw In Indonesie, 1870–1970* (Zutphen: De Walburg Pers, 1990).

03 Maclaine Pont used the term "Indian Gothic" in documents for patent applications in the late 1940s. In English translations it became "Indies Gothic" (Indian in the plural), and "Indonesian Gothic," the former translation being preferred by Indonesians, as it refers to the colonial conditions.

04 Charles P. Wolff Schoemaker, "Kunst en Wetenschap Indonesische Bouwkunst," *Bataviaasche Nieuwsblad* (October 20, 1922).

05 Sutan Takdir Alisjahbana, *Indonesia; Social and Cultural Revolution* (Oxford: Oxford University Press, 1966), 67.

06 Friedrich Silaban, "Idealisme Arsitektur dan Kenyataannya di Indonesia," The Second National Congress of the Indonesian Institute of Architects, Yogyakarta, December 3, 1982.

07 The Indonesian National Parliament issued a definition of "Indonesian national culture" in the 1998 legislative resolution (TAP MPR No II, 1998) based on a concept developed by Indonesian experts, such as scholar Ki Hajar Dewantoro and anthropologist Koentjaraningrat.

08 The event by Lembaga Sejarah Arsitektur Indonesia was officially called *Lokakarya Nasional Pengajaran Sejarah Arsitektur* (National Workshop on Architectural History Teaching) and was held in 1995 at Universitas Kristen Petra in Surabaya.

ISTIQLAL MOSQUE
Friedrich Silaban

Photos: © Moritz Henning

View into the courtyard of Istiqlal Mosque, Jakarta. With the tall facade pillars (left) and arcades (right).

The main prayer hall is surrounded by four levels of galleries.

Text: Setiadi Sopandi

In 1953, the government of the Republic of Indonesia launched a competition for the design of a new national mosque in Jakarta. As a symbol of postcolonial national identity, the project was considered of the utmost importance. Its site would be the northeast corner of Merdeka Square, designated by President Sukarno to be the epicenter of the capital city. Of the 27 entries, Friedrich Silaban's modernist design won the competition, but the realization of his colossal vision proved more difficult than expected. The state's funds were limited and construction works dragged on for years. The colossal scale of the project required enormous amounts of steel and concrete, a supply that was partly imported from abroad, but which also greatly stimulated the emergence of domestic production. Although the lack of local technical

expertise posed a challenge at the time, Istiqlal Mosque was nevertheless constructed with the most up-to-date technology. The prayer hall—a huge space lined with galleries running over four levels—is topped by a breathtaking reinforced concrete dome, the casting of which required the assembly of a complex polyhedron steel-frame structure built with the help of steel pipes and ball joints manufactured in West Germany. Because religious protocol mandates that the prayer hall be oriented towards the Qibla— slightly off the axis of Merdeka Square—Silaban rotated the mosque's inner courtyard, known as a *sahn,* by 20 degrees to have the colonnade facing directly onto the National Monument, in the middle of the square. Silaban conceived the sahn of the Istiqlal Mosque as an intimate patio offering worshipers refuge

from the tropical rain and scorching sun between its slim, deep rectangular columns. Similarly proportioned, but four times as tall, the majestic columns on the main facade rise up uninterrupted over the whole height of the building, conveying a severe sense of monumentality. Frequented daily by hundreds of people and often used as the backdrop for official state visits, the semantic power of Silaban's design remains unchallenged and makes the Istiqlal Mosque a highly charged national symbol projecting Sukarno's original vision for Indonesia as a unitary, modern, independent state, both nationally and internationally.

MONUMEN N

R. M. Soedarsono

ASIONAL

Text: Setiadi Sopandi

A competition for a new national monument to rise in the middle of Jakarta's Merdeka Square (Independence Square)—formerly Koningsplein (King's Square) during Dutch colonial rule—was announced by President Sukarno in 1955. At that time, the area was surrounded by rows of villas belonging to European dignitaries who sought to avoid the hustle and bustle of the old town of Batavia, which was full of mosquitoes and considered unsanitary. Friedrich Silaban— who had already designed both the square itself and the Istiqlal Mosque there—was awarded first prize in the competition. His proposal, however, left Sukarno and the committee uneasy about its suitability to represent the nation, as well as about its economic feasibility. By the end of the 1950s, while the government's attention was consumed elsewhere and public resources were running low, Silaban's design had still not been realized. Around 1961, after a long and troubled process, a new, less ambitious but radically modern design by R. M. Soedarsono was selected. This consisted of an obelisk-like tower emerging from a pyramid-like podium that has been turned upside-down, with its point sunk into the ground. Covered in gold foil, the tip of the obelisk resembles a huge flame, which rises 115 meters high. Inside the podium are the Indonesian National History Museum and the Hall of Independence, which host respectively a collection of 51 dioramas depicting key events in Indonesian history, and a collection of relics commemorating the country's struggles for independence.

This iconic monument is amicably referred to as "Monas." For decades Monas and Merdeka Square were the objects of continuous restructuring. The square's symbolic function as the epicenter of the nation, however, often collides with that of a public space serving a city of ten million people. Highly charged with political meaning, Merdeka Square is where rallies and demonstrations typically take place. The number of participants at such events are like a barometer, accurately measuring levels of political unrest in the country. In 2002, the former Governor of Jakarta, Sutiyoso, ordered that Monas be enclosed within a fence, in order to better control the vast square and ward off illegal street vendors. As a result, Merdeka Square and Monas today remain highly contested places that attract hundreds of thousands of visitors every year but are not freely accessible as truly open public spaces.

© Moritz Henning

VISUALIZATION OF NATIONAL HISTORY FROM, BY, AND FOR WHOM?

Text: Hyphen —

On the outside, the National Monument of Indonesia (Monumen Nasional, abbreviated as Monas) in Jakarta is a gold-topped obelisk surrounded by an incredibly vast, green, lush park. Most of the park area is open for visitors. The impression we get from the exterior of this monumental structure is that it is majestic yet convivial and open to everyone.

Inside the monument is the Monas museum, which contains 51 dome-covered dioramas narrating the history of the Indonesian struggle going back to prehistoric times. Similar to dioramas used in other museums on Java, these dioramas present a reconstruction of past events, using figurines and objects with a backdrop depicting the surrounding landscape, be it outside in nature, indoors, or cityscapes.

The dioramas at the Monas museum were created by one of Indonesia's most famous sculptors, Edhi Sunarso. Sukarno, the first president of the newly independent Republic of Indonesia, commissioned him in the early 1960s to develop hundreds of dioramas in order to summarize and relate the history of Indonesia to the public. In 1965, General Haji Mohamed Suharto took over control of the government, and in 1968 he was named the second president of the Republic of Indonesia. Under President Suharto, the construction of this symbolic and eminent monument of the Indonesian nation continued.

In July 1966, amidst the turmoil of massive political shifts, Edhi Sunarso was summoned to Jakarta to oversee the construction of Monas. At the time, a number of dioramas had already been installed in the museum. The call to Jakarta was an indication that the installation of dioramas was to continue, with Edhi still overseeing the process. The remaining few were being completed by Edhi at his studio in Yogyakarta together with his students from ASRI (Fine Arts Academy of Indonesia). However, the new commissioner ordered that changes be made to the narratives told by the dioramas. You might wonder: whose version of history do the dioramas tell? Can you change history?

Nearly ten years later, in 1977, the Monas museum finally opened to the public. As part of the project *From, by, and for whom?* audio guides were produced which enable visitors to immerse themselves in the museum's dioramas while listening to alternative versions of the historical events they depict.

Excerpted and adapted from Hyphen –'s introductory curatorial text for the exhibition Contested Modernities.

The audio guides were produced as part of the project From, by, and for whom? *curated by Hyphen —, initiated by Gudskul: Contemporary Art Collective and Ecosystem Studies, and commissioned by Encounters with Southeast Asian Modernism. The original archive exhibition* Visualization of National History, *held at Gudskul in 2019, investigated the diorama-making process of Indonesia's eminent national sculptor Edhi Sunarso. The workshop* (Re)Producing Fear and Joy, *conducted by Grace Samboh with lectures from Vera Mey and Jati Andito, explored the role and function of historical dioramas, our contemporary perception of them, and the various forms of critical storytelling that may be derived from them.*

In 2021, Visualization of National History (2) *will be presented as part of* Contested Modernities *in Berlin. The exhibition was created in collaboration with Akmalia Rizqita, Alghorie (Arie Syariefuddin), Ary "Jimged" Sendy, Grace Samboh, Nissal Nur Afryansah (Lindung), Rachel K. Surijata, and Ratna Mufida. Hyphen – thanks Griya Seni Hj. Kustiyah and Edhi Sunarso in Yogyakarta for their invaluable support.*

All photos: © Christian Hiller

Gusmarian (Acong): The Imam Bonjol War, 1821–37.

Laksmi Lilu Herlambang: Raden Adjeng Kartini, 1879–1904,
Indonesian women's rights activist.

Duta Adipati: Internment camp in Digul, where rebels from the communist
insurrection of 1926–27 were imprisoned.

Ratih PN Ardianti: The role of the Roman Catholic Church
in nation-building efforts in Indonesia.

Jennifer Augusta (Sol Cai): Decree of March 11, 1996.

Maria Zevonia Fernandez Vieira and Ratna Mufida:
Integration of East Timor, 1976.

Indonesia becomes
a member of the
United Nations,
September 28, 1950.

Pancasila State
Doctrine prevails,
October 1, 1965.

A NEW TROPICAL ARCHITECTURE

Since its founding in 2001, Indonesia-based architectural practice d-associates has drawn widespread acclaim for projects such as the Tamarind House in South Jakarta and the DRA House in Bali. In preparation for the 2018 Asian Games, the architects were commissioned with the renovation of the Gelora Bung Karno Sports Complex in Jakarta, which was originally commissioned by President Sukarno for the 1962 Asian Games. The work of d-associates is characterized by the use of a climate-sensitive, tropical language that reflects the sensibilities of a new generation of Indonesian architects that has emerged on the global scene since the 2010s.

Photos, unless otherwise stated: © Davy Linggar

Built in 1962 for the Asian Games, the Gelora Bung Karno Sports Complex in Jakarta underwent a major overhaul in 2018. Participating architects included d-associates as well as Andra Matin, Boy Bhirawa, Adi Purnomo, Deddy Wahjudi, Bambang Wicaksono, and Adjie Negara.

Gregorius Yolodi and Maria Rosantina, partners of the Jakarta-based architects d-associates, in conversation with Moritz Henning and Christian Hiller

Retrofitted ticket booths on the ground floor were removed to restore accessibility. A new lighting concept was implemented and new seating was added to the main stadium. Gregorius Yolodi of d-associates was responsible for the renovation of the stadium.

MORITZ HENNING: Gregorius, you founded d-associates in 2001, at the age of 27. Maria joined soon after. What was it like for young architects in Jakarta in the early 2000s?

GREGORIUS YOLODI: I graduated in 1998. The economic situation was very bad back then. After the Asian financial crisis of 1997, the entire economic system was on the brink of collapse. There weren't many career opportunities at the time. When I had nothing to do, I would go to the shopping mall, sit in the food hall and draw, hoping that someone would pass by and say, "Oh, you are an architect! Do you want to design my house?" It never happened, of course [laughs]. The mall was next to the Gelora Bung Karno Sports Complex, so in the afternoon sometimes I went jogging there. One day at the mall, I ran into a friend. He asked me if I wanted to set up an interior design firm together. I said, "Yes, let's do it." That's how it all started. Our first jobs were for a few wealthy clients, the kind who would hire an architect to decorate their home but who want to have a say in every aspect of the design. At some point I told my friend, "Listen, I cannot only do interior design, because my heart is calling for architecture."

In the early 2000s, I started working on my own projects and founded d-associates in 2001.

MARIA ROSANTINA: I studied architecture at the Parahyangan Catholic University in Bandung, like Gregorius. At the time, many architecture practices had to close because, after the crisis, there wasn't much work. After graduating I tried to set up my own practice with some friends, but it didn't last long, which motivated me to work with Gregorius.

GY: Between 2000 and 2002 we had a few interesting projects. In 2003 I invited Maria to join the practice as a partner. We started

A new cantilevered roof made of reinforced concrete was installed over the stands in the athletics stadium.

out with quite modest projects, like renovations of apartments and restaurants, but eventually we took on bigger jobs. Who would have imagined that one day we would win the competition to renovate the very same sports complex where I used to go jogging 15 years before?

MR: The first major project by d-associates was the design of a new highway rest area in Central Java, which won the 2008 Indonesian Institute of Architects (IAI) Prize. That was the turning point for us.

CHRISTIAN HILLER:

Let's come back to the Gelora Bung Karno Sports Complex. Being involved with its renovation and redesign is one of your newest and biggest projects. Can you tell us more about the history of the complex?

GY: The complex was designed in 1959, when Jakarta bid to host the 1962 Asian Games at the behest of president Sukarno. It was a huge political move and a crucial aspect of Sukarno's national and international agenda. He wanted to use the Games to present Indonesia as a rising power, but the state treasury was not in a good shape to host them. Sukarno sought financial and technical aid from the Soviet Union because Indonesia did not have the technical expertise to build a world-class Olympic stadium. Friederich Silaban, Sukarno's favorite architect, helped the responsible minister to choose the site, but the design and build were assigned to a team of Soviet architects and engineers. The area had been designated to become a new urban center, located between the old Dutch colonial town in the north and Kebayoran, a satellite town south of Jakarta, which is now fully integrated into the city. To realize the complex, they had to relocate a huge number of residents further south. Along the new north-south axis, a new global business

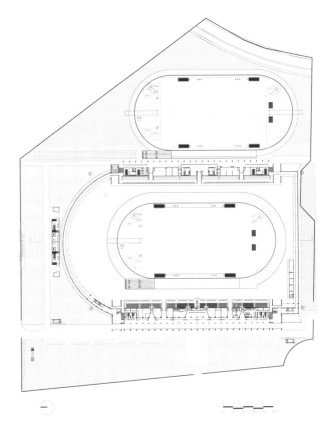

Athletics stadium, floor plan of the ground floor zone.
© d-associates

and governmental district emerged, with embassies, banks, hotels, and so on. The famous Hotel Indonesia was designed in a monumental modernist style to impress the international Olympic delegations and to project an image of prestige to the world.

MR: This was all part of Sukarno's grandiose cultural and political program. But now, the athletes' village, located right next to the complex, is being demolished, and will be replaced by a shopping mall.

CH: The sports complex has had various names over the years. Can you explain why and when the name changed?

MR: Its first name was simply the Asian Games Complex. In 1984, in an attempt to erase the memory of the Asian Games and the glory attached to Sukarno's name, President Suharto changed the name into the more neutral Gelanggang Olahraga Senayan [Senayan Sports Complex]— Senayan is the name of the area. In 2000, President Abdurrahman Wahid changed the name again, to Gelanggang Olahraga Bung Karno (Comerade Karno Sports Complex), in honor of Sukarno, who is considered the founding father of the modern Indonesian state.

CH: As the host for the Asian Games in 2018, why did Jakarta choose to renovate the old stadium instead of building a new one? Governments usually like to have new facilities built for international games as a kind of monument to themselves. Do you think the decision was politically motivated?

GY: I think it was rather an economical choice: the sports complex was already there and it was still suitable for hosting the Games, and so they figured it would be best to invest the

money into renovating the old complex, rather than building a new one that would be abandoned after the Games. The city of Palembang, on the island of Sumatra, which cohosted the games together with Jakarta, also had a large preexisting stadium.

MH: I think this was a very sensible decision, compared to what Sukarno did in 1962, and what many countries still do today. In 1963, in Phnom Penh, they built a huge stadium that was far too big and expensive for a small country like Cambodia. At the time, the idea was to use architecture as way to say, "Look at us, we are an up-and-coming country; we are our own masters; we are no longer a colony."

GY: The wish of the current president, Joko Widodo, was that the Gelora Bung Karno Complex will become a better public space, a place that Indonesian people can actually use and be proud of.

CH: This collective sense of

pride for the postcolonial heritage appeared to be very much alive during our visit to Jakarta in 2019. After the end of Suharto's New Order regime (1966–98), people seemed to recall the euphoria of the period of independence and decolonialization, and perhaps the wish to preserve and revive the architecture from this time is related to that. This is not always the case in other Southeast Asian countries. Maybe this is why Widodo decided to renovate the old stadium: to bring back that sense of euphoria from the period of independence and to inspire new generations who didn't experience it personally.

MH: Tell us more about your design for the main stadium.

GY: You have to keep in mind that the entire Gelora Bung Karno complex is a heritage site, and so we were not allowed to build any new structures, with the exception of the baseball stadium. Our first design idea for the main stadium was to add new ramps on the

outside to make the upper floors more accessible, because at the moment there are only two elevators. The design for the ramps had already been approved by the board of directors of the complex and by the Olympic Committee, but the heritage conservation board firmly opposed it. Their argument went along the lines of: "If you want it to be more accessible, then make a new building." This conservative approach prevailed and so I had to proceed with a more discreet design to make the building more functional, but without changing the look too much. In previous years, a lot of elements were added that clashed with the original design. For example, the ground-floor gallery had been completely obstructed by too many box offices. We removed them to restore the original sense of openness, accessibility, and clarity. We also developed a new lighting concept that is carefully tailored to the architecture, to enhance the beauty of the structure. And

The roof of the athletics stadium is supported by reinforced concrete columns, which also serve to structure the outdoor area on the ground floor.

finally, we put in new seats, as requested by the Olympic committee; they asked for individually numbered seats. Before, there were benches, making it impossible to accurately measure the stadium's capacity, which fluctuated between 95,000 and 100,000, depending on how close people sat next to each other. For safety reasons, the heritage board allowed us to change the seats. The new ones are in the colors of the Indonesian flag—white and red—but instead of using the classic stripes, we wanted to have a delicate and dynamic red whorl going all around the tribunes.

MH: Maria, you designed an additional roof above the tribunes of the athletics stadium, as well as the new baseball stadium, which is the only new building realized for the 2018 games. I was amazed at how your interventions fit so well into the original complex. They are bold designs but they speak the same rationalist architectural language of the original buildings. What were the main ideas behind them?

MR: The main idea was to create a timeless architecture that respects the heritage site. The baseball stadium is relatively small, with only 1,500 seats, and with an additional 1,000 temporary seats just for the Games. I decided on a very linear, horizontal structure, with low tribunes that gently adapt to the old complex. The second idea was to make it a tropical stadium. It has to provide plenty of shade, but it also has to allow in natural light and air, which is achieved by a textured skin made of perforated splayed concrete tiles. The stepped profile of the canopy is my personal reinterpretation of the original modernist architecture.

CH: Jakarta is a very chaotic city. You have high-rises everywhere

and multilevel motorways running through the entire city, and there is hardly any public space. The Gelora Bung Karno complex is one of the few large public spaces in the city. Entering it is like stepping into another world entirely. Everything is green and quiet, and there are people everywhere enjoying themselves. Not only is the complex for sports but also for music festivals and other events. Was it so popular before the renovation as well?

GY: Before, each of the buildings was enclosed by a fence, protected by security guards, and accessible only by car. The complex was divided into compounds, each managed by a different sport association with its own facilities for athletes and its own offices. It was a mess. It did not feel like a place for people to spend their leisure time. They went there either because they were a member of

one of the sport associations or because they had to attend an event. The first thing we did when we started working on the master plan was very simple: we removed as many fences as possible. Then we designed a pedestrian-friendly landscape that connects all the buildings with one another, so people can simply stroll through the complex, not just go to a sports event. The main goal was to bring people in. Most sports complexes cannot sustain themselves only with sports events; they need to offer a wider variety of leisure-time uses. Take, for example, the aquatics center designed by Andra Matin: it is always very busy; kids love it, they are always in the pools, jumping off the platforms. Everyone likes to swim, but not everyone plays baseball or basketball, or does athletics. These buildings need to have a more flexible program in

The baseball stadium, designed by Maria Rosantina, is the only entirely new building added as part of the renovation.

order to finance themselves. They have to host things like concerts and other public events.

MR: One important aspect was that every architect who worked on the individual buildings agreed to have built-in gates, so that access controls start at the buildings themselves. For example, you can walk all the way up to the entrance of the main stadium and only need to pass a gate when you enter the actual building. This way, the space around the stadium is freely accessible to everyone and you can walk from one building to the other, moving through a landscaped park with plenty of seats and small leisure areas to linger and rest.

GY: This is the first time that Jakarta has 1,000 or more hectares of open public space right in the middle of the city.

MH: Why aren't there more parks like the Gelora Bung Karno complex in other parts of the city?

GY: That's our question as well! The understanding of public space is very different here to what you have in Europe. It's evident even in the terminology that the government uses: here green spaces are called "gardens," that is to say, a green space without activities. When you say "garden" you think of something very different than when you say "park." Urban planning here is not human-oriented, it is real estate-oriented. The goal is never to make a space for people to enjoy it; it is "development," whatever that means. You have buildings, you have roads, and in between you have gardens. But the gardens are not for the people, they have no facilities. Gelora Bung Karno attracts 15,000 to 20,000 people every weekend. People are starting to realize that they can use it in different ways. This is something that was simply not available before.

Jakarta is completely car-oriented. The bigger the roads are, the less space you have left for people, and if you don't give space to people, people will not use it—it's as simple as that. First you have to provide a good public space, and then the space will determine the behavior. So, to answer your question: It's not that there is no demand for public space, it's just that, until now, there was no political will to provide more public space, and so people learned to live without it.

MH: What kind of impact did the renovation of the Gelora Bung Karno complex have on people's understanding of modernist architecture in general? How do people, and architects, relate to modernist buildings from the postcolonial era? Do you use them as a reference in your work?

GY: I don't think that "postcolonial" is a category that many architects are interested in. We admire the work of Friederich Silaban and respect the iconic

View inside the baseball stadium. The perforated facade of concrete blocks forms an intermediate climatic layer that provides shade while allowing in air and natural light.

modernist buildings of the post-independence era, but I don't think that many architects are necessarily using them as references in their work. There are many different ways in which one can relate to the modernist heritage. One way is to historicize it, which is to treat it merely as a historical style: the architectural expression of a given moment that is recorded in history as such. Another way is to politicize it, to reference it with a specific political agenda in mind. The Gelora Bung Karno complex is a post-colonial architecture that speaks a completely different language than, let's say, the architecture of

Friederich Silaban. The structure of the stadium is itself the architecture. It is brutal. It's as pure and rational as it gets. This stadium could be anywhere. It speaks the global language of the Cold War era. The architecture of Silaban, on the other hand, speaks the language of Indonesian national identity. Yet another way to relate to the modernist architectural heritage is to look at it through the category of tropicality, which is a geographical and climatic category. I think this is how most Indonesian architects relate to modernist architecture nowadays: we try to find a language that combines the tropical vernacular

with today's programs and materials—something that Silaban himself did in the years after independence. Silaban is not a direct reference, though we are part of the same tradition, in a way: we use new technologies, we build with modern materials like glass and concrete, but instead of copying and pasting a building that was designed somewhere else, we design it in a way that makes sense for the tropical context. In this way, we are defining a truly new tropical architecture.

Above
The new roof of the aquatics center, designed by Andra Matin, is an open steel truss, covered on the inside with a perforated membrane.

Left
The diving tower of the aquatics center.

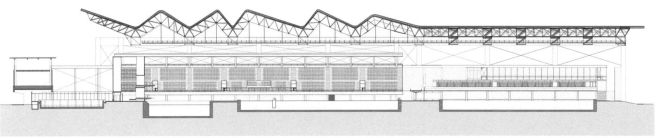

Section of the aquatics center with its new folding roof.

ARCH+
features

ruangrupa, Total Football, and the Modern Project

'LUMBUNG'
Lumbung is the Indonesian word for
a collectively governed 'rice-barn'
where harvest surplus of farmers
is share for common good.
It serves community's well being
on longer term through shared
resources and mutual care.

And it's
organised   Wooden
through a set   Structure
of values, collective rituals and
organizational principles.

Sasak Trib   Lumbun

WE DON'T HAVE ANY MESSAGE TODAY

FARID RAKUN is one of the core team members of the Indonesian collective **ruangrupa,** which will curate DOCUMENTA FIFTEEN in 2022. CHRISTIAN HILLER, EDUARD KÖGEL, and MIRKO GATTI spoke with him about Jakarta, modernism, and ruangrupa's vision for documenta.

CHRISTIAN HILLER: *You are one of the core members of the artist collective ruangrupa and of the Gudskul project, in Jakarta. You work across many fields and combine different professions: you are an artist, curator, editor, and researcher, but originally you trained as an architect. Why did you choose to study architecture?*

FARID RAKUN: The simple answer to your question is that I went to architecture school because I thought it would give me the opportunity to continue doing what I loved: drawing. I started at University of Indonesia in Jakarta in 2000. If I had wanted a more technical education, I probably would have gone to Parahyangan University in Bandung, or to Bandung Institute of Technology (ITB). It was only after my studies that my interest turned to things like philosophy and writing. I never regretted my decision to study architecture: it gave me a different perspective on artistic practice, a sort of pragmatism about getting things done.

CH: *Did you also work as an architect?*

FR: After graduating, I worked for five years in dull professional architecture offices, where I learned how to manage things that artists usually cannot manage: contracts, safety standards, budgets, etc. During that time I became completely disillusioned with the profession, and realized that it wasn't for me. I was not drawing anymore. There was hardly anything creative about my work. There was maybe ten percent creativity and the rest was just reading contracts and such.

CH: *At what point did you discover the interests that inform your current artistic practice?*

FR: When I was in college, I discovered ruangrupa, a group of artists who were talking about many of the things that interested me, such as the politics of space and the city. They addressed these things from a completely different perspective than what I was learning in architecture school. There were also other groups at the time, such as AMI, an acronym for *Arsitek Muda Indonesia* (Young Indonesian Architects), which emerged in the late 1990s, in the midst of the Asian economic crisis. Some of its members later became internationally well known, such as Andra Matin and Yori Antar. But I found the work of ruangrupa much more appealing. ruangrupa is more punk rock. I started hanging out with them around 2003/04, while still a student. The issues we discussed in the group inspired my work in architecture school.

Gudskul in Jakarta, pictured from above. © Jin Panji

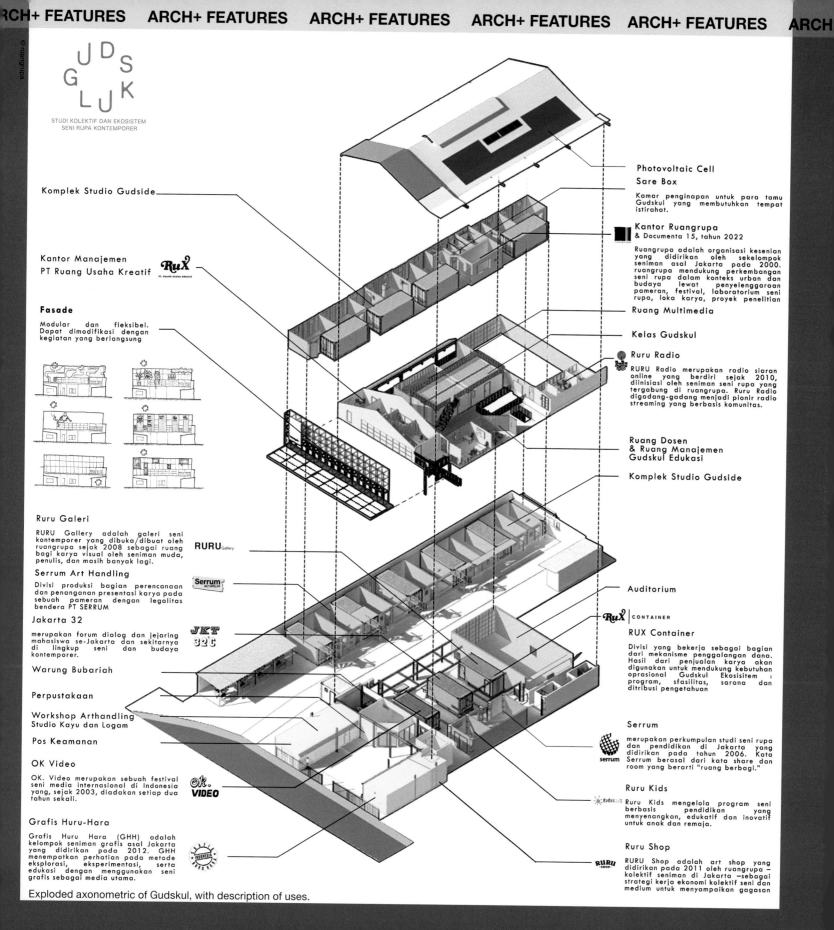

G U D S
G L U K
S K

STUDI KOLEKTIF DAN EKOSISTEM
SENI RUPA KONTEMPORER

Komplek Studio Gudside

Kantor Manajemen
PT Ruang Usaha Kreatif

Fasade

Modular dan fleksibel.
Dapat dimodifikasi dengan
kegiatan yang berlangsung

Ruru Galeri

RURU Gallery adalah galeri seni
kontemporer yang dibuka/dibuat oleh
ruangrupa sejak 2008 sebagai ruang
bagi karya visual oleh seniman muda,
penulis, dan masih banyak lagi.

Serrum Art Handling

Divisi produksi bagian perencanaan
dan penanganan presentasi karya pada
sebuah pameran dengan legalitas
bendera PT SERRUM

Jakarta 32

merupakan forum dialog dan jejaring
mahasiswa se-Jakarta dan sekitarnya
di lingkup seni dan budaya
kontemporer.

Warung Bubariah

Perpustakaan

Workshop Arthandling
Studio Kayu dan Logam

Pos Keamanan

OK Video

OK. Video merupakan sebuah festival
seni media internasional di Indonesia
yang, sejak 2003, diadakan setiap dua
tahun sekali.

Grafis Huru-Hara

Grafis Huru Hara (GHH) adalah
kelompok seniman grafis asal Jakarta
yang didirikan pada 2012. GHH
menempatkan perhatian pada metode
eksplorasi, eksperimentasi, serta
edukasi dengan menggunakan seni
grafis sebagai media utama.

Photovoltaic Cell

Sare Box

Kamar penginapan untuk para tamu
Gudskul yang membutuhkan tempat
istirahat.

Kantor Ruangrupa
& Documenta 15, tahun 2022

Ruangrupa adalah organisasi kesenian
yang didirikan oleh sekelompok
seniman asal Jakarta pada 2000.
ruangrupa mendukung perkembangan
seni rupa dalam konteks urban dan
budaya lewat penyelenggaraan
pameran, festival, laboratorium seni
rupa, loka karya, proyek penelitian

Ruang Multimedia

Kelas Gudskul

Ruru Radio

RURU Radio merupakan radio siaran
online yang berdiri sejak 2010,
diinisiasi oleh seniman seni rupa yang
tergabung di ruangrupa. Ruru Radio
digadang-gadang menjadi pionir radio
streaming yang berbasis komunitas.

Ruang Dosen
& Ruang Manajemen
Gudskul Edukasi

Komplek Studio Gudside

Auditorium

RUX CONTAINER

RUX Container

Divisi yang bekerja sebagai bagian
dari mekanisme penggalangan dana.
Hasil dari penjualan karya akan
digunakan untuk mendukung kebutuhan
oprasional Gudskul Ekosisitem :
program, sfasilitas, sarana dan
ditribusi pengetahuan

Serrum

merupakan perkumpulan studi seni rupa
dan pendidikan di Jakarta yang
didirikan pada tahun 2006. Kata
Serrum berasal dari kata share dan
room yang berarti "ruang berbagi."

Ruru Kids

Ruru Kids mengelola program seni
berbasis pendidikan yang
menyenangkan, edukatif dan inovatif
untuk anak dan remaja.

Ruru Shop

RURU Shop adalah art shop yang
didirikan pada 2011 oleh ruangrupa –
kolektif seniman di Jakarta –sebagai
strategi kerja ekonomi kolektif seni dan
medium untuk menyampaikan gagasan

Exploded axonometric of Gudskul, with description of uses.

"ruangrupa combines art with other disciplines
to open up a critical perspective on contemporary
urban issues in Indonesia."

Romo Mangun worked with residents to expand and renovate the former squatter settlement, which had illegally spread along the Code River.   Photo: Gregorius Antar © Aga Khan Trust for Culture

"We yearned to go back to the roots of community and build kampung architecture."

Due to the steep topography and muddy soil, most of the bamboo homes at Kampung Kali Code were elevated and anchored in concrete foundations.

Yusuf Bilyarta Mangunwijaya (aka Romo Mangun): Kali Code Kampung
(Kali Code settlement) in Yogyakarta, 1985. Photo: Gregorius Antar © Aga Khan Trust for Culture

CH: *You have a good international network. Tell us about some of your international experience.*

FR: During the short time I worked as an architect, I practiced outside of Jakarta. Having been born and raised in Jakarta I wanted to get away. This city is not an easy place to live. I tried to escape three times. First I worked in Bali, and then in Phnom Penh. In 2010, I ran into the folks from ruangrupa again, and they invited me to become an editor for their online journal, and so I officially became a part of the collective. After that, I went to the United States to do a masters at the Cranbrook Academy, in Michigan. Now I am back in Jakarta.

CH: *Tell us more about Cranbrook Academy. How was it different from the University of Indonesia?*

FR: Cranbrook played a key role in the early years of American modernism. Its campus was designed, and later presided over, by Eliel Saarinen. His son, Eero Saarinen, later became an apprentice at Cranbrook himself. In the 1930s, Eero met Charles Eames there; Eames was studying furniture design and started teaching there soon thereafter. Florence Knoll also attended the academy, and met Ray Eames there. Many of the key figures of American modernism passed through Cranbrook in those years. When I attended the academy, there were ten departments ranging from painting to sculpture, 3D design, architecture, print media, metalsmithing, ceramics, and more. Each department has an artist, designer, or architect in residence as the program mentor. There are no standard classes or grades; basically, I could do whatever I wanted and also explore different departments. I spent time with a lot of non-architects, and everything was very open. People in the 2D-design department, which basically combines graphic design and illustration, were doing more painting than those in the painting department, who were producing installations instead. At Cranbrook, I also delved into art history from a Western perspective, because how we talk about art in Asia and how it is taught in Europe and in the US is very different. Being an artist in Indonesia is also very different. In 2013, I decided to come back to Jakarta, and have been active in ruangrupa ever since. Sometimes I also teach at the University of Indonesia.

EDUARD KÖGEL: *Did the difference between education systems influence how you think about architecture and art? Upon your return from the USA, did you look at Indonesia through a different lens?*

FR: Yes, studying abroad influenced my practice very much. Had I stayed in the

Gudskul, view into a hallway on the ground floor. © Karya Tabaru

United States, maybe I would be a proper artist now, you know, not someone who is confused and confusing, like I am. In the USA, my background was very valuable. The values and insights that I developed growing up in Indonesia played out differently in the States. There was a special interest in my work, and so it was also easier for me to draw attention to my work as an Indonesian artist living abroad. Here in Jakarta, everyone shares similar sensibilities. Had I remained in Indonesia all along, maybe I would not see my work as something unique, but being in the States showed me that it is unique somewhere else.

CH: *Is modernism something you addressed as an architecture student? For example, the way modernism was perceived across Southeast Asia and how modernist architecture and urban planning were used as a means of national representation in the post-independence period?*

FR: Yes, it was addressed. New generations of architects are still heavily influenced by the ideal of Indonesian modernism. The members of AMI, for example, are essentially its direct successors. Modernism is still popular, even if is only treated as a style. Some call it "tropical minimalism" and vehemently campaign for it. Personally, the first thing that comes to mind when I think of modernism is that it was the architectural style introduced by our first president, Sukarno, who used it as a propaganda tool to build national monuments.[01] He hired Friederich Silaban, his favorite architect, to design the most representative buildings of the newly independent Indonesian state in a bold modernist style. Of course, there is also another kind of Indonesian modernism, that of Yusuf Bilyarta Mangunwijaya, for example, who is also known as Romo Mangun (Father Mangun), and who trained at the RWTH in Aachen, Germany. I love his work.

EK: *Architecturally speaking, his work is very interesting. You can see that he was influenced by Hans Scharoun. It's impressive how creatively he adapted some of Scharoun's ideas to the Indonesian context, such as the floating space.*

FR: Romo Mangun is a very important reference for ruangrupa. What we find especially interesting about his work is how he combined his background as an architect and his institutional role as a priest to realize projects like the settlement by the Kali Code River, in Yogyakarta. He lived there with a marginalized community and, together with its residents, built a modern *kampung*,[02] a kind of urban village. With this project, he fundamentally challenged the traditional role of the architect. He didn't even draw proper floorplans, but drew directly on site, in the sand. Mangun was a writer as well. In addition to a lot of fiction, he wrote a book that has been very important for Indonesian architecture students, called *Wastu Citra*.[03] It has never been translated into English. We want to translate it for documenta fifteen— let's see if it will actually happen.

EK: *What significance does modernism hold for your generation?*

FR: The legacy of Sukarno is a heavy one. Modernism and its aesthetic language— that of Friederich Silaban, for example—holds a certain power of association here. Sometimes it is not about the idea behind the building but the way it looks and its semantic power. Modern architecture in Indonesia conveys a certain political message. After 1965, when the whole country turned against communism, and Suharto established the New Order (*Orde Baru*) in 1967, a lot of tension developed between modernist buildings and the new ideology.[04] It became more "eclectic," as one would say in the architecture history books. I grew up under the New Order regime, so for me, modernism is the language of Sukarno, while the language of the New Order era was the opposite of modernism. I started working professionally, like the other members of ruangrupa, in the years after the New Order imploded in 1998. So for me, it's interesting to see how we could start to see modernism not only as a language, but also as a concept. It is also interesting to see how the concept of modernism plays out differently for the post-1998 generation. There was a certain moment when we yearned for a kind of architecture like that of Mangunwijaya: we yearned to go back to the roots of community and build *kampung* architecture. Suddenly there was this empowering idea of an architecture that you can build from the bottom up. This kind of approach entails an implicit critique of modernism and of the modern project, which has never been fully

successful in Indonesia. The critique is no longer about a formal style, but about the failure of modernism as a project. That is why ruangrupa combines art with other disciplines, like the social sciences, politics, technology, and media—to open up a critical perspective on contemporary urban issues in Indonesia.

MIRKO GATTI: *Your response to the top-down thinking of modernism has been to do projects*
that focus more on non-hierarchical logics—one example being Gudskul, the educational platform that ruangrupa co-initiated. Can you tell us more about that?

RF: Gudskul is a horizontal educational platform, initiated in 2018, by three Jakarta-based collectives: ruangrupa, Serrum, and Grafis Huru Hara. The program lasts for one year. Participants collaboratively develop different artistic practices, from music to writing, cooking, curating, designing, print-making, and more. We consider ourselves to be an art ecosystem where we put all our resources—money, the program, technical equipment, books, etc.—into a collective pot.

CH: *Can you also tell us about the building? How does its architecture reflect Gudskul's collec-*

tive structure?

RF: Believe it or not, you are actually the first person to ask me about the building! People in the art world always ask complicated questions about our practice; they don't really see the architecture. But in a way, what we do can be understood through the architecture. In fact, I think that analyzing the building is a very nice way to understand our practice.

Initially, we asked other collectives to join us in a big warehouse that we had purchased in Jakarta. It has about 6,000 square meters of indoor space—it's huge. In that moment we understood how this new environment represented a jump in scale, not just spatially, but for the practice itself.

CH: *So in a way, the architecture changed how you work?*

FR: Yes, even though the Gudskul building was the product of a series of semi-accidental opportunities. The first one was the roof: one of the main reasons we bought the property is because it already had a roof. It was like a small soccer field covered by a big roof. Building regulations in Jakarta are quite lax, but building a roof is one of the things you must have a permit for. Once the roof was secured, we had to build something

Gudskul, work area between containers, which structure the space. © Jin Panji

Eko Prawoto: Community Learning Center in Ujung Alang, Cilacap, 2005
© Eko Prawoto Architecture Workshop

under it as fast and as cheaply as possible. The shipping containers came from our previous space, while a lot of the wall panels were recycled from previous Jakarta Biennale exhibitions. Everything kind of happened organically afterwards.

The main steel framework was already there, but a lot of the secondary beams were added later, following a kind of organic-growth construction logic, rather than a rational construction logic. In some places we have double beams, because the old beams were no longer sufficient and we simply added another to stabilize it. Another aspect that reveals the process is the padlocks on the studio doors: they are all installed from the outside. That means you can't lock the door from the inside. Originally the site was for storage, not private studios. This pre-existing logic determines the collective use of the space: with the padlock attached on the outside, it means that this is a space you can open and use, and afterwards lock it behind you, so the tools and materials are not stolen. But it is never a private space where you lock yourself inside to work on your own. This kind of

intrinsic logic, which you can read in the architectural details, shows what kind of designers we are, and what kind of educational institution we are.

CH: *I remember that you once said that architectural education needs to be "de-modernized." As I understood it, you see modernism as a system of values that puts things into boxes, which is something you try to challenge with your educational approach at Gudskul, right?*

FR: I learned the term "de-modernization" from two people: the curator Charles Esche[05] and the semiotician Walter Mignolo. I don't use it in the same way, though. They come from a more intellectual background than I do, and have been teaching at prestigious American and European universities. We also have different cultural backgrounds. For me, de-modernization means unlearning what we were taught before, which is that the path for us to become postcolonial must go through the nation-state. That is what Sukarno did after independence: he used modernist architecture to build the Indonesian national identity, like Oscar Niemeyer did in Brazil.

But now, 40 or 50 years later and after everything that we have been through, our generation knows how absurd and awkward that goal was in the first place.

Because the modern project was never fully successful here, because it never significantly improved our quality of life, we don't understand why we need it. Why should we sustain certain social or economic systems? Why do we need to believe in a growth-oriented economy? These aren't just questions that we are asking as a bunch of radical artists with too much time on our hands. It's also the people who are not benefitting from modernism—the farmers, the fishermen, the street vendors—who are asking themselves the same questions.

And they are creating collective modes of production to get around the problematic system that was imposed on them. This is also why we are interested in unauthored design and on how we can hack certain systems within the design world. Design hacks are not even about participatory or collective authorship. They get rid of authorship and of designers all together.

MG: *I see that you are very skeptical of modernist architecture, because, like you said, for Indonesians these buildings are associated with a certain idea about nation-building embodied in the political figure of Sukarno. But isn't it possible to think of the "modern project," as you call it, as a collective project? Can you think of modern architecture as collective and bottom-up, like Gudskul, but on a bigger scale? Aren't there any modernist buildings in Jakarta that are not primarily an expression of Sukarno's agenda, but which can be seen as representing a broader notion of collectivity?*

FR: If you look at architecture through time and read all the traces of history, even a building like the national monument on Merdeka Square can tell a collective story. It was commissioned by Sukarno in a monumental modernist style. On the ground floor, inside the big hall, there are dozens of display windows exhibiting cheesy dioramas of significant moments in Indonesia's history. Some of these dioramas were commissioned later, by Suharto, and they frame the story so as to comply with the official narrative of the Suharto regime. And then there is a whole new layer about how the monument and the dioramas are perceived today. For example, now there are security gates all around the monument complex. Taken together, all of these different historical traces form a collective idea of Indonesia. The monument itself does not express this collectivity, only the layering of symbolism over time does.

EK: *Building on this idea, I would like to go back to Mangunwijaya, because I think it would be interesting to try and build a counter-narrative about Indonesian modernism. The main narrative is that modernism is the heavy concrete stuff that was built by the state. But what Mangunwijaya did was to take countermeasures. He was also a modernist, but he went to the people and worked with the communities. He went there with very avant-garde, modernist designs and he worked on them with the local people on site. This is a fascinating counter-narrative to the official history of modernization as a nationalist project, don't you think?*

FR: Yes, I think so too. But I see him more as a solo genius, like Friedrich Silaban. We worked with one of Mangunwijaya's students, Eko Prawoto, a few times. We learned a lot from him, because he has a very special sense for things like low-tech passive cooling systems suitable for the tropical climate, and for vernacular technologies. We absolutely love his work in terms of the architecture. But for me, being younger than Eko Prawoto,

"What interests me much more is swarms of people coming together, to the point where suddenly it's no longer clear whose idea is being implemented."

RURU Gallery, run by ruangrupa, has been exhibiting work by emerging Indonesian artists since 2008.
© Karya Tabaru

Exhibition space during the Open House Days at Gudskul, September 2019. © Jin Panji

Festival poster, 2009.

OK.Video, an international media art festival launched by ruangrupa in 2003, is also present in Jakarta's public space. Pictured here during the festival's third edition, 2007.
© ruangrupa

Festival poster, 2007.

Film still from DODOL (Holiday Dos and Don'ts: Do not take pictures of accidents while on vacation), a promotional video for the Gudskul Holymarket, 2020.

WE DON'T HAVE ANY MESSAGE TODAY

Installation by ruangrupa for the 4th Gwangju Biennale, 2002. © ruangrupa

RURU, an installation by ruangrupa at the 31st São Paulo Biennial, 2014. © ruangrupa

"As a collective, we like to think of ourselves as a football team, playing according to the 'total football' strategy. No one has a predetermined position."

KAOS, installation by ruangrupa at the 9th Istanbul Biennial, 2005. © ruangrupa

I don't aspire to follow in Romo Mangun's footsteps because I see him as a single architect of something in particular. What interests me much more is swarms of people coming together, to the point where suddenly it's no longer clear whose idea is being implemented. Of course, that means you have to go through a lot of talking, negotiating, and wasting time. This type of practice is time- and energy-consuming, it is neither efficient nor economical, but it makes me feel more alive, both personally and artistically.

CH: *Mangunwijaya's approach differs from yours because he went there and activated the place himself. But the idea behind ruangrupa is that the activation process is triggered by the people themselves. So the people are not participants in the project but its co-initiators?*

FR: Yes, at least, that's our intention. That's why we like to challenge ourselves when it comes to authorship. As a collective, we like to think of ourselves as a football team, playing according to the "total football" strategy—are you familiar with that idea?

CH: *Isn't that the tactical system used by Johan Cruyff and the Dutch national team in the 1970s?*

FR: Yes, exactly. Total football is when any player can take over the position of any other player in a team. No one has a predetermined position. It is a fluid system, in which every team member can become an attacker, a midfielder, or a defender at any point in the game, and every player is always ready to substitute another's position. This kind of strategy confuses the opponent and creates unexpected opportunities in which even the goalkeeper might suddenly run up and score a goal. But in order for this strategy to succeed, every player has to be highly versatile and everyone on the team has to know each other as well as possible, understanding each other's strengths and weaknesses. Sometimes I try to imagine what it would be like if we were to get into proper architecture. Maybe after documenta fifteen we will put this into practice and apply the total football strategy to the design of an actual building. We have already done many such experiments with art before, also in collaboration with people from theater, dance, etc.—design and architecture would be the next level.

The auditorium was spontaneously used for the production of various protective equipment at the beginning of the pandemic. © Jin Panji

CH: *In a way, Gudskul is already a building that was designed with the total football strategy. How does it work in practice? Are there different departments located in specific parts of the building? Or is everything always in flow?*

FR: We have tried to introduce some differentiation: we have spaces that are designated as classrooms, but in practice it often blurs organically. The auditorium, for example, is really good for holding our assemblies, which are very important for us. But functions can shift. Since working on documenta, we have been moving around a lot in the Gudskul because we have different kinds of needs. How we function to run documenta is different from how we function when we offer classes. At one point, we needed a meeting space just for documenta, but then, all of a sudden COVID-19 came, and so we moved the documenta space into a virtual one. For a short period of time, at the start of the pandemic, our auditorium became a mini-manufacturing site for health equipment. Another time, our store went from selling artistic merchandise to selling vegetables and other farm products.

CH: *How have you been coping since the start of the pandemic? It must have had a huge impact on an institution like Gudskul, where everything is about togetherness and exchange, not only in terms of ideas, but also manual skills. How was the switch from face-to-face to online teaching?*

FR: It is very challenging. Not only for Gudskul and our educational program, but for everything. We are really dependent on people coming together in physical space; that is the fundamental requirement of our kind of practice. On the bright side, Gudskul now has a regular program that is fully available online, which means that we are accessible to many more people because they don't have to come to Jakarta to attend sessions. Our original goal was to have participants from the entire Indonesian archipelago. But for a lot of students, leaving their own city or village to spend a year in Jakarta is financially very difficult. Jakarta is one of the most—if not the most—expensive cities in Indonesia.

EK: *Tell us more about the relationship between space and ruangrupa. What is your idea of spatial production?*

FR: The name ruangrupa is made of two words: *ruang* means space and *rupa* roughly means form. It's a play on words and didn't already have a specific meaning. But it contains the word "space" because space has always been important to us, from the very beginning. Space is something that is

Repurposing of Gudskul for the production of COVID-19 protective equipment, April 2020. © Jin Panji

With the help of a 3D printer, the collective produced self-designed protective visors. © Jin Panji

"The notion of public space as somewhere that everyone can access and spend time in is new here. Public space has always been contested in Jakarta."

contested, which we have to occupy. We started out transforming rented homes from domestic spaces into public spaces, because they don't really exist in cities like Jakarta. The notion of public space as somewhere that everyone can access and spend time in is new here. Public space has always been contested in Jakarta. Questions like, "What does it mean to be public?" and "Who has the right to be in a public space?" are still very important questions for us because they bring underlying class conflicts to the surface.

EK: *What influence has your work had on the local neighborhood and community?*

FR: At Gudskul, we think of ourselves as a resource. This is essentially the basic idea behind it—we are a bank of physical and intellectual resources that are available for collective use. Space is one these resources; we often welcome people to use our space. But of course it is also a question of who our audience is. The first audience we address is ourselves and our friends—those who want to get involved. Our neighbors are the second: street vendors, people who live nearby—they use our space, too. A lot of our projects have the format of markets, concerts, public screenings, etc. We often show well-known Indonesian films that everyone can watch and laugh with. These events are also popular outside the collective.

We also have projects about collective waste management, to collect waste from our surroundings and turn it into something else. With this kind of project, one of the most important things is the relationship we create with our surroundings. For example, when we collect plastic bottles for a project, we speak with housewives, street vendors, and all the other people in the neighborhood. It's an excuse to talk to them and introduce them to our work, so next time they won't ask "Are we allowed to go inside?"—they will just come. This kind of thing is much more important for us than the product itself.

EK: *One thing that is very interesting about this approach is that it challenges the typical family-based social structure at the level of the neighborhood. Groups like ruangrupa come together in different ways and take a different position in society than the family. There are free individuals, and there is the collective; the family doesn't play a role here, and this idea of a society that is not based on the traditional nuclear family is another, very important aspect of modernism that we should build our counter-narratives on.*

FR: That's true. The nuclear family was an invention anyway.

CH: *Coming back to the topic of public space: when I was in Jakarta, it seemed like many public services are now being provided by digital platforms. Grab, for example, is an extremely popular ride-hailing app across Southeast Asia.*

It's one of the most reliable options to get from point A to B, because there is hardly any public transport in Jakarta. It also offers food delivery, cashless payments, hotel reservations, cleaning, and more. It's a super app that offers multiple services. Are there any alternative projects that provide the same services but as grassroots initiatives, focused less on pure profit and more on actual sharing? Like the work at Gudskul, but scaled up to the city level?

FR: In fact, there are several apps that are gaining more traction in Southeast Asia. Gojek, Grab, and Tokopedia are perhaps the most popular ones. Digitalization is happening very fast, following the Chinese model. Of course, Chinese capital plays a huge role in these technological developments. But there are also many digital activists dealing with other issues, such as women's reproductive rights in small villages.

CH: *Let's conclude by talking about documenta fifteen. The exhibition will take place in 2022 and ruangrupa will be the curators. Tell us a bit about what you have in mind.*

FR: documenta fifteen is still a big work in progress. We have a lot of thinking to do on how to translate our ideas into space. One thing we are thinking about is turning the Fridericianum into a school. But before that,

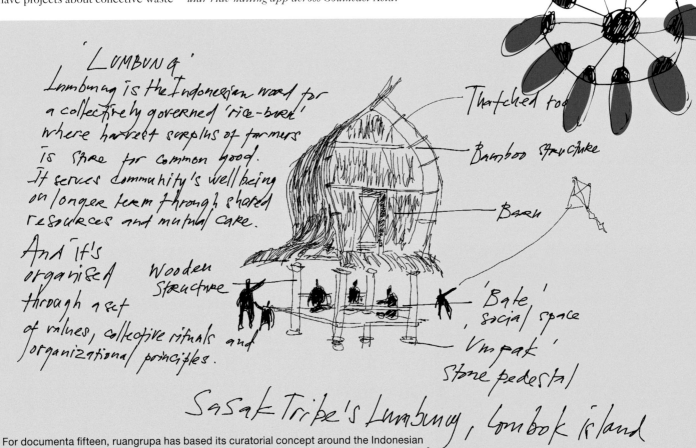

'LUMBUNG'
Lumbung is the Indonesian word for a collectively governed 'rice-barn' where harvest surplus of farmers is share for common good. It serves community's wellbeing on longer term through shared resources and mutual care.

And it's organised through a set of values, collective rituals and organizational principles.

Wooden Structure

Thatched roo

Bamboo Structure

Barn

'Bale' social space

'Umpak' Stone pedestal

Sasak Tribe's Lumbung, Lombok island

For documenta fifteen, ruangrupa has based its curatorial concept around the Indonesian word *lumbung*, which literally means "rice barn." In rural Indonesia the term refers to storage chambers where surplus crops are stored as a common resource for the future.

Newly designed facade of ruruHaus in Kassel, a former sports equipment shop. The site is already being used by ruangrupa in the run-up to documenta fifteen and will serve as one of the exhibition's main venues.
Photo: Nicolas Wefers © documenta fifteen, ruruHaus

we have to understand our audience. The big question is: how do we understand the audience, not just as people who paid a ticket to see a show, but so they have a more active role in shaping the exhibition? I am thinking about a real school, with an actual educational program, and people attending regularly, rather than paying a ticket for a single visit and then never coming back. Whether it can be done that way remains to be seen.

EK: *I was a university student in Kassel in the 1980s and 1990s. Back then, there were constant attempts to establish a new relationship between documenta and the local public. For the people from Kassel, the locals, the one hundred days of documenta is associated with a feeling of anxiety. It's as if something is looming over the city, something from the outside, which is occupying the city and causing all sorts of strange things to happen.*
FR: I don't know whether we will be able to overcome that fear. What we can do is try to avoid being like a spaceship that lands and then tries to compete with all the existing initiatives. What we have done for now is to set

up ruruHaus, a former department store that is now functioning as a meeting space for the artistic direction of documenta fifteen, but also as an open, collective space for encounters and discussions with guests, researchers, curators, and, most importantly, with local people and local initiatives who want to get involved.

To be honest, I don't know what the parameters for success should be in terms of local participation, but one thing is for sure: this fear that you mention is definitely not something that we want to provoke. Rebelliousness, criticism, or protests would be so much better. If the people in Kassel want to hack us, for example, that would be amazing! But that would put us in a very awkward position, of course—if we ask people to hack us, well, then we are missing the whole point, aren't we?

01   Sukarno was the leader of the Indonesian nationalist movement during the final years of Dutch colonial rule, and the first president of Indonesia after the country obtained independence, serving continuously from 1945 to 1967.
02   *Kampung* is an Indonesian term that refers to traditional villages, but is also sometimes used to refer to neighborhoods or communities within towns, or urban villages. The term is often erroneously used in a derogative way because historically *kampungs* were labeled as slums, especially during the time of Dutch colonialism.
03   Y. B. Mangunwijaya, *Wastu Citra* (Jakarta: Gramedia Pustaka Utama, 1988).
04   Suharto was a military general and the second president of Indonesia, serving from 1967 to 1998. His administration is commonly referred to as the "New Order" (*Orde Baru*), as opposed to the "old order" of Sukarno. Suharto was regarded by most foreign observers as a dictator. In the two years before his election in 1967, acting as a general of the Indonesian National Army, he participated in an anti-communist purge in which an estimated half a million political dissidents were killed and as many as 1.5 million were imprisoned.
05   Charles Esche was member of the International Finding Committee that selected ruangrupa as curators of documenta fifteen.

Open House Day at the Gudskul, December 2019   © Jin Panji

ARCH+
features

Platform for discourse
by ARCH+ and Siedle

SSS SIEDLE

© 2021 ARCH+ Verlag GmbH,
and the authors
archplus.net/features

PUBLISHER: ARCH+ Verlag GmbH
EDITOR-IN-CHIEF: Anh-Linh Ngo
EDITORIAL TEAM: Mirko Gatti,
Christian Hiller, Nora Dünser,
Leonie Hartung
CREATIVE DIRECTION:
Max Kaldenhoff
MANAGING EDITOR ENGLISH
EDITION: Mirko Gatti
ART DIRECTION: Mike Meiré
DESIGN: Charlotte Cassel,
Jeremias Diekmann,
Meiré und Meiré
TRANSLATION & COPY EDITING:
Alisa Kotmair
PROOFREADING: James Copeland
PREPRESS: max-color, Berlin
PRINTING: Medialis Offsetdruck
GmbH, Berlin

COVER: The central photo shows
the courtyard of Gudskul
in Jakarta © Christian Hiller

ARCH+ features is a series by
ARCH+ that explores the current
conditions of the production of
space. *ARCH+ features* is curated by
Anh-Linh Ngo and made possible
by Siedle as an initiating partner.

This special edition is part of the
international exhibition and discourse project *Contested Modernities.
Postcolonial Architecture in Southeast
Asia.* The project is a continuation
of *Encounters with Southeast Asian
Modernism,* which began in 2019
in several countries in Southeast Asia
and is now being discussed in a
German context.

INITIATORS AND ARTISTIC
DIRECTORS: Sally Below,
Moritz Henning, Christian Hiller,
Eduard Kögel
VISUAL IDENTITY AND
EXHIBITION DESIGN:
Constructlab – Peter Zuiderwijk,
Alex Römer
PROJECT MANAGEMENT AND
COMMUNICATIONS: sbca

Contested Modernities is funded by

www.seam-encounters.net

AM

RESIDENCE
Andra Matin

View from the garden to the second floor,
with the open living area below.

Above
The transition is fluid
between the
garden and the living/
dining area on the
first floor.

Right
Street view.

Photos, unless otherwise stated:
© Paul Kadarisman, courtesy
arsitekturindonesia.org
Drawings: © andramatin

Text: Mirko Gatti

The AM Residence stands upon a trapezoidal-shaped plot in the residential district of Bintaro, in South Jakarta. It was built from 2008 to 2013 by Andra Matin for himself and his family. Despite its unapologetically modern bare concrete volumes, the house establishes an almost symbiotic relationship with the surrounding environment and provides the ideal habitat in the hot and humid climate of Jakarta.

A narrow gate at the short edge of the plot leads over a gently sloping ramp into a semi-open, ground-floor space that includes a car port. Here, shaded from the afternoon sun between two rows of pilotis are the library and service rooms, enclosed within individual volumes. A hedge of lush tropical vegetation wraps around the intimate triangular garden, whose lawn slants gently toward the house,

naturally mitigating temperatures and carrying rainwater down along a draining groove into a small basin. Next to it, a ramp leads upstairs to the first upper floor, where a large open space includes the kitchen, dining, and living areas. Only shielded by the cantilevers of the concrete box above, this level is completely open to the elements and enjoys an all-round view onto the garden and swimming pool. The ramp continues at a steeper angle up to the second floor, where three small capsule-like bedrooms for the children share a large collective playroom, which, unlike the living space below, is snugly protected within concrete walls. Daylight enters through a low ribbon window running along the floor length and small skylights scattered along the ceiling, thus keeping the room temperature comfortably cool.

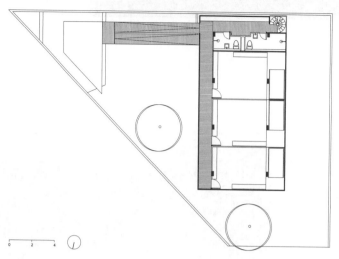

Floor plan,
second floor.

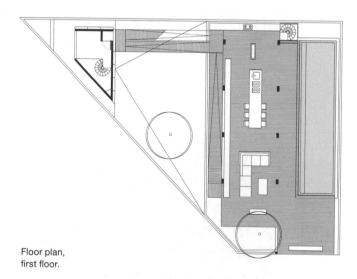

Floor plan,
first floor.

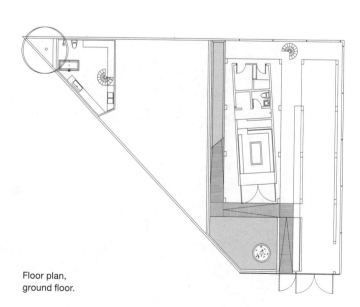

Floor plan,
ground floor.

117

Above
The master bedroom is in a separate pavilion, located across the gently sloping garden. It is connected to the main house by a walkway.

Below
The master bathroom is located in the basement of the pavilion; a skylight provides natural light.

Above
The second floor is accessed by a ramp.

Below
The corridor on the second floor leads to the children's bedrooms. Light and fresh air enter through thin horizontal slits, keeping the area from becoming too hot.

Right
Sketch showing how rain-
water flows along the
garden's gentle slope into
a small water basin.

Below
Interior, second floor.

View through the living
room on the first
floor to the garden beyond.

The master bedroom is located in a small independent pavilion across the garden, with an en-suite bathroom and dressing room buried below and accessible via a small spiral staircase.

The bold purist design of the AM Residence synthetizes the language of a young generation of Indonesian architects, who, since the early 2000s, have stoutly reinterpreted tropical modernism with the same empowering optimism of Brazilian masters like Mendes da Rocha or Lina Bo Bardi. The work of Matin, formally powerful, structurally rational, and deeply mindful of climatic conditions, proves how universalist design principles can be successfully adopted to the specific requirements of the local environment.

Myanmar (formerly known as Burma) gained independence from British colonial rule in 1948. In 1962, General Ne Win violently seized power, with his new military government declaring a "Burmese way to socialism." In the aftermath of the coup, Myanmar was cut off from the rest of the world for decades. The country now has a population of around 52 million inhabitants, divided into more than 135 ethnic groups. Post-independence ethnic conflict has been a constant challenge for the Myanmar state.

After the British withdrawal, important commissions in engineering and architecture initially went to British figures, including Raglan Squire and James Cubitt, and to Americans like Benjamin Polk and Oswald Nagler. Among the first Burmese architects to come back from studying abroad was Bilal Raschid, who had studied in Liverpool in the 1950s. An architecture faculty was founded at Yangon University in 1954, and the first five architects graduated from the program four years later. In 1963, the US-trained architect U Myo Myint Sein took over as dean of the Department of Architecture in Yangon; he had previously worked with Minoru Yamasaki in the United States. The new buildings completed in Myanmar at this time—libraries and cinemas, as well as public buildings for education and health care—reflected hopes for a new, emancipated society, however, these hopes would go unfulfilled.

After decades of military dictatorship, Aung San Suu Kyi's National League for Democracy won an absolute majority in parliament in 2015, in the country's first-ever free elections. Suu Kyi became de facto head of government, although the constitution enforced by the military formally denied her office. Under her leadership, the country gradually began to open up and saw increased foreign investment, especially from Singapore and China. These developments are now rapidly changing the cityscape of the former capital city, Yangon. A series of initiatives are now attempting to protect British colonial architecture from demolition, but it is still early days in terms of the general awareness of postcolonial modernism.

Recently, the country has created headlines due to another military coup, which took place on February 1, 2021. Again, it seems, democratic development in Myanmar is literally under attack by the military.

SB/MH/CH/EK

Text: Benjamin Bansal

Designed by the British architect Raglan Squire, the former Engineering College in Yangon was built in 1954–56.

CONCRETE BATTLEGROUND

When Burma (today Myanmar) gained independence in January 1948, Rangoon (today Yangon) was still reeling from the destruction and chaos of the Second World War.[01] Bombing raids by the Japanese in 1941 and 1942 (before they captured the city) as well as lawlessness and looting ahead of the Allied re-capture in 1944 had permanently changed the face of the city.

Wall mosaic by the
artist Aung Soe.
© Moritz Henning

Two Western architects in Myanmar

The new government headed by prime minister U Nu struggled to keep the young multiethnic and multireligious nation together. As early as 1949, armed factions representing various groups advanced to Rangoon's doorstep. A semblance of domestic stability only returned to the country in the early 1950s. Some construction took place in the city, financed primarily by the Western bloc on the one side, and by the Soviet Union and China on the other. In the early 1950s, from an American perspective, Burma, just like nearby Vietnam, was strategically important as one of the "dominoes" that would have fallen to communism had the Americans not become more politically involved in the region. Because the Soviets had supported communist rebels in the civil war before, the USSR did not open an embassy in Rangoon until 1951. From then on, official relations between the two warmed consistently.

Nevertheless, Burma always emphasized its neutrality within the power games of the Cold War. The Western bloc channeled financial aid to Burma via foundations and multilateral organizations in order to extend their influence in the region while avoiding outright meddling in internal affairs of a self-proclaimed neutral country. The Soviets, for their part, treaded carefully, trying not to alienate non-aligned countries. Between Rangoon and Beijing, however, there was a relationship of mutual distrust, with China being highly concerned about the Americans' influence on its immediate neighborhood. In this complex geopolitical situation, the process of nation-building for newly independent Burma was fraught with pitfalls, as the country would later learn at great cost.

Nation-building was a formidable challenge also for more mundane reasons. For example, there were hardly any Burmese architects in the country, as no universities offered architectural programs in Burma before the war. It was not until 1954 that one could study architecture in Rangoon, which explains the dearth of local professionals in the years after independence. During this time, architecture was often used as a political and ideological weapon in Southeast Asia, turning the region quite literally into a concrete battleground. It is in this context that the work of two Western architects, Raglan Squire and Benjamin Polk, was so important for the development of architecture in Burma. Their works in Yangon reveal contradictions of

a sort: they are foreign impositions often dictated by Cold War politics, the high point of international postwar modern architecture; yet, at the same time, the buildings are deeply connected with the local context and they quickly turned into symbols of an increasingly inward-looking nation-building process.

Born in London in 1912, Raglan Squire became an architect in the interwar years. He founded his own practice in 1937 and soon after began looking for work in the former British colonies. Peter Murray calls him the first of the British "global architects" whose cosmopolitan lifestyle was made possible thanks to the introduction of the jet engine on commercial flights in the 1950s.[02] It was during this time that he received his first overseas commissions outside of Great Britain. The Ministry of National Planning approached him and asked him to design an important set of educational facilities, including the well-known Engineering College in Yangon (today University of Medicine). The complex was realized between 1954 and 1956 with American financial support provided via the Colombo Plan. The Colombo Plan was a regional organization set up under the auspices of the Commonwealth in 1950, one year after president Truman had given his famous second inaugural speech, which is regarded by many historians as the beginning of international development policies. Truman's goal was to battle communism in South and Southeast Asia with development assistance programs rather than weapons. When he was assigned the design commission for the Engineering College, Raglan Squire arrived with more than 30 engineers and surveyors, with whom the government hoped to facilitate the transfer of technical expertise to local partner firms. The British contractors Taylor Woodrow Construction, together with United Engineers Ltd.—a Singapore-based company with a branch in Burma—employed Burmese as well as Indian workers.

The Engineering College comprised several buildings, the biggest of which, the library, was the tallest modern structure in Rangoon at the time. Its design adheres to some of the fundamental principles of the modern movement, such as the use of pilotis, flat roofs, and ribbon windows, yet inspiration was also drawn from local climate conditions. For example, roofed galleries connect the different wings of the building on all levels, providing shelter from the tropical sun and

Above
In late 1956–57, the American jazz musician Benny Goodman and his band gave a series of concerts in Rangoon, pictured here in the assembly hall of the Engineering College, which has since been demolished.

Right
The library's honeycomb windows, made of prefabricated concrete elements, were originally colored red and green.

Below
Perspective drawing of the Engineering College complex; the assembly hall is on the left.

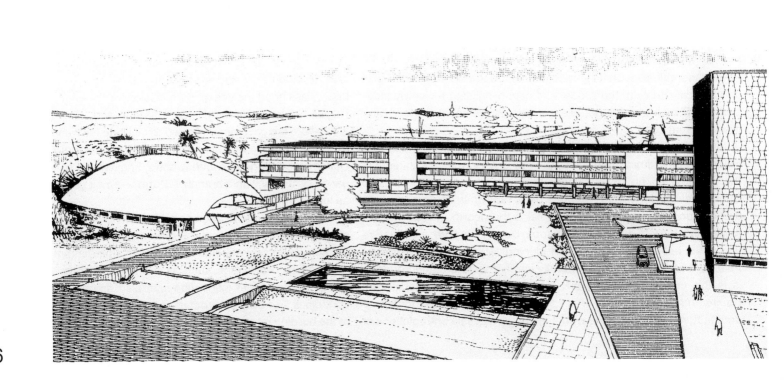

Mechanical Engineering wing of
the former Engineering College.

monsoon rains; the precast honeycomb elements of the library's facade facilitate cross-ventilation and reduce direct sunlight exposure; large courtyards provide naturally cool outdoor spaces that were indispensable in the days before air conditioning. The laminated teak wood vault of the assembly hall was the pride of the college. It was a marvelous piece of engineering, to which Ove Arup also contributed. Jazz legend Benny Goodman performed in the hall in front a rapturous audience during a tour organized by the United States Agency for International Development (USAID) in 1956–57. *The Architectural Review*'s praise of the building briefly put Yangon on the cutting edge of the international architectural scene.[03]

Burmese artists were hired to realize a series of bas-reliefs adorning the outer walls of the college in a similar fashion to their Socialist Realist counterparts around the world. But while the idea of hiring local artists to decorate the building with optimistic messages of self-determination was noble, from today's perspective it seems permeated with a sense of postcolonial condescension, especially given that the building itself was entirely designed and built by foreign companies. Nevertheless, for the first architecture students in post-independence Burma, as well as for many other future professionals, the Engineering College was an inspiration. It was here that many Burmese students had the opportunity to train for high-skilled positions for the first time in their home country. Some of the curricula were developed together with American instructors during exchange programs financed by the Ford Foundation. In contrast to all the dramatic policy failures of the time, buildings such as the Engineering College should be regarded as a successful chapter in the history of Western aid programs in the region, inasmuch as the college actually produced long-term change and effectively trained a new generation of home-grown professionals.

A few kilometers to the northeast of the Engineering College there is a less visible yet equally symbolic building: Tripitaka Library, designed by American architect Benjamin Polk. After completing a diploma in regional planning in London in 1950, Polk and his wife traveled to India in 1952. At unease about the widespread conservativism and the repressive political atmosphere in the US during the McCarthy era, Polk decided to stay in India. In 1955, he opened an architecture practice in Delhi with Joseph Stein. Tripitaka Library stands at the edge of a large religious compound built for the Sixth Buddhist Council, which between 1954 and 1956 brought 2,500 international monastics to Rangoon. For the occasion, several buildings were built north of the Inya Lake, including the Kaba Aye Pagoda, the dormitories for the guests, a cavernous assembly hall, a museum, and the library.

Funds for the construction again came from the Ford Foundation, with the mission of providing "cultural development assistance" to support the arts and humanities. Financing projects with religious purposes was anathema to most development organizations, but the Ford Foundation argued that showing sensitivity to indigenous spiritual values would contradict the popular notion that Americans are only guided by their economic benefit, and that anyway "Buddhism is inherently in opposition to the tenets of Communism."[04]

Benjamin Polk's connections at the Ford Foundation secured him the commission for the library. Upon first meeting Burmese prime minister U Nu, Polk had been advised by Nu to study the traditional Burmese architecture in the ancient city of Bagan, where Polk drew invaluable inspiration for his own work, particularly for Tripitaka Library. At the same time, the use of reinforced concrete allowed Polk to reinterpret traditional Burmese architecture through the implementation of very bold formal solutions, for example through the use of cantilevers and gently recessed arches that lean towards the center

Right
Section, Tripitaka Library
main building, Yangon.
From: Benjamin Polk, *Building
for South Asia: An Architectural
Autobiography* (New Delhi:
Abhinav Publications, 1994).

Below
The main building is adjoined
by three wings: the public
library, the museum of
religion, and the auditorium.

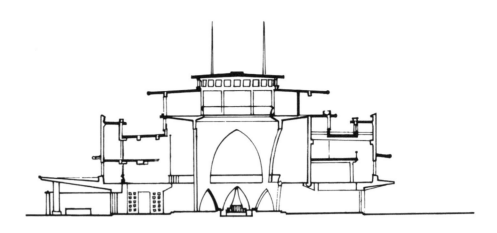

Photo of model from: Benjamin Polk, *Building for South Asia: An Architectural Autobiography* (New Delhi: Abhinav Publications, 1994).

of the library "like the stamen and pistil forms of a flower."[05] His design is rife with symbolism. The central round building is inspired by the classic hemispherical stupa, the Buddhist architectural equivalent of a mausoleum. The overall layout, composed of four interconnected wings, is a reference to the four noble truths of Buddhist teachings, while the threefold vertical partition of the building follows the three principles of existence.[06] In Polk's own words—in accordance with Anagarika B. Govinda's writings on the symbolism of stupas, "weight and mass became a living reality and a latent energy—a magic substance full of hidden activity."[07]

Polk was a pioneer in reconciling modernism with his deep insights on Buddhism. Tripitaka Library is a place of study and meditation, inherently modern and traditional at the same time. It conveys the bygone optimism of the young nation-building project, but it also speaks for traditional Buddhist values, embodying U Nu's choice to declare Buddhism the official state religion—a choice that alienated minorities and sparked much political tension. The library represents one of the few successful syntheses of modern architecture and vernacular tradition in the region—perhaps because it was designed by an American architect who deeply detested the illiberal atmosphere of his own country.

Both the Engineering College and Tripitaka Library therefore represent more than just foreign, Western impositions. These buildings are deeply tied to the culture and political history of Myanmar. They tell the stories of the early years of independence; they are a living testament to the world's opposing postwar ideologies and to the complex political transition that is still in process today. Myanmar's much-touted international opening under former president Thein Sein, started in 2011, has transformed the face of Yangon. The generic and de-contextualized architecture of shopping malls and private condominiums has sprouted up everywhere in the city. In this context, visionary public buildings like the Engineering College and Tripitaka Library, albeit rife with symbolism of past ideologies that might have been surpassed, still constitute an invaluable source of reflection and inspiration for the present and future of Myanmar.

Main entrance of Tripitaka Library, designed by Benjamin Polk, Yangon, 1954–56.

01   Burma was officially renamed Myanmar (Republic of the Union of Myanmar) on June 18, 1989, by the new military government under General Saw Maung. Many places in the country were also renamed at this time, including the capital city, from the English colonial name, Rangoon, back to its precolonial name, Yangon.
02   Peter Murray, "Globe Trotting Designers," *Archinect,* April 24, 2017, accessed July 15, 2021, archinect.com/features/article/150003726/globe-trotting-designers.
03   Due to a substantial lack of maintenance, the assembly hall of the Technical College was torn down in the 1980s.
04   Kathleen D. McCarthy, "From Cold War to Cultural Development: The International Cultural Activities of the Ford Foundation, 1950–1980," *Daedalus* 116, no. 1 (1987), 93–117; 101.
05   Benjamin Polk, *Building for South Asia:*

An Architectural Autobiography (New Delhi: Abhinav Publications, 1993), 5.
06   The four noble truths form the core of Buddhist teachings and include *the truth about suffering* (1), *cause of about the cause of suffering* (2), *the truth about the cessation of suffering* (3) and *the truth about the way that leads to the cessation of suffering* (4). The three characteristics of existence, also known as the Dharma Seal, refer to

the characteristics that are common to all phenomena of "existence":
1. *annica* ("Everything is transient and nothing of eternal continuance. Everything is subject to change.");
2. *dukkha* ("Everything is subject to suffering.");
3. *anattā* ("All things and phenomena exist without an unchanging essence. There is no separate, permanent *ego* and no eternal soul.").
07   Polk, *Building for South Asia* (see note 5), 6.

© Moritz Henning

© Manuel Oka

Above
Window of the
library's rear
wing, with lotus
ornament.

Left
Curved reinforced
concrete canopies
on the library's
main building.

Right
Atrium in the main
building of
Tripitaka Library.

© Moritz Henning

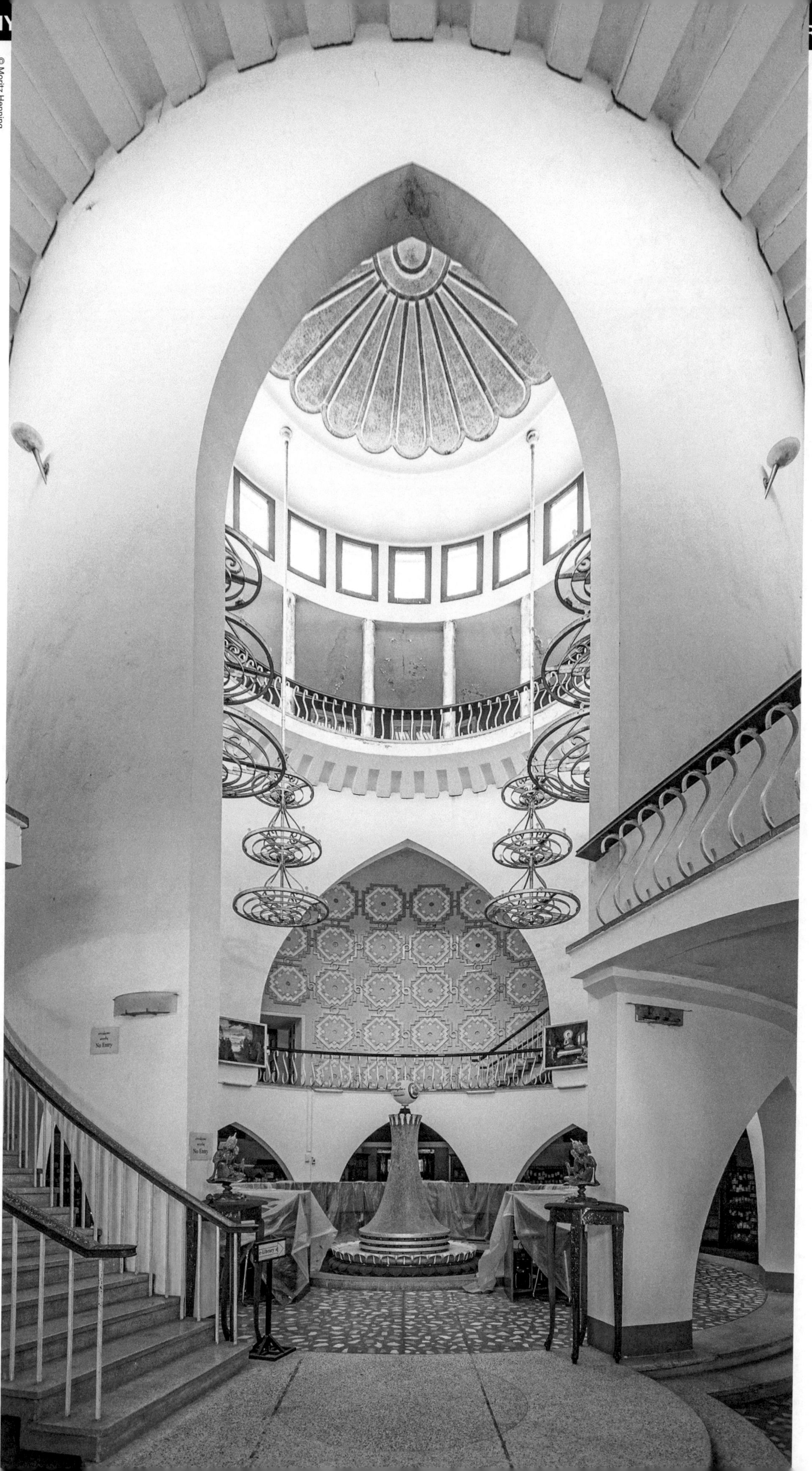

The tripartite division of the facade follows classical motifs.

ENVIRONMENTAL EDUCATION CENTRE, HLAWGA
NATURE CONSERVATION AND NATIONAL PARKS PROJECT, BURMA.

Perspective drawing of the
Environmental Education
Center at Hlawga Zoo Park,
Rangoon, 1980.

A MODERN BURMESE STYLE

In 1979, when he was still in his mid-twenties, U Sun Oo launched his first practice, Architect Sun Oo and Associates, in Yangon. In 1994, he cofounded Design 2000. For the last 30 years he and his practice have been responsible for key projects such as the Environmental Education Center, the National Martyr's Mausoleum, and the complex around the Sule Pagoda. By interweaving traditional and modern elements, he led Myanmar architecture into a new era and shaped the architectural landscape of the fledgling nation.

A conversation with U Sun Oo for *Encounters with Southeast Asian Modernism*

ENCOUNTERS WITH SOUTHEAST ASIAN MODERNISM: You studied architecture at the Rangoon Institute of Technology (RIT) in the 1970s. What was it like to be an architecture student in Rangoon back then?

U SUN OO: U Myo Myint Sein was my professor and Lwin Aung was the head of the department. Both were already famous architects. From U Myo Myint Sein I learned a lot about modernist architecture, while Lwin Aung taught me about Burmese traditional architecture and about the essence of Burmese culture and art. My ideas about architecture were strongly influenced by their teaching. Artist U Aung Soe also made a big impression on me. While in India, U Aung Soe learned how to combine tradition and contemporary art in order to find new ways of expression. From him I learned how to think creatively and to unify different forms of artistic expression, like mixing different ingredients to cook a good curry. A country's culture is constantly evolving and so one always has to think ahead.

ENC: Did you study the work of foreign architects too?

USO: Kenzo Tange, I. M. Pei, and Louis Kahn are three architects whom I greatly admire. Their buildings served as models for my own architectural creations. They were among the most influential architects for my generation.

ENC: How did you start practicing architecture?

USO: In the 1970s, the university was often closed because of the frequent uprisings that were taking place in Rangoon at the

time, and so I asked my teachers if they had any work for me to do while I was still a student. U Myo Myint Sein sent me to Yae Nan Chaung to work on the design of a memorial park with a bronze statue of General Aung San. After that, I worked for about a year as an intern for the architect U Kyaw Win Hman. There were not many architecture firms at that time. If you didn't want to work on your own, there was only the Ministry of Construction and the Architect Group II, which was run by Captain Kyu Kyaw. After my internship, I founded my own company, U Sun Oo and Associates.[01] It was not easy. In school they did not teach us many practical aspects of the profession and so in the beginning I had to face a lot of challenges. When I started practicing architecture, most of my clients did not understand my projects. They were too innovative for them. People in Rangoon had been cut off from the world for a long time. I went to great lengths to convince my clients, but once my first projects were completed things changed, because seeing is believing. This is how I established my reputation as a professional architect.

ENC: How did you get your first commissions? Were there any architectural competitions?

USO: When I launched my firm in 1979, the memorial park at Yae Nan Chaung I had designed was already under construction. Afterwards, I was commissioned for another memorial park in Magway, the capital of the Magway Region, in central Burma. That led to another commission, for the Magway central market. In the 1980s, we won three key public

competitions in Rangoon: first the Environmental Education Center at Hlawga Zoo Park in 1980, then the National Martyrs' Mausoleum in 1984, and finally the complex surrounding the Sule Pagoda in 1986.

ENC: How did people react to the modern architecture in Rangoon built in the years after independence?

USO: After independence, people in Burma not only got a taste for modern architecture, they were proud of it! After becoming independent from the British, the country's economic situation improved steadily. Modernist buildings, inspired by those of famous international architects, were being built everywhere. Between 1948 and 1962,[02] Singapore, Malaysia, and Thailand were far less progressive than Burma in terms of architecture. Our country cherished and accepted modernism undeniably. The Mingaladon International Airport, for example, was once the best airport in Southeast Asia.[03] The dome of the assembly hall of the Rangoon College of Engineering, the Nat Mauk Technical High School,[04] the new Secretariat Office, the Myanmar Radio and Television Station[05]... those modernist buildings were the pride of the country.

ENC: Did the government issue recommendations on how the buildings should be constructed and in which style? It seems that Burma's new identity was symbolized by modernist architecture; is that right?

USO: Yes, that's right. Political leaders of that period had an international perspective. They understood what was going on in the world, and as modernist architecture flourished after the Second World War, they adopted modernist architectural language to represent the new Burmese state. Both decision makers and the public embraced a new generation of modern buildings. They enjoyed them and were proud of them.

ENC: How did Myanmar modernism differ from western architecture of the same period and from that of other Southeast Asian countries?

USO: During the rule of the Burma Socialist Programme Party,[06] from 1962 to 1988, the Burmese economy was not in good shape. The lack of building materials was a big challenge for architects. As one of my senior architects once said, the government asked for 20th-century architecture but they could only provide 18th-century building materials. How could we create new designs with just brick and timber? Cement, steel, and clear glass had to be imported, but there was not enough foreign currency to spend. Only a few lucky architects—mainly the architects from the Ministry of Construction and from Architect Group II—had the opportunity to experiment with modern materials.

ENC: From 1980, with the Environmental Education Center, you also worked with concrete. This is a unique design that delicately combines modern materials and traditional Burmese architecture. What was the main idea behind this project?

USO: This was a competition launched by the Burma Forest Department and the UN Food and Agricultural Organization (FAO). The brief specifically required that the new educational center should reflect the Burmese

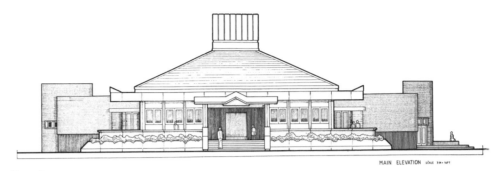

Front view.

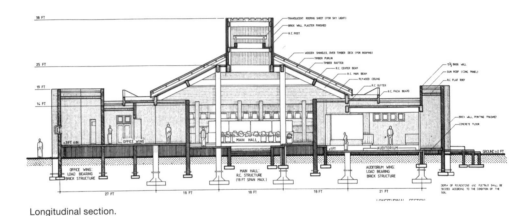

Longitudinal section.

Environmental Education Center, main entrance.

national character. Neither a traditional building nor a typical international-style building was expected, so we tried to integrate Burmese archetypes with modern materials. To do so, we simplified the classic features of traditional Burmese architecture and embedded them into a functional design. The concrete rectangular element on the roof is essentially a shikhara[07] (or *kundaung* in Burmese), the Hindu equivalent of the European spire. In this case, it functions as a skylight for the central hall. The four triangular concrete elements placed at each of the roof's eaves, in Burmese traditional architecture, are called *tu yin*. The small masonry walls running around the podium are called *tha yet kin*. Such unique features and components of Burmese architecture were carefully embedded into the design. The great Japanese

architects of the 20th century used a similar approach, translating Japanese traditional forms into a new architectural language.

ENC: Was there an exchange of ideas with architects from abroad? How did you get information? Were there any professional networks?

USO: At the time, international professional networks were out of the question. From 1962 to 1989 Burma was behind the "teak curtain," like China was behind the "bamboo curtain." The citizens of Burma rarely had a chance to get a visa to travel abroad. They were not even allowed to talk to foreigners freely. Only a few foreigners were permitted to visit Burma at that time. There was only a handful of TV channels and no internet—but we had some books and magazines, which gave us a window to look

at what was happening outside of the country. The architecture department library was a rare opportunity for students to access international magazines, such as *Progressive Architecture, AD, JA, A+U,* and more.

ENC: Please tell us more about the design of the Martyrs' Mausoleum (see feature on the Mausoleum in the following pages). This was a very symbolic building for the regime. Did the government specifically ask for a modern design, or was this your own proposal?

USO: The original design we submitted for the Martyrs' Mausoleum competition had a striking diagonal roof structure placed on a high podium, which was intended to incorporate the pre-existing tombs. It was a totally modern design, as requested by the government. However, just as

we were about to proceed with the planning, there was the tragic bombing of 1983—a failed attempt orchestrated by North Korean agents to assassinate the prime minister of South Korea, Chun Doo-hwan, during a state visit to the old mausoleum. The blast killed 21 people. Immediately after the accident, the cabinet requested that we revise the design: we were to remove the roof and only keep the podium. Within a few days, we presented a new design. We decided to transform the original shape of the roof ridge into a sculpture emerging from the podium. In terms of materials, we didn't have much choice. The country was on the verge of bankruptcy and expensive materials like stone, etc., were simply out of question. Brick and reinforced concrete were really the only options.

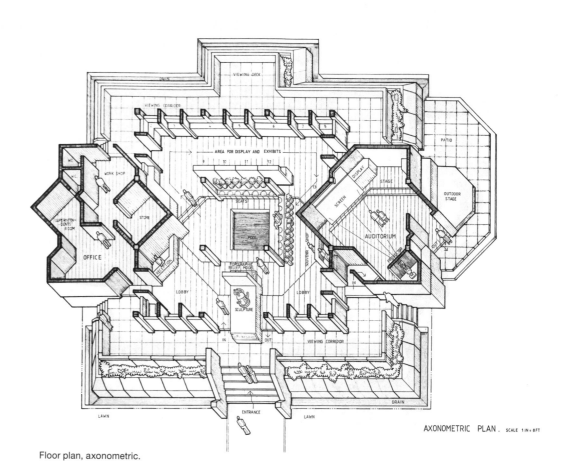

Floor plan, axonometric.

AXONOMETRIC PLAN. SCALE 1 IN = 8FT

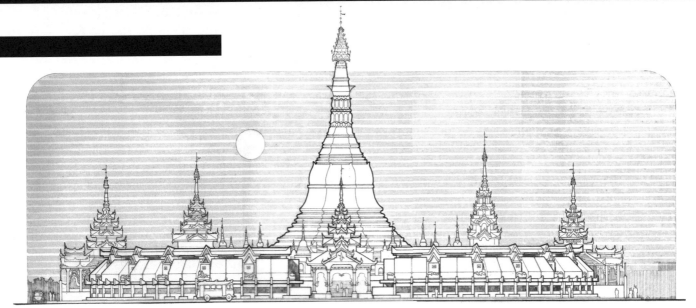

တောင်ဘက်-မတ်ရပ်ပုံ
SOUTH ELEVATION scale _ 1 IN = 16 FT.

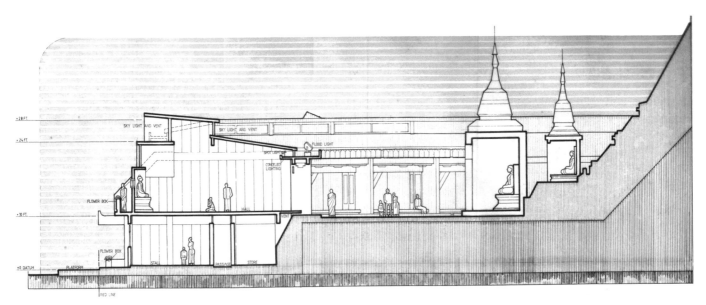

ဖြတ်ပိုင်းပုံ
SECTION scale _ 3 IN = 16 FT.

Above
South view of the complex
around Sule Pagoda, 1986.

Below
Section: The ground floor
has street-facing shops.
The rooms on the second
floor are connected to
the pagoda courtyard.

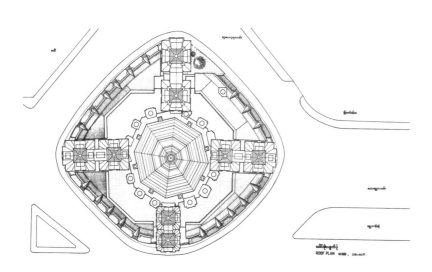

ခေါင်မိုးရှုတ်ပုံ
ROOF PLAN scale _

Roof, top view.

ENC: Your 1986 design for the complex surrounding the Sule Pagoda is fascinating. It integrates a bold modern architectural language with a highly symbolic historical site. What was the original brief for this project? How did people react to seeing such a modern design next to the ancient pagoda?

USO: The Sule Pagoda board of trustees asked for a modern-style podium that would harmonize with the existing stupa and the four traditional tiered roof pavilions at each entrance. Luckily, the majority of the trustees were very open-minded and we won the competition. They understood that modern architecture also had the power to transport a nation's culture. Of course, there were also some opponents among the general public, people who believed that the new complex clashed with the traditional style of the existing structures. But overall, the new building was welcomed with enthusiasm, because it pulled together the whole site and spoke for its time. People saw it as a symbol of progress, bridging the old with the new.

ENC: What is it like today for architects in Myanmar?

USO: These days, good design is not appreciated in Myanmar. There is no long-term vision. Clients and decision makers do not have any aesthetic ambitions that adequately represent the country today. They would rather have buildings that look similar to the ones they have seen on their trips to Singapore, Malaysia, or Australia. Nor do architects have a vision; they aren't thinking about what it could look like to continue the country's 1,600-years-long architectural tradition. They don't think about how they could narrate the great changes that Myanmar has gone through. Today in Myanmar, if you are

going to build a public or a religious building in the local style, you are probably going to have the tiered spire made by a traditional craftsman in Tanpawadi, a quarter in Mandalay known for its artisans who produce traditional arts and crafts. Especially during the time of the military rule, under the State Law and Order Restoration Council (SLORC, 1988–97) and the State Peace and Development Council (SPDC, 1997–2011), people thought that in order to build truly Myanmar architecture they had to replicate the same designs from the Konbaung era. They built pagodas like the Shwe Dagon Pagoda. But the design of pagodas in Myanmar has evolved. The general public has forgotten that, while we need to create designs that are truly Burmese in style, we also have to speak for our own time. We cannot limit ourselves to copying 200-year-old designs.

ENC: Was that attitude different in the past?

USO: Nowadays we are importing materials from all over the world. They have become part of our society and culture. During the socialist era, the country wasn't wealthy enough to import materials. Modernist architecture was not lavish, but primarily functional. After the uprisings of 1988, when the Burma Socialist Programme Party was deposed by a new coup, Myanmar started importing new materials. But due to the Asian financial crisis of 1997 and the Myanmar banking crisis of 2003, changes in the industry were slow to come about. From 2000 onwards, building standards generally improved. But even more important than the quality of the materials and workmanship is the design quality. Even if everything else is good, people won't like a poor design.

KCN: What are your personal ambitions for the future?

USO: Throughout my career, I always explored the idea of a Myanmar-specific modernism, which combines the principles and aesthetics of Myanmar tradition with modernism in new, creative ways. Unfortunately, I seldom meet clients who are open to such ideas. During my 40 years working as an architect, I've had maybe ten opportunities to build something in a truly modern Myanmar style, and I cherish each one of them.

This conversation is an excerpted from a video interview conducted on November 15, 2019 with documentary filmmaker Christopher Chan Nyein in Yangon. The questions were developed by Moritz Henning, Pwint, and Win Thant Win Shwin and later added to by Mirko Gatti and Moritz Henning in an email correspondence with U Sun Oo.

01   U Sun Oo and Associates included partners U Wint Khin Zaw (B. Arch., RIT 1979), now in Australia; U Gavin Tun (B. Arch., RIT 1980), now in Spain; and U Khin Maung Lat (B. Arch., RIT 1982), a founding partner of Design 2000 architects in Yangon.
02   On March 3, 1962, the government led by prime Minister U Nu was overthrown by a military coup led by commander Ne Win. This date marks the start of Burma's transition towards a one-party socialist state.
03   Mingaladon International Airport was built in 1947 by

the Calcutta Metropolitan Airports Authority on the site of the former Mingaladon Airfield used by the British Royal Air Force. Before Burma isolated itself internationally, Mingaladon was regarded as the primary hub in the region. It was later superseded by other hubs such as Singapore, Bangkok, and Jakarta.
04   The assembly hall of the Rangoon Engineering College and the Nat Mauk Technical High School in Yangon were designed by the British architect Raglan Squire and both completed in 1956.

05   The Burma Broadcasting Service Station (now the Myanmar Radio and Television Station) was completed in 1960.
06   From 1964 onwards, the Burma Socialist Programme Party was the country's sole legal political party.
07   Shikhara (literally "mountain peak") is the term used in South India to indicate the top element of the elongated, domed tower of traditional Hindu temples; in North India, the term is sometimes used to indicate the entire dome tower.

139

Sule Pagoda, said to date back to the 5th century BCE, along with its modernist extension,
is now located on a large, heavily trafficked roundabout.

BOGYOKE AUNG SAN MAUSOLEUM
(MARTYRS' MAUSOLEUM)

The Martyrs' Mausoleum in its present state with Shwedagon Pagoda in the background.

U Sun Oo and team, Rangoon Institute of Technology

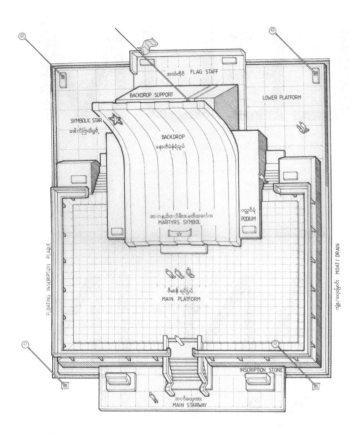

Above
Floor plan, axonometric.

Below
Perspective drawing, back
of the mausoleum.

Text: Moritz Henning with
Brian Win Thant Win Shwin

On July 19, 1947, shortly after negotiations were held securing the independence of Burma, now Myanmar, Burmese nationalist leader and now national hero, Aung San,[01] along with seven other ministers, were assassinated during a cabinet meeting in Rangoon. To commemorate the victims, a small pavilion was erected at the foot of the famous Shwedagon Pagoda in the early 1960s, which was to be replaced by a new mausoleum in 1982. The competition was awarded to the design team at Rangoon Institute of Technology (RIT), led by the young architect U Sun Oo, who envisaged an open pavilion based on traditional building forms and constructed mainly of wood. However, the plans were not implemented in this form. In 1983, the old memorial was the site of a bomb attack on South Korean President Chun Doo-hwan, who was about to lay a wreath there during a state visit. While the president survived the assassination attempt perpetrated by North Korean agents, 21 people died and 47 were injured. U Sun Oo was asked to revise his design for the mausoleum to ensure more security in the event of another attack. This included changes such as the removal of the roof.

U Sun Oo soon submitted a new proposal, but that, too, had to be revised due to a personal intervention by the socialist President Ne Win, a general who came to power following a coup d'état in 1962. Some of the planned details were left out

in the implementation of the design, which is why—as U Sun Oo later commented—the monument lacked the spirit it was intended to convey.[02] It was not until the monument's renovation in 2016 that some of the originally planned elements were added, such as the biographies of the martyrs and the symbolic star perforating the ramp. Under Ne Win, the monument was dedicated only to anonymous national martyrs, as the legacy of Aung San and the ministers were to be erased from the country's collective memory.

What remained of U Sun Oo's original plans was a modern, curved structure of reinforced concrete and brick, referencing the form and dimensions of Burma's traditional religious monuments. U Sun Oo's efforts to create an iconic, modern monument are recognizable, but were ultimately not fully realized due to the political circumstances. The Martyrs' Mausoleum is therefore a material reflection of the history of Myanmar's independence since colonial rule—infused with great pathos.

01 The Mausoleum was originally dedicated to Aung San, the father of Nobel laureate and later de facto head of government, Aung San Suu Kyi, who was arrested in February 2021 following a military coup.
02 Kyaw Phyo Tha, "Rangoon's Martyrs' Monument Revamped to Highlight Aung San," *The Irrawaddy*, July 12, 2016, accessed June 17, 2021, www.irrawaddy.com/ news/burma/rangoons-martyrs-monument-revamped-to-highlight-aung-san.html.

Al Mansfeld
with David Yanai

A MAUSOLEUM FOR AUNG SAN IN RANGOON

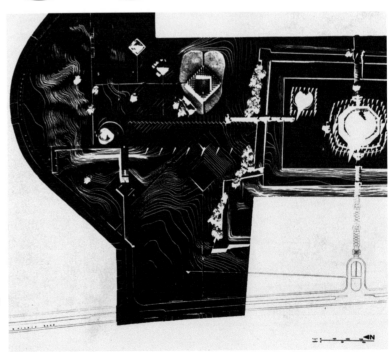

Site plan with the mausoleum design by Al Mansfeld (left) and the existing Shwedagon Pagoda (right).

Images, unless otherwise stated, from: Alfred Mansfeld, "Mausoleo a Rangoon," *L'Architettura: Cronache e Storia* 115 (May 1965): 27.

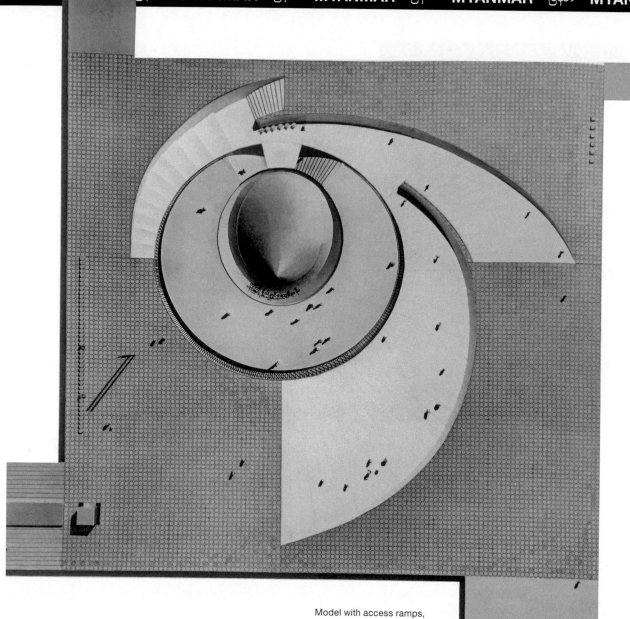

Text: Eduard Kögel

Model with access ramps, photographed from above. From Anna Teut, ed., *Al Mansfeld: Architekt in Israel. An architect in Israel* (Berlin: Ernst & Sohn, 1999), 72.

In 1961, Burma's prime minister U Nu approached the Israeli government for help in planning a mausoleum for General Aung San, who had been shot dead during a cabinet meeting 14 years earlier.[01] The Israeli architect Al Mansfeld (1912–2004), who grew up in Berlin, was proposed for the project, for which he joined forces with his colleague David Yanai. However, their design never came to fruition. In March 1962, General Ne Win took power in a coup d'état and did not continue the project as planned. Nevertheless, the design for the mausoleum occupies an outstanding position within Mansfeld's work and demonstrates the architect's sensitivity in making the country's cultural foundations the starting point of his approach.

The first time Mansfield traveled to Rangoon was to sign the contract, during which time he visited the intended building site located in the immediate vicinity of Shwedagon Pagoda. Considered the religious center of the country, the pagoda is said to be more than 2,500 years old, and made a great impression on Mansfeld. Realizing that he would have to delve deeper into local history and culture for this project, the architect returned to Asia a short time later.[02] During this extended tour he visited, among other places, Burma's historic temple complexes in Mandalay and Bagan as well as the cave temples of Ellora and Ajanta in India. In the process, he made an observation that was instrumental in shaping his design: he saw pilgrims moving in a strictly clockwise direction around the sacred sites as part of their ritual practice. He applied this circumambulation, called *pradakshina*, as a basic principle to the interior and exterior of the mausoleum, bringing it into a radically modern but timeless form.

The mausoleum was to be laid out on a square terrace and entered through a slightly lower main entrance reached by a circular ramp. With its open interior, the building differs from the traditional Buddhist monuments, stupas, from which Mansfeld drew inspiration for the form. The upper end of the cone-shaped mausoleum was cut at an angle, with which the architect wanted to symbolize the sudden death of Aung San. The missing part of the volume protruded into the interior as a negative form, the tip of which almost touched the actual tomb, which was also

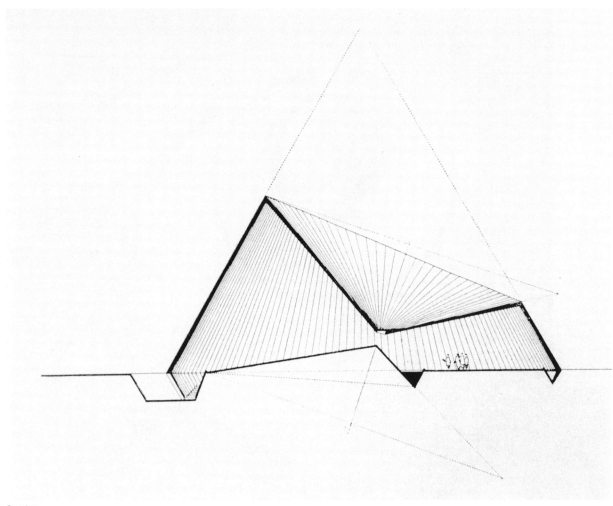

Section.

conical and was sunken diagonally into the ground. At the tip of the cone was a small opening, allowing natural light to penetrate the interior. During the monsoon, masses of water were expected to flow through this hole onto the tomb, thereby connecting heaven and earth. A surrounding basin would collect the rainwater. Mansfeld wanted to cover the interior's surface with matt white ceramic tiles, which would reflect the diffuse light and reference the traditional color of mourning. The exterior wall of the truncated cone, on the other hand, was to be covered in golden-brown mosaic tiles—establishing a link with the gilded cone-shaped

pagodas in Burma and, not least, with the Shwedagon Pagoda.

Even though Mansfeld's mausoleum for Aung San was never realized, the design was met with a positive response at the time. When the Association of German Architects awarded Mansfeld its plaque of honor in 1969, Gerhart Laage wrote, "Architecturally speaking, an attempt was made to bring the outlines and forms of the memorial in dialogue with the monuments of the region, but without imitating them."[03] Julius Posener, in his citation at the award ceremony, noted, "The tomb and monument may confidently be called unique. ... We have seen that the

mausoleum may also follow the rules of masterful building. ... Mansfeld has made great strides in the way of architectural artistry."[04]

The military, which came to power with General Ne Win, clearly did not appreciate the abstract transformation of religious motifs, and Mansfeld's design disappeared into a drawer.

01   Burma was the first Asian country to establish friendly relations with Israel in the 1950s. The first diplomatic representative they sent was David Hacohen, a former senior manager at the Solel Boneh construction company. It is certainly no coincidence that this company, which operates in many developing countries, is also active in Myanmar with joint ventures, particularly in housing construction.
02   "The impression was overwhelming," Mansfeld later wrote. See Anna Teut, ed., *Al Mansfeld: Architekt in Israel. An architect in Israel* (Berlin: Ernst & Sohn, 1999), 94.
03   "Ehrenplakette des BDA für Alfred Mansfeld," *Der Architekt* 11 (1969): 380–88; 384.
04   Julius Posener, "Laudatio, aus Anlass der Verleihung der Ehrenplakette für ausländische Architekten an Al Mansfeld," *Der Architekt* 12 (1969): 413f.

Above
Model of the interior;
a single light source
illuminates the top of the
cone-shaped tomb.

Below
Model of the exterior.

U Maung Maung Gyi and team

YANGON REGION PARLIAMENT (FORMER PEOPLE'S CONGRESS)

01   Renaud Egreteau, "Power, Cultural Nationalism, and Postcolonial Public Architecture: Building a Parliament House in Post-Independence Myanmar," *Commonwealth & Comparative Politics* 55, no. 4 (2017), 531–50, accessed June 17, 2020, doi.org/10.1080/14662043.2017.1323401.

© Manuel Oka

Yangon Region Parliament, view from the southwest.

© Moritz Henning

Left
View into the inner courtyard.

Below
Plenary hall.

Text: Moritz Henning,
Pwint and Win Thant Win Shwin

© Moritz Henning

In 1922, the Legislative Council in British Burma was recast as a partially elected body for the first time. For its meetings, a modest pavilion was erected in the courtyard of the Secretariat, the seat of British colonial and administrative power in Burma since the late 1880s. Another 52 years would pass until the parliament, then called the People's Congress, received its own building. The first democratic government after independence under Prime Minister U Nu failed due to a variety of conflicts—not least over the design of the future parliament building. Ironically, the construction of the People's Congress did not take place until after the military seized power in 1962, establishing the one-party dictatorship of General Ne Win. Four teams of architects, including U Shwe with the Rangoon Institute of Technology, were invited to submit a design, with U Maung Maung Gyi's group winning the bid.

Ne Win's Burma Socialist Programme Party (BSPP) favored the proposal that adopted the traditional architectural language of the Konbaung dynasty (1752–1885), which had wruled the country before the British. The traditional stepped roof (*pyatthat*) used in Myanmar architecture was thus applied to the People's Congress, while the concrete slab-column construction system exposed on the façade reflects the modern and functional character of the new parliament building. Courtyards provided natural lighting and ventilation as well as passive cooling of the building. Inside the building, the regime under Ne Win continued its efforts to erase the colonial legacy by changing the seating arrangement from two tiers facing one another, inherited from the British Parliament, to an amphitheater. This also reflected the regime's choice to override the bicameral system introduced by the Government

of Burma Act in 1935 and revert to a unicameral parliament, with the People's Congress serving as the country's supreme legislative body.[01]

Ne Win, head of state during the military dictatorship, used this new building as the main seat of government and considered it to be the architectural embodiment of the "Burmese path to socialism," a strictly isolationist course that led to the impoverishment of the population. In 2005, Myanmar's capital was moved to Naypyidaw. The parliament moved into the newly planned city in a palatial building with exuberant, historicist

embellishments. In comparison, the old People's Congress, despite its exterior expressing the power of the Ne Win regime, seems downright modest and reserved. With the move, the People's Congress in Yangon lost its central importance. Today it is where the Yangon Region Parliament holds its meetings.

Left
Design for a prayer hall in
Dhammaryon, 1996.

Below
Design for the Golden
Pavilion, Bagan Hotel, 1994.

THE TRADITION OF MODERNITY

GOLDEN PAVILLION.

A conversation with U Shwe for *Encounters with Southeast Asian Modernism*

The architect U Shwe trained in Japan before returning to Burma in 1972. In his native country, became a teacher of architecture at the Rangoon Institute of Technology, working there until his retirement in 1990. His career as a teacher exerted a decisive influence on several generations of Burmese architects. One of his major preoccupations was teaching Burmese modernism as a synthesis of local traditions and Western influences.

ENCOUNTERS WITH SOUTHEAST ASIAN MODERNISM: You grew up in Myanmar when it wasn't yet possible to study architecture there. So how did you get into architecture?

U SHWE: After I finished school, I applied for a scholarship in Japan. The recipients of the Japanese government scholarship were selected by the Burmese government. During the interview, I was asked what field of study I would like to enter. At first, I chose textile engineering. But during my first year in Japan, when I was mainly just learning Japanese, it was still possible to change subjects. A Brazilian friend, who was also a student there, told me about Brasília and showed me pictures of the big modern buildings which were soon to be built. I looked at them and asked him, "What is the name of the subject when you learn how to build big buildings?" He said, "The subject is architecture." This piqued my interest in architecture, although I knew almost nothing about it: I was about 17 or 18 years old at the time. The next day I went to the embassy and told them I no longer wanted to be a textile engineer, that I wanted to study architecture instead.

To study architecture, I went to Maebashi Municipal College of Technology [today the Maebashi Institute of Technology], a technical college with a strong focus on structural engineering. But the school was not good for design training. And since everything was taught in Japanese, I had failed an exam. Since my scholarship was only guaranteed for four years, I would have to finance my final year out of my own pocket, so I took a year off to work and make some money. I also knew the knowledge I had acquired so far would hardly have any relevance in Myanmar, so I decided to switch to Yokohama National University, which at the time was known for its strength in design and other artistic subjects. So that's where I graduated from.

ENC: You did not come back to Myanmar straight away after graduation—you stayed on in Japan and gained practical experience. What did you do during that time?

US: After graduating from college, I was able to do a one-year internship in Japan. I thought about Kenzō Tange and Yoshinobu Ashihara for this, but ultimately I chose Ashihara, because he thought very seriously about

how to combine traditional Japanese simplicity with modern architecture, whereas other architects often only imitated modernist styles from other countries. After my internship, I spent another six months in the design department of the construction company Kajima. In the 1950s, Kajima had played a key role in building Myanmar's biggest hydroelectric power station, at Lawpita Falls in Kayah, which the Japanese government financed as reparation for the occupation in World War II.

ENC: Can you describe your architectural approach? You are obviously influenced by Japanese architecture, among other things.

US: The essence of Japanese architecture is simplicity. In Japan I learned that the concept of simplicity still holds true. When Frank Lloyd Wright finished the Imperial Hotel in Tokyo in 1923, he said he learned something fundamental from Japanese architecture, which was to leave out what was unimportant. This idea shapes my thinking to this day. We can also learn from the simplicity of traditional Burmese architecture. The temples of Bagan may well contain useful lessons for the future. In being open to other influences,

we should not lose sight of our own local needs and traditions. This is the only way to create architecture which is sustainable for the future.

In addition to Japanese architecture, I was heavily influenced by my encounter with modern Western architecture. I read a lot about Walter Gropius, Marcel Breuer, and Frank Lloyd Wright. Gropius's 1955 essay collection, *Scope of Total Architecture,* made clear to me the great influence of the Bauhaus on modern architecture. I learned about the importance of the interplay between space, form, and construction.

ENC: You came back to Myanmar in 1972. What was the situation in the country like?

US: At that time, architects basically had three job opportunities: first, at the Rangoon Institute of Technology (RIT); second, with Architect Group II, a semi-state planning office which built many industrial, research, and educational institutions in the early 1970s, under Captain Kyu Kyaw; and the third possibility was joining the Ministry of Construction, part of the government. I went for RIT, where I taught Fundamentals of Drawing and Fundamentals of Design for

Right
Design for the studio of a
watercolor painter, 1989.

Below
Design for a big house,
2003.

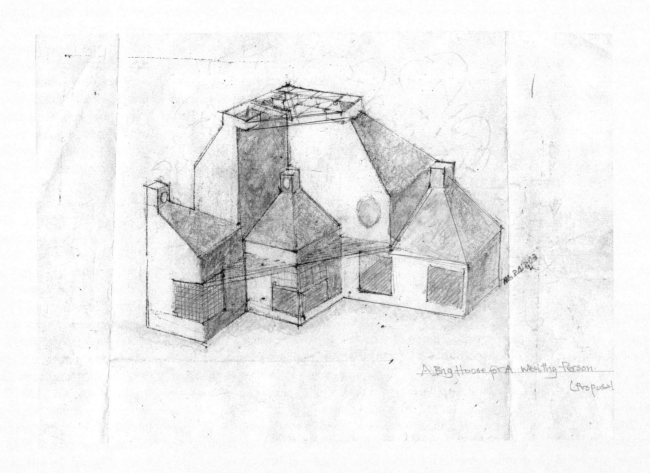

Right
Design for an office
building in Yangon, 1988.

Below
Design for a high-rise with
condominiums and a
supermarket in Yangon, 1997.

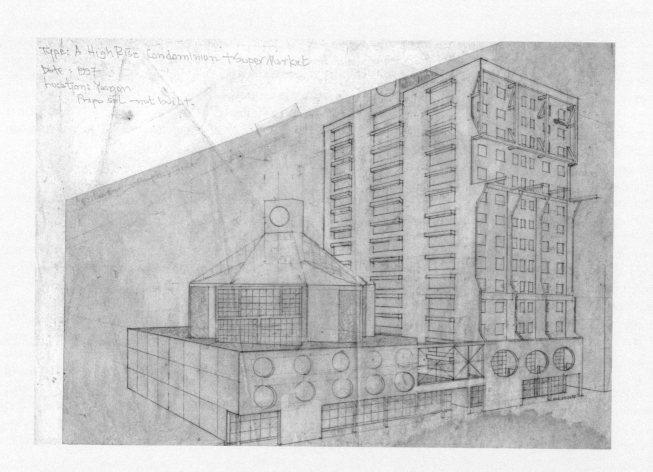

153

nearly 20 years. Since the architecture department at the RIT Engineering College was still relatively new when I started, there were not enough teaching materials, and no proper curriculum. It was also unclear whether we wanted to be aligned with the Soviet Union, the United States, or Britain. At the time, German and Japanese textbooks seemed to me to have the most depth, as they were very precise and well written. So I started translating lessons from Japanese textbooks into Burmese, and using them to teach.

ENC: Did you also carry out your own architecture projects during this period?
US: Getting my ideas implemented in practice was not easy. I was only able to build two private houses the way I wanted. With other building designs, to a large extent I had to adapt to the wishes of the client, who also asked for discounts. There were very few independent architects at the time, since almost nothing was being built except by the government. The few people who could afford to build took a lot of time and were subjected to special rules. The situation was quite different from Japan, where architects could work more independently. In Myanmar there was little appreciation for architects' work; people were simply unfamiliar with it and did not understand its qualities. This was also because all construction management was still in the hands of civil engineers, who had controlled the building process since colonial times. They had a very big influence on construction, and thus on architecture too.

ENC: Can you still remember the names of the architects of your time?
US: The Architect Group II,

which I already mentioned, certainly had the most influential role purely in terms of construction activity across the country. It was led by the architect Kin Maung Lwin, along with Captain Kyu Kyaw, who died recently. They built more than 500 buildings in total, all of which had a similar, non-specific style: flat roofs, a couple of colors, marble tiles. This was linked to a very superficial understanding of modernism; it made no significant contribution to modernist architecture in Myanmar, which we now seek to recall as important cultural heritage.

Three or four other people were influential, including Sithu U Tin (1890–1972), who built the Yangon City Hall, and U Kin Maung Yin, who was a painter and a filmmaker as well as an architect. U Kin Maung Yin was too busy to focus on his architecture work, but he contributed to shaping the Burmese modern art movement in the 1960s and 1970s.

ENC: Were there women architects too?
US: There was a married couple. They were both architects. She was the first female architect in Myanmar. Unfortunately, I wasn't able to follow her work closely, since I was studying in Japan during her creative phase.[01]

ENC: Can you tell us how modern architecture first came to Myanmar?
US: Among the first modern buildings in Yangon were the impressive dome designed by Raglan Squire for the assembly hall of the Engineering College, built with financial support from the USA in 1954–55 (see Benjamin Bansal's article in this issue); the Nat Mauk Technical High School, also by Squire, built in 1956; and the Yangon International

Airport, which opened in 1947. Those three buildings opened our eyes; they were the first important steps toward modern architecture in Myanmar. They were all very different from typical buildings of the time, and everyone was very impressed: *Wow, this is how you can build today!* Other modern structures were built with Soviet assistance, like the Rangoon Institute of Technology, built in 1961 by Pavel Stenyushin; the Sao San Htun Hospital in Taunggyi, also known as the "Russian Hospital," built in 1961; and the Inya Lake Hotel, built in 1962 by Viktor Andreyev and Kaleriya Kislova. But these buildings were much more conservative.

ENC: Did the government have any influence on architectural design? Did architecture change with independence?
US: In the colonial era, architects had a status like that of civil servants. British architects could ask for a lot of money when they applied for such a position with the authorities in countries like India or Myanmar. The British only commissioned civil engineers in those places, but didn't hire anyone to work on design. After all, it was master masons who made the temple complex at Bagan, the historic royal city, not civil engineers.

The foundation of the Engineering College in 1954 finally put architecture on the curriculum, alongside mining, mechanical, and civil engineering. At the time, teachers of architecture mostly came from India, from the University of Calcutta, but they too did not understand modernism. No one understood what terms like "modern" or "not modern" really meant. So they mimicked the forms of modernism without truly understanding the ideas, the underlying philosophy. Even now,

I think one of the main tasks of the universities is to impart this knowledge to students.

ENC: What do you understand by modernism and modernity?
US: Modernism is not just a Western phenomenon. Regardless of which country we're talking about, modernism for me, beyond particular stylistic tendencies, is associated with a way of thinking that is future-oriented and based on reason. So we should not just have Europe or the United States in mind when we talk about modernism. Modernity had an impact all over the world. People who are committed to modernist ideas and principles today should not be afraid to put them into practice. But to be modern does not mean being opposed to tradition.

Maybe modernity will only be realized in Myanmar if society, economy, politics, and architecture again come together in a single "project" driving society as a whole. The old royal city of Bagan emerged from a strong desire to create forms of expression for the new religion. Today we face a completely different situation: for decades, our society has been wasting its entire energy in simmering political and ethnic conflicts. Nothing new can emerge from this.

ENC: How do you think modernity and tradition can be reconciled in Myanmar?
US: It's hard to say, and the combination of the two has indeed produced strange fruits. Often plans were made for a functional building, but then later a *pyatthat*—a multitiered roof—was added on top, and this was sold as being part of Burmese tradition. The word for this kind of roof is derived from *prasada*, which comes from Sanskrit and in Hinduism refers to the buildings where the gods live. That kind of

Above
KMK House in
Mandalay, 1992.

Below
KMK House,
design sketch.

roof was put on the main station in Yangon, built by U Hla Gyaw in 1954; on the Yangon City Hall, built by U Tin in 1925–40; and on the parliament building, built in 1974 in Yangon by U Maung Maung Gyi; among other examples. At the time, a critic referred to this type of building as being in the style of Princes Myin Kun and Myin Khondaing. These two princes had rebelled against King Mindon Min in the 19th century, but lost the fight, and fled to Saigon. In Vietnam, they dressed in Western clothing but kept the traditional Burmese bun in their hair. Smart shoes, western suits, but with a bun. And this is how these buildings were constructed, with their lower sections located in the West, but with a pyatthat stuck on top. That was a very astute criticism. The style still exists today.

ENC: Were there conflicts between tradition and modernity?
US: After the British took over

Myanmar in 1886, the importance of traditional Burmese architecture quickly diminished. The new colonial rulers built public buildings in the style of their own country; nobody thought of building in the Burmese style. The Western influences on many public buildings of the time can still be clearly seen: for example, the bank buildings along Pansodan Road.

Most people today think that buildings from this time are not part of our culture. But that is a problem, since both of these things—the Burmese architectural tradition, and the influence of Western modernity—are now part of our culture. It should be about finding a synthesis.

Raglan Squire was a pioneer in this regard. He based the dome of the Engineering College assembly hall on the round huts built by the Shans, an ethnic group in eastern Myanmar. When the dome fell into disrepair, myself

Interior of the KYK House in
its current state.

© Moritz Henning

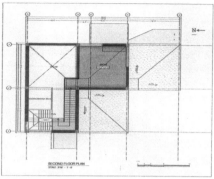

Floor plan,
second floor.

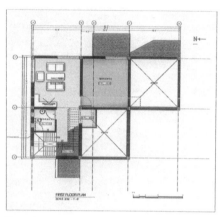

Floor plan,
first floor.

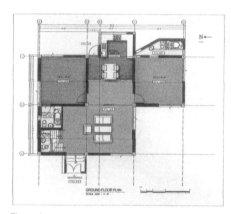

Floor plan,
ground floor.

and my colleague Nyi Hla Nge, director of Civil Engineering at RIT, wrote an essay to convince the people in charge of the building that they should maintain the dome. The essay was entitled, "We Preserve Our Tradition," but we could have added: *by preserving the legacy of modernism.* We argued that the dome did not follow an English design, and that it was actually derived from the shape of huts at Inle, in the Shan state. But the officials in charge did not want to oppose the government's decision—they were afraid they might get into trouble. So eventually, the dome was demolished, and now the building is lost. The Burmese do not know about their own building traditions. This lack of appreciation

is also a societal problem. Only by teaching these complex inter-relationships can we find a balance between the different forces that impact a culture.

This is an excerpt from a video interview filmed in Yangon on November 14, 2019, by the documentary filmmaker Christopher Chan Nyein. The questions were developed by Pwint, Win Thant Win Shwin, and Moritz Henning.

01   The couple he is referring
to are Daw Thin Thin Aye
and her husband U Win Myint.

KYK House in Yangon,
watercolor, 2005.

157

GAPORE 新加坡 *Sing*

ngapura சிங்கப்பூர் *S*

加坡 *Singapura* சிங்

SINGAPORE 新加坡 *Sin*

சிங்கப்பூர் SINGAPOI

Singapura சிங்கப்பூர்

新加坡 *Singapura*

apura சிங்கப்பூர் SIN

SINGAPORE 新加坡

The Republic of Singapore is a city-state located on an island off the southern tip of Malaysia. It currently has a population of over 5.7 million. Since independence in 1965, the country's politics has been determined by the People's Action Party (PAP). Singapore is one of the wealthiest countries in the world, but also has a particularly high cost of living. The island's area is limited, which presents a series of particular economic, ecological, social, and cultural challenges.

Singapore's modern history began with the foundation of the British East India Company by the Englishman Stamford Raffles in 1819. Until then, the island had been sparsely populated. In 1867, Singapore, along with the Malay peninsula, was declared a British Crown colony. During the Second World War, Singapore was occupied by the Japanese, who surrendered in 1945, returning the island to British rule. In 1959, Singapore became a self-governing Crown colony. In the first elections, the PAP emerged as the winner, with Lee Kuan Yew becoming prime minister. In 1963, Singapore merged with Malaya, Sabah, and Sarawak to form the Malaysia Federation and in this way gained formal independence from Britain as a colonial power. But the federation only lasted a short time; Singapore was expelled from Malaysia in 1965, and has since existed as an independent city-state.

Under Lee Kuan Yew, who ruled until 1990, the PAP launched a campaign to modernize the country. Within a single generation, Singapore went from being a developing country to being a highly industrialized one. In the early 1960s, the Housing and Development Board (HDB) was established, with the task of creating modern, affordable homes for slum dwellers and, in doing so, to contribute to economic growth. Given the limited area of the state, dense high-rise settlements were constructed. These would eventually receive international attention, and many political delegations arrived to visit the new buildings from neighboring Asian countries, but also from West Germany, for example. Today, around 80 percent of Singapore's population still lives in HDB housing. The homes are subject to a leasing system, whereby the land remains in public hands. Since the 1990s, the early developments have been renovated or completely rebuilt. However, the future of these iconic modern buildings is now uncertain, and many have already fallen victim to profit-oriented new construction projects. SB/MH/CH/EK

TIONG BAHRU
A modernist district in the tropics

Courtesy *The Straits Times* © SPH

Opening celebration for Tiong Bahru Community
Centre, Singapore, July 8, 1951.

Text: Ho Puay-Peng

Tiong Bahru was the first housing estate by the Singapore Improvement Trust (SIT), designed and built between 1936 and 1950. Created during British colonial rule with the passing of the Singapore Improvement Ordinance of 1927, SIT's main mandate was "to provide for the improvement of the Town and Island of Singapore" by clearing the slums, redeveloping the narrow back lanes of the traditional shophouse neighborhoods, and generally improving the conditions of dwellings, notoriously unsanitary and overcrowded.[01]

01 James Milner Fraser, *The
Work of the Singapore
Improvement Trust 1927–47*
(Singapore: Authority of
Singapore Improvement Trust,
1948), 2.

The dwellings built between 1936 and 1941 are based on the traditional shophouse typology. The backyards are used collectively and separated by thin, high walls.

among the first to introduce modernist principles in housing design in Singapore. After briefly working in the housing department of the London County Council and West Ham Borough Council, Fraser spent almost the entirety of his professional career in Singapore, serving the SIT first as an architect, then as manager, and finally as the chairman of the board. Before leaving Singapore, Fraser helped to draft the legislative framework that led to the setting up of the Housing and Development Board (HDB), which replaced the colonial SIT after British disengagement in 1958, and which has played a crucial role in the development of independent, modern Singapore ever since.

The two construction phases of the Tiong Bahru estate are clearly visible in the different urban layouts. The pre-war blocks are arranged in clusters around large courtyards, while the later ones are strictly aligned along neat rows. The buildings are by-the-book reproductions of the modern housing estates realized for workers in North and West London in the same years, like the Ossulston Estate (architect: George Topham Forrest; completion: 1931) or the iconic Kensal House (architect: Maxwell Fry; completion: 1937). The large horseshoe cluster is reminiscent of the famous *Hufeisensiedlung* in Berlin-Britz (architect: Bruno Taut; built 1925–33). These European models, however, were implemented with consideration given to Singapore's hot and humid tropical climate as well as the local building tradition. Modernist elements in the design include flat roofs, ribbon windows, slit-vents below the windows, and round-edged brick balconies. But while the buildings appear unquestionably modern from the outside, the internal layouts of the units—especially those of the pre-war period—follow quite closely those of the traditional Asian shophouses.

The layouts realized during the first phase of construction feature small staircases that lead directly from the sidewalk onto a landing on the first floor, granting access to two units each. Bedrooms are at the front, facing the street, and utilities at the rear. Like in the traditional shophouse, the rear of the units is cut in half so to obtain a small backyard space next to the kitchen and washroom. In order to meet modern fire-safety standards, the courtyard space is partially occupied by a fire escape staircase. The pre-war portion of the Tiong Bahru estate was among the first social-housing projects realized in Singapore. It proved very successful in terms of the high living standards and became a source of pride for the Singapore Improvement Trust. Photos of the estate featured on the cover of the yearly SIT report for

The plot of land where Tiong Bahru stands today used to be a cemetery at the fringe of the city, occupied by around 2,000 squatters. In 1927, the land was acquired by the SIT, which cleared the site and built roads in an attempt to make it more attractive for private developers. But because no one expressed interest in the project, the SIT decided to develop the area itself. This resulted in the construction of 20 housing blocks, including 784 apartments, during an initial phase from 1936 to 1941, plus a further 55 blocks, including 1,258 apartments, completed after the Second World War, in 1954. The design of the complex is attributed to the Scottish architect James Milner Fraser, who was

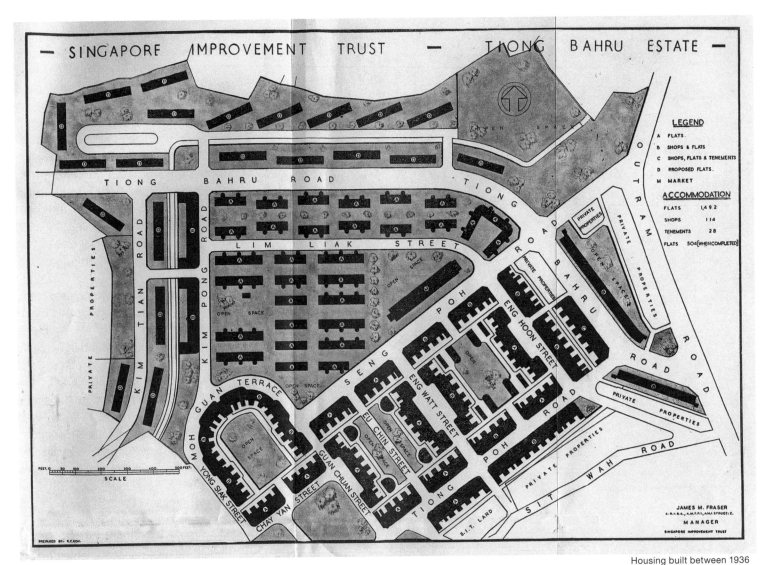

- SINGAPORE IMPROVEMENT TRUST - TIONG BAHRU ESTATE -

LEGEND
- A FLATS.
- B SHOPS & FLATS
- C SHOPS, FLATS & TENEMENTS
- D PROPOSED FLATS.
- M MARKET

ACCOMMODATION
FLATS	1,492
SHOPS	114
TENEMENTS	28
FLATS	504 [WHEN COMPLETED]

JAMES M. FRASER
A.R.I.B.A., A.M.T.P.I., A.M.I.STRUCT.E.
MANAGER
SINGAPORE IMPROVEMENT TRUST

Housing built between 1936 and 1941 was arranged in blocks and based on the traditional shophouse typology (lower right), while postwar apartment buildings are laid out in rows (upper left).

many years, and foreign dignitaries were often invited to visit Tiong Bahru as one of the most successful public housing programs in Southeast Asia. Several other SIT estates in Singapore, partially realized before SIT was disbanded in 1960, such as Queenstown and Toa Payoh, were planned according to the Tiong Bahru prototype.

The blocks realized after the war are very different in character from the pre-war ones. They consist of four-story blocks with three external semi-circular staircases projecting from the facade, each one serving two flats per floor. The units are not as large as the pre-war types, but they are better lit and ventilated. All of them benefit from large balconies and verandas, providing cool semi-open spaces that are well-suited to the tropical climate. The perfectly orthogonal north-south exposure of these later blocks breaks completely with the preexisting urban fabric, representing an entirely new direction in urban planning compared to earlier approaches.

Today, according to the Urban Redevelopment Authority's master-plan, 20 blocks of the Tiong Bahru estate are protected as listed heritage. To this day, the high standards offered by Fraser's design remain unchallenged, but the estate has changed remarkably in character since its conception almost 100 years ago. Low-rise housing complexes with a distinct urban character like Tiong Bahru are uncommon in Singapore, and the estate has gained a reputation as a desirable and culturally vibrant district. The apartments are now occupied by a mix of long-term residents and a cosmopolitan young crowd attracted by its popular cafes and restaurants. Preservation of the estate is now secured, also thanks to its commercial success, but it remains to be seen if the complex will succeed in staying diverse and accessible to low-income dwellers. Singapore's own tradition of progressive public housing policies and its groundbreaking 99-year property rights system offer the legal infrastructure to save Tiong Bahru from real estate speculation. But it is essential that, along with the buildings themselves, a collective memory of their original social ambition is also preserved, in order to inspire a new generation of Singaporean architects.

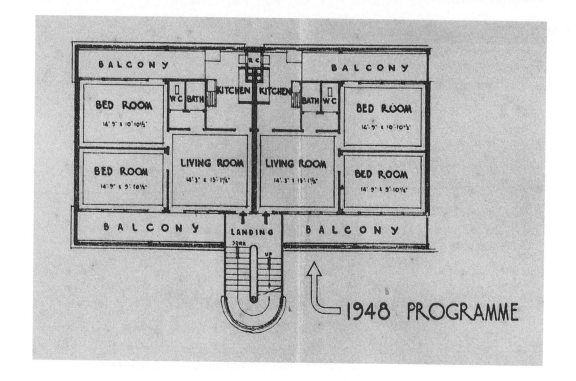

Floor plan of a prewar apartment unit, featuring street-facing bedrooms with a balcony or porch. Bathrooms and kitchens face the backyard.

Above
Housing built after 1948 featured rational floor plans oriented to both sides of the building, accessed via an exterior stairwell.

Below
Guests at the opening of Tiong Bahru Community Centre, Singapore, July 8, 1951.

Courtesy *The Straits Times* © SPH

Above
Tiong Bahru, with its many
small shops and cafés,
is one of Singapore's most
popular districts today.

Below
Art Deco elements, such as
rounded balconies,
verandas, and cantilevered
canopies are not only
stylistically interesting, but
also serve to adapt the
architecture to Singapore's
tropical climate.

All images © Darren Soh

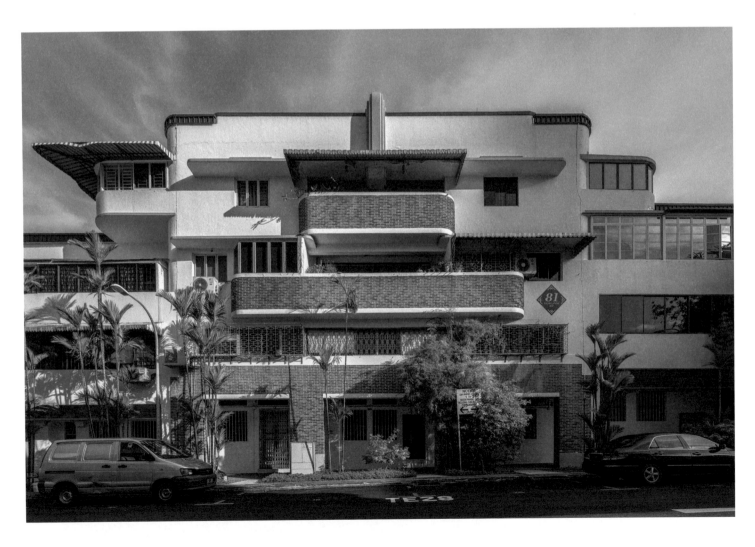

The apartment buildings built after 1948 have striking rounded, open stairwells.

Block 34 Whampoa West was completed in 1971 as part of the urban redevelopment around Kallang Basin, after the former marshland was drained by the Housing and Development Board (HDB).

The building has the longest continuous shared corridor of any HDB building in Singapore.

PUBLIC HOUSING

IN

Photo essay: Darren Soh

SINGAPORE

Text: Mirko Gatti

The jungle of residential high-rises extending across the whole island is a defining feature of the Singaporean urban landscape. Land is very expensive here and, due to its unique leaseholds system, more than three quarters of Singapore's land is state-owned. The majority of residential buildings are developed by the Housing and Development Board (HDB), the public authority in charge of housing policies since the dissolution of the colonialist Singapore Improvement Trust, in 1960. The very idea of home ownership is radically challenged by the Singaporean model, in which most private properties are in fact 99-year leaseholds that will eventually go back into the hands of the HDB once the

leaseholds have expired. In practice this has not yet happened. Instead, many of the units, built in the 1960s or later, have already been sold back to the state, demolished, and redeveloped before the leaseholds even came close to the expiry date.

Photographer Darren Soh has captured the soul of Singapore's public housing architecture, saving many of these buildings from anonymity, yet not always succeeding in saving them from demolition. The iconic Pearl Bank Apartments, for example, featured in Darren Soh's 2018 exhibition *Before It All Goes: Architecture from Singapore's Early Independence Years*, are probably the most eminent victims of Singapore's fast and

furious development agenda (see Soh's photographs accompanying Ho Weng Hin's article in this issue).

The photographs collected in this short photo essay aim to expose the HDB's vast yet discreet architectural output, offering visibility to Singapore's home-grown modernism as well as to the progressive public housing policies that changed the face of the city, radically improving housing standards for hundreds of thousands of Singaporeans.

Above
Block 52 Lorong 6, completed in 1966, was one of the first social housing buildings in the new town of Toa Payoh.

Right, above
Block 19 Jalan Sultan, completed in 1974, is one of two identical blocks in Precinct North 1, a large-scale HDB development project undertaken in collaboration with Norwegian architect Erik Lorange.

Right, below
Selegie House was the HDB's first major urban redevelopment project in the city center. At the time of its completion in 1963, it was the tallest HDB building in Singapore.

Block 82 Commonwealth Close, completed in 1964, was the HDB's first leasehold property as part of its home ownership program. Prior to this, all HDB units were for rent only.

THE FUTURE OF SINGAPORE'S RECENT PAST

It is only in the last 20 to 30 years that an awareness has developed in Singapore of the importance of conserving its postwar modern architectural heritage. This has hardly been a smooth process, but one fraught with difficulties and tensions between authorities, civic groups, and the public.

Text: Ho Weng Hin

The divergence of views over historical buildings has highlighted the inherent conflict between the state's developmentalist ethos shaped by its 1960s modernist urban renewal agenda, and the public desire for a more inclusive approach to urban planning that takes into account intangible values such as social memories.

This was the case with the old National Library on Stamford Road, a modern structure completed in 1960 and demolished in 2004 to make way for a traffic tunnel in anticipation of a new university campus. The announcement of the imminent demolition was met with a groundswell of dissent and sparked an unprecedented public debate on topics of conservation and cultural heritage in Singapore. Pro-conservation advocates argued for the library as an important shared civic space imbued with collective memories of generations of Singaporeans, transcending religious, ethnic, and cultural differences. For the authorities, however, the building did not possess sufficient architectural merit or historical value to be considered worthy of conservation. Many pioneering public housing projects with historical, social, and architectural significance are now confronted with a similar destiny to that of the old National Library. A notable case is that of the Dakota Crescent Estate, an early modern housing estate built in 1958 by the Singapore Improvement Trust (SIT)—the colonial predecessor of the current Housing and Development Board (HDB). Large parts of the estate have been demolished over the years, partly under the Selective En bloc Redevelopment Scheme (SERS), an urban redevelopment strategy employed by the HDB since 1995 to optimize land use in the city. In 2017, after three years of campaigning by the citizen group Save Dakota Crescent, six housing blocks were designated for conservation. Yet this small triumph was an exception rather than the norm, with many modern iconic housing complexes in Singapore still being threatened with demolition.

Modern architecture in Singapore is the tangible legacy of the visionary leadership of politicians, planners, developers, and architects who reinvented the future of the city-state after it obtained independence in 1965. The buildings realized during this period are a manifesto of Singapore's experimental urban renewal policies realized under the government Land Sales Program—Singapore's unique system of leasing public land to private developers for 99 years while retaining public ownership of it. For this reason, public housing is synonymous with Singapore's own identity. Today, 80 percent of the locals still live in HDB estates and they own their homes on a time-limited basis, usually through a 99-year strata leasehold.[01] The modernist jungle of heroic skyscrapers rising above the colonial historic districts was the engine of the socioeconomic growth of Singapore. It offered high-quality living spaces, fundamentally transforming the way Singaporeans live. Many of these buildings have high architectural and historical value. Nevertheless, in the past few years, they have been the object of ever more frequent *en bloc* redevelopment schemes.

An *en bloc* sale is when a developer strikes a deal with the individual owners of the units to collectively sell their strata titles and redevelop the land altogether. This is becoming increasingly common for modern housing blocks in central locations, where much of the land has increased in value several times since the blocks were originally built. The deteriorating conditions of some of these buildings—often due to inadequate maintenance—together with the fact that most of the units have already reached the midpoint of their 99-year leases, make *en bloc* sales highly attractive for strata-title owners, who are often easily convinced to give up their homes in exchange for better deals somewhere else. With this system, developers can make huge profits by redeveloping prime, central locations before the previous land leasehold has even expired. But the recent *en bloc* fever poses great challenges to the Singaporean land development system and raises fundamental questions about its long-term sustainability. The speed at which property values have risen, and the fact that the public sector is itself largely profiting from land speculation, means that demolition is sometimes inflicted on buildings that are only 20 years old. The system is now reaching an impasse, encouraging an endless acceleration of urban renewal cycles to the extent that it is urgent to rethink the logic behind it.[02]

The best example of this tendency is the case of the Pearl Bank Apartments, a modernist icon, which, at the time of its completion, was one of the world's most densely populated apartment blocks and the tallest housing complex in the whole of Asia. Despite being a dense, residential high-rise, this 113-meter-high building was designed by Tan Cheng Siong to optimize exposure to natural light and to ensure privacy. Its massive shear walls were constructed using a groundbreaking slip-form technology, able to support 38 floors of

Demolition of the iconic Pearl Bank Apartments, designed by Tan Cheng Siong, began in 2019. The building was first wrapped in a protective synthetic fabric to prevent debris from scattering.

interlocking maisonettes. The layout of the units, each one distributed over three split-levels, was incredibly sophisticated, with clearly separated living and sleeping areas and windows on both sides to enable cross-ventilation. The gracious "broken cylinder" shape of the building captures the breeze in its semicircular courtyard and prevents the hot afternoon sun from shining directly into the apartments. With about 1,500 people over 280 units, the Pearl Bank Apartments achieved spectacular density without compromising on living standards or the quality of the surrounding urban environment. This tower became a prototype for residential high-rises worldwide, embodying the pioneering and progressive spirit of post-independence Singapore.

The first *en bloc* sale attempt for the Pearl Bank Apartments was made in 2007, and then again in 2008 and 2011. In 2012, Tan Cheng Siong, together with some of the strata-title owners, proposed a renovation project that would leave the original building substantially intact, while adding 150 new units with privately accessible hanging gardens stacked above a preexisting carpark. The new units would finance the costs of maintenance and refurbishing the historic building and guarantee a margin of profit for the developer. When put forward for voluntary conservation in 2015, the Urban Redevelopment Authority (URA) acknowledged the heritage value of the building and publicly signaled willingness to back Tan's proposal, but in order to proceed with the plan Tan had to obtain the support of all the strata-title owners in the block.[03] The proposal fell short by about 10 percent, and so, as the attempt failed, many owners went back to the original

Left
The split-level units at the Pearl Bank Apartments were arranged along semicircular corridors. Each unit had a small private balcony and some of them could only be accessed by floating staircases.

Below
Completed in 1976, the building was one of the first residential high-rises erected under the pioneering Government Land Sales program.

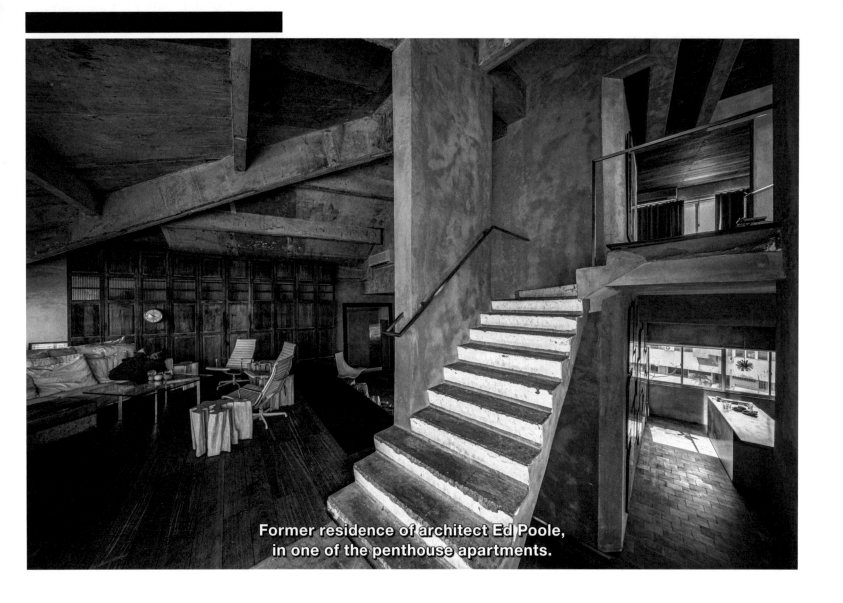

Former residence of architect Ed Poole,
in one of the penthouse apartments.

en bloc sale offer. In 2018, the entire complex was sold to CapitaLand for 728 million Singapore dollars (about 550 million euros). Many Singaporean architects and heritage advocates rallied to save the building and launched public petitions suggesting alternative proposals. The nonprofit organization Docomomo International suggested a multigenerational co-housing scheme with collective care and co-working facilities distributed over the lower floors.[04] The Singapore Heritage Society published a seminal position paper, titled "Too Young to Die: Giving a New Lease of Life to Singapore's Modernist Icons," which identified not only the Pearl Bank Apartments but also the People's Park Complex (1973) and the Golden Mile Complex (1973) as important monuments to postwar modernist architecture.[05] Despite these efforts, the Pearl Bank Apartments were demolished in March 2020, and a new development is already under construction. But the building did not die in vain: after the dismay caused by the demolition of this iconic building, a new consensus emerged that a comprehensive set of planning, financial, and regulatory incentives coordinated across different government agencies need to be formulated in order to encourage and promote the proper maintenance, rehabilitation, and adaptation of modern housing complexes and of other buildings of historical and social value. These can be economic incentives, as well as more flexible zoning or the topping-up of old

leasehold contracts. Existing conservation policies, developed primarily for fine-grain urban districts like Chinatown or for standalone institutional buildings and monuments are difficult to apply to large housing complexes like the Pearl Bank Apartments, where a multitude of stakeholders are involved, including residents' associations, developers, project consultants, heritage groups, and government agencies. Engagement and dialogue is critical to shift the emphasis of conventional conservation negotiations towards an approach that is positive, collaborative, and strategic.

The demolition of the Pearl Bank Apartments raised collective awareness about the state of affairs of real estate speculation in Singapore and cast new light on the future of other modernist housing blocks that are currently threated by *en bloc* sale attempts. On October 9, 2020, in an unprecedented move, Singapore's Urban Redevelopment Authority (URA) announced a conservation scheme for the famous Golden Mile Complex, designed by Design Partnership and completed in 1973, citing its historical and architectural significance (see feature on the Golden Mile Complex in this issue). However, this decision will not save the building from *en bloc* sale; quite the opposite: the government announced conspicuous economic incentives for the developer willing to purchase the entire block and embark on a renovation project that will preserve the building's original design.[06]

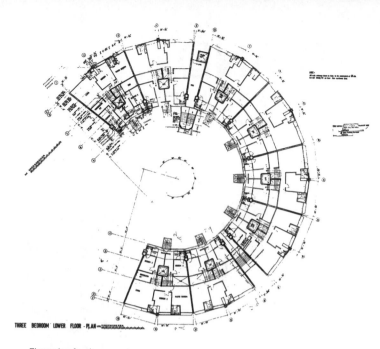

THREE BEDROOM LOWER FLOOR PLAN

Floor plan for the
standard floors.
© Archurban Architects
Planners

© Archurban Architects Planners / Tan Cheng Siong

In 2012, in an attempt to
save the building from
demolition, Tan Cheng
Siong submitted a design
that left the existing
structure untouched but
added 150 new units
with privately accessible
hanging gardens.

Should the plan be successful, the Golden Mile Complex will be the
first privately developed strata title complex from Singapore's post-
independence era to be preserved, potentially writing a new chapter
in the Singapore's heritage conservation movement.

As of today, with the *en bloc* trend resulting in ever-shortening
cycles of demolition and rebuilding, Singapore needs to rethink its
tabula rasa mode of urban redevelopment. This paradigm is increasingly environmentally and socially unsustainable, causing ruptures in
the social and cultural development of the city, which is indispensable to
a vibrant and livable city. It has become imperative to establish a new
agenda for Singapore, one in which existing buildings with social
and historical value are preserved, not only for the sake of
Singapore's historical memory, but also to slow down Singapore's
fast and delirious building cycles in the name of the city's social and
ecological future.

01   What in Singapore is often
referred to as "home owner"
is, in fact, just the owner of a
99-year strata leasehold
title ("strata title" for short).
While the use of the property
belongs to the apartment
owners for this duration,
ownership of the property itself
remains with the state.
Because of this system, the
state owns about 80 percent
of the land in Singapore.
02   Several global and local
movements have appeared
in the past years—also in
response to more widespread
awareness of climate change
issues—calling for a radical
transformation of the
Singaporean building industry.
Examples include the petition
Singapore Architects
Declare Climate and Biodiver-
sity Emergency (sg.archi-
tectsdeclare.com); the British
Architects' Journal campaign,
Retrofirst (www.architects-
journal.co.uk/news/retrofirst);
and the Climate Heritage
Network (climateheritage.org).
03   An *en bloc* sale only
requires the backing of owners
holding 80 percent of the share
value of the entire property.
If those owners agree, the
owners holding the remaining
20 percent are forced to sell.

04   Docomomo International
(International Committee for
Documentation and Conservation of Buildings, Sites and
Neighbourhoods of the Modern
Movement) is a nonprofit
organization founded in
Eindhoven in 1988, dedicated
to the preservation of modern
architecture, landscape,
and design around the world.
05   Singapore Heritage Society, "Too Young to Die:
Giving a New Lease of Life to
Singapore's Modernist
Icons," 2018, accessed July
19, 2021, www.singaporeheri-
tage.org/wp-content/
uploads/2018/08/SHSPosition-
Paper-Too-Young-To-Die-Aug-
2018.pdf.
06   Urban Redevelopment
Authority, "Supporting the
Conservation and Commercial
Viability of Golden Mile
Complex," October 9, 2020,
accessed July 19, 2021,
www.ura.gov.sg/Corporate/
Media-Room/Media-Releases/
pr20-28.

Sectional perspective
through one of
the three-story units.

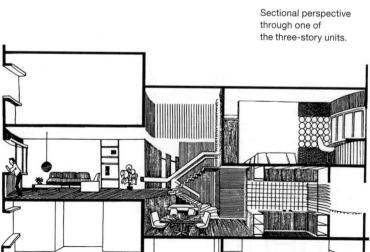

© Archurban Architects Planners

BIGNESS AND THE SEARCH FOR IDENTITY

SPUR's programmatic design for a linear mega-structure: the building rises from a podium that holds a dense, multi-layered network of public spaces and is connected to the subway system.

Illustration from the article "Our Cities Tomorrow: Sky-High Structures May Solve Population Problems," *Asia Magazine* (May 1966).

Courtesy William S. W. Lim

Think tanks in an emergent Asian modernism

Text: Wee H. Koon

Since the 1950s, the soft power of the United Nations—often exercised in the form of economic and technical aid for the "Third World"—legitimized the implementation of aggressive policies of urban renewal by newly formed governments as a tool to modernize postcolonial societies. The search for new architectural and urban forms corresponded with the search for new national identities.

The institutional framework around this process had strong intellectual and cultural allegiances to the European, American, and Japanese urban development discourse, often through the formation of international think tanks. These were frequently financed by the private sector as a way to keep socialism and communism at bay. Two pan-Asian think tanks played a key role in the process of urbanization and modernization in Asia from the 1960s onwards: the Singapore Planning and Urban Research Group (SPUR) and the Asian Planning and Architectural Collaboration (APAC).[01] These two groups were empowered by national and international institutions to foster urban modernization in Asia. At the same time, they raised critical questions regarding the cultural and economic hegemony imposed on Asia through foreign aid policies and lobbied for a more proactive participation by the local private sector in matters of urban development.[02] Despite deep political anxieties, in the 1960s liberal formations of nongovernmental think tanks were allowed to proliferate in Asia because they were often considered associations of purely technical professionals and thus apolitical by nature. Later on, the visions of SPUR and APAC were partly coopted into the state's nationalist narrative of modernization, as well as into a neoliberal agenda aiming to use urban planning as a means to build and sustain an affluent middle-class population.

SPUR and APAC formed separately. They attracted members of the architecture "intelligentsia" from Singapore, Japan, Hong Kong, Thailand, and India, who shared the same elite educational backgrounds and the same ambitions to pursue greater civic engagement as professionals. SPUR brought together a group of young and passionate architects and planners in Singapore, including William S. W. Lim, Tay Kheng Soon, and Koh Seow Chuan, who were also members of the successful Singaporean office Design Partnership. APAC was formed in 1969 as an alliance between Design Partnership and Maki & Associates, in Japan. Koichi Nagashima was working for Maki at that time and remained a core member thereafter. APAC later came to include Sumet Jumsai, Likit Tri & Associates (Thailand), TaoHo Design Architects & Designers (Hong Kong), and Charles Correa (India). The core members of APAC (Lim, Maki, Nagashima, and Tao Ho) were all students at Harvard between the 1950s and 1960s. It was there that they were strongly influenced by the teachings of Jaqueline Tyrwhitt, who was also an editor of Constantinos Apostolos Doxiadis's journal *Ekistics* and an influential figure in the shaping of the UN Habitat developmental strategies. APAC members—Maki in particular—were themselves active at the international Delos Symposia organized by Doxiadis, as well as at other Ekistics conferences.[03] Lim and Nagashima belonged both to APAC and SPUR, so that the groups' ideas often overlapped. Tyrwhitt passed through Singapore,

Cover of *SPUR 65–67*, a booklet published by the group on their own initiative, with an updated version of the article previously published in *Asia Magazine*, retitled "The Future of Asian Cities."

Indonesia, and Japan on various occasions during her career and she was able to cultivate connections with her former Harvard students. Maki described APAC as an Asian approximation of Team 10, an idea that was encouraged by Tyrwhitt herself.[04] The pervasiveness and inventiveness of APAC and SPUR revealed new ways that transnational intelligentsia could influence urban policies across Asia, while each individual member pursued artistic practices and urban research unique to their national sensibilities and local complexities.

When the British granted self-government rights to Singapore in 1959, a great part of the local population was living in very precarious conditions. The inner district of Chinatown was overcrowded and large portions of urban and suburban land were occupied by illegal squatters. After the Second World War, modernist principles of urban renewal were famously brought to Singapore by a United Nations team of experts composed of the American Charles Abram, the Japanese Susumu Kobe, and the German Otto Koenigsberger, who had advocated for the formation of think tanks as a way to supplement the limited resources of the public sector.[05] In this context, there are legitimate claims to reassess the work of SPUR as part of a nation-building process in which the genuine need for modernization, as prescribed by the UN experts, went hand-in-hand with the search for a new national identity expressed through urban forms. These forms were naturally ambitious and large in scale, because large in scale were the challenges faced by Singapore in terms of economic and demographic growth.

One of the most iconic architectural symbols of this search for a new identity is the Golden Mile Complex, a huge hybrid residential and commercial building conceived in the late 1960s by Design Partnership (see feature on the Golden Mile Complex in this issue). The Golden Mile Complex is the result of a new concept for pedestrian-oriented urban centers, which some critics consider one of the most characteristic elements of a specifically Asian type of modernism. The building is the material realization of one of the core elements of SPUR's visionary high-density linear city, a utopian urban concept famously illustrated in the article, "Our Cities Tomorrow: Sky-High Structures May Solve Population Problems," in *Asia Magazine*, published in Hong Kong in 1966.[06] A reworked version of "Our Cities Tomorrow" was included in the journal *SPUR 65–67*, under the title "The Future of Asian Cities." When Lim and Tay departed from Design Partnership in the 1970s, the younger Koh Seow Chuan, Gan Eng Oon, and Chan Sui Him continued their legacy and formed DP Architects. As recalled by Chan, the high-density linear city depicted in the drawings, immediately adjacent to a row of vernacular shophouses, was in fact a proposal for an urban renewal strategy to be implemented on Upper Cross Street, above Singapore's historic Chinatown district. Lim, Tay, and the rest of the group advocated for a high-density development adjacent to the colonial shophouses to be carried out with little or no demolition of the historic fabric because, in their view, the "demolition of these buildings does not and cannot solve the problems of slum dwellers."[07] Lim argued that it was "slum psychology" that prevented modernist planners from properly addressing real urban issues, such as the lack of incentives for landlords to upkeep their properties, and a general lack of income and poor education among the working-class tenants. At the same time, SPUR relentlessly advocated for the linear mega-city as a new, technologically innovative urban form specific to the Asian context that would be able to accommodate unimpeded growth. At the core of this idea was an obsession with modes of transportation and continuous circulatory systems. SPUR deplored regressive social utopias like the anti-urban Garden City of Ebenezer Howard, which its members scorned as "cultural obsolescence."[08] Making no apology for the necessity of a super-dense Asian city, they advocated for urban density as a specifically Asian value: "If we look into our own Asian cities you will find that Asians have been conditioned to live in a highly concentrated manner. What we want is to find the right living pattern for our present needs and the right symbols to satisfy our present cultural aspirations."[09] The density and size of buildings proposed by SPUR may have been shocking to people in the mid-1960s, but these attributes were also positioned to make claims about a unique demographic, cultural, and climatic response for Asia. In the feasibility study for the Golden Mile District, for example, Design Partnership proposed a one-mile-long linear Megastructure of 21 interconnected blocks along the strip of land between Nicoll Highway and Beach Road, with retail on the lower floors and housing above. This unbuilt masterplan was supposed to be entirely pedestrian. Private automobiles would be parked in a diamond-shaped car park "terminal"

to the southern entrance of the complex, much like in a suburban shopping mall. SPUR described the adoption of the linear city model as a response to "how industrial working-class cities have been freed [from traditional constrains] with the progress of modern technology—road transportation, piped supply."[10] In these words, SPUR shows a docile affinity with techno-utopian ideas of technological progress as an object of class struggle and as a vehicle to attain social equality. Design Partnership's first built projects, such as the People's Park Complex and the Golden Mile Complex, were concrete realizations of these avant-garde tendencies that were intelligently embedded in the government's socialist agenda at the time.[11] There was a discernible connection between the work of Design Partnership and the socialist sensibility of Singapore's early nationalist ambitions, evidenced in the institution of the Housing and Development Board (HDB) and in its unwavering public housing program.[12] On the other hand, it is also important to note that, even if SPUR's vision did not necessarily portray shopping as its primary activity, the deployment of mass forms of shopping, present in both the podiums of the Golden Mile Complex and of the People's Park Complex, are the expression of Singapore's will to actively partake in the emerging globalized consumerist economy.

In this respect, SPUR shared the same optimistic faith in the social leveling power of economic growth and technological innovation as the British avant-garde group Archigram. But while Archigram's visionary plans stayed for the most part only on paper, Lim and Tay were able to command a great deal of control over urban development in Singapore. This is partly because Design Partnership were highly practical professionals who were able to advise clients and governments on topics of land sales and budgets. Lim had extensive knowledge in urban economics and understood the importance of persuasion, administration, and careful budgeting. Lim was the first of a new breed of multidisciplinary administrator-planner-architects able to operate at all scales.[13] The sectional drawings of the Golden Mile District reveal that Lim was experimenting with strata titles as a special form of property ownership as early as 1968. The Golden Mile Complex was among the first test grounds in Singapore for a strata-titled mixed-used property after the passing of the Land Titles (Strata) Act in 1967.[14] According to Chan, at the first Urban Renewal Department land sales in 1967, the private contracting firm Woh Hup Pte. Ltd. was able to bid on the land because of Design Partnership's proactive role as both architects and development consultants.[15] Construction costs were considerably lower than those of conventional buildings of the same type, despite the fact that the Golden Mile Complex made use of pioneering structural systems developed together with Ove Arup and Partners.[16] High levels of professionalism across the board allowed contractors and developers to pull off many large-scale projects with broad urban implications. These contractor-developer business conglomerates were the fundamental prerequisite for the emergence of a new category in modern Asian architecture, that of bigness.[17]

The capacity to think and design big was shared among many Asian architects, who were confronted with the challenges of an urbanization driven by unprecedented demographic growth and rural-to-urban migration. In this respect, the formation of APAC was remarkable inasmuch as it created a platform for these architects to

Courtesy William S. W. Lim

SPUR's programmatic design shows the back of a stepped, linear mega-structure rising above Singapore's Upper Cross Street across from Chinatown's historic shop-houses.

Illustration from the article "Our Cities Tomorrow: Sky-High Structures May Solve Population Problems," *Asia Magazine*, May 1966.

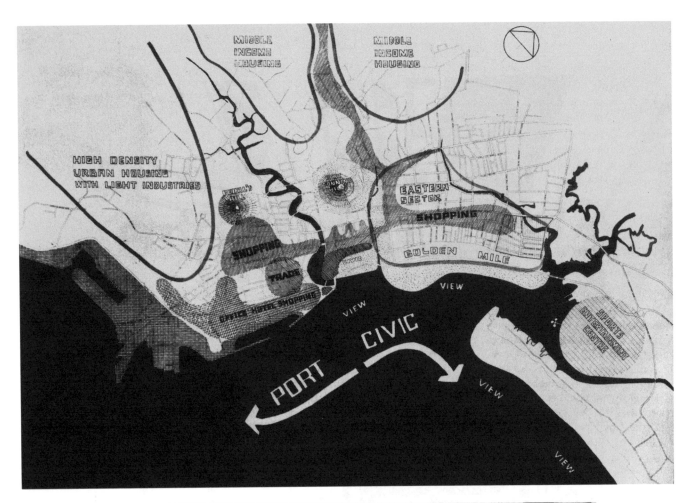

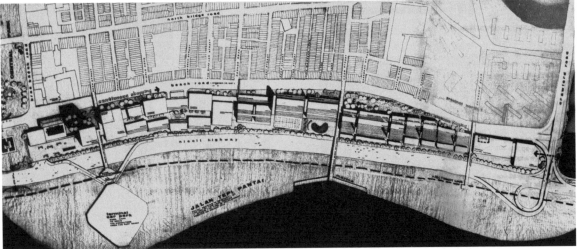

Above
Feasibility study for
Singapore's city center
and Marina Bay by Design
Partnership and SPUR
from 1973, with the so-called
Golden Mile along Beach
Road.

Below
Design Partnership's unrea-
lized master plan for the
Golden Mile District originally
envisioned a linear
megastructure consisting of
21 interconnected blocks.
The Golden Mile Complex,
completed in 1973, is the
only one of these buildings
that was actually realized.

Sectional perspective of the Golden Mile Complex: twelve terraced residential floors rise above the podium, which holds shops, restaurants, cafés, and offices.

Courtesy DP Architects

share a pan-Asian perspective on problems of mass urbanization. Koichi Nagashima describes the work of APAC as representing "what looms larger and larger in the group's approach to problems," and this was magnified by the fact that Asia was undergoing a massive change in which "architecture cannot be separated from larger issues of environmental design."[18] Maki's firm in Tokyo boasted of similar urban scale expertise as Design Partnership did in Singapore, with a highly integrated understanding of urban design and architecture.[19] In their respective writings from the 1970s, both Maki and Lim articulated a similar concept of bigness, referring to megastructures as new forms of "environmental design."

APAC specifically targeted the developmental needs of "Third World" countries that were in search of an appropriate architectural and urban language in a period of rapid decolonization. The think tank also sought to steer these countries away from ready-made urban solutions that were conceived in, and for, the West, fundamentally challenging the narrative of a "Third World" that must grow up to

meet "First World" standards—a process that often entailed borrowing funds and services from the latter. In a brochure from the 1970s, APAC reports that, "many of the developing countries in the East and Southeast Asian regions are in the process of rapid modernization and urbanization. These countries have until now relied largely on specialists in the field of urban development programs. At the same time, these countries have been developing a professional capacity of their own, particularly through their national educational institutions. APAC intends to harness this professional expertise and to maximize its creative contribution in the region."[20] APAC thus legitimized Asian professional expertise as the preferred solution for Asian urbanization. It also maintained an unapologetic approach towards large-scale developments and high urban density all through the 1970s, an approach that at the time was not shared by most Western counterparts, who were more concerned with finding a middle ground between the urban and the suburban. To their detriment, however, APAC did not succeed in translating any of its intellectual work into

183

Above the commercial podium is a large common terrace, accessible to the residents of the units above.

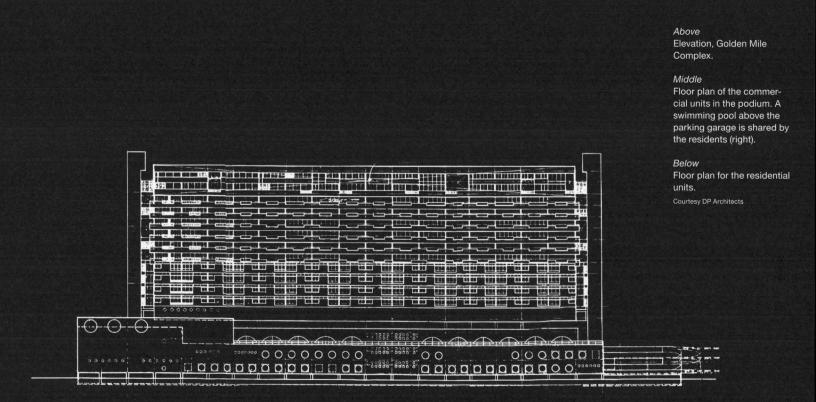

Above
Elevation, Golden Mile
Complex.

Middle
Floor plan of the commer-
cial units in the podium. A
swimming pool above the
parking garage is shared by
the residents (right).

Below
Floor plan for the residential
units.
Courtesy DP Architects

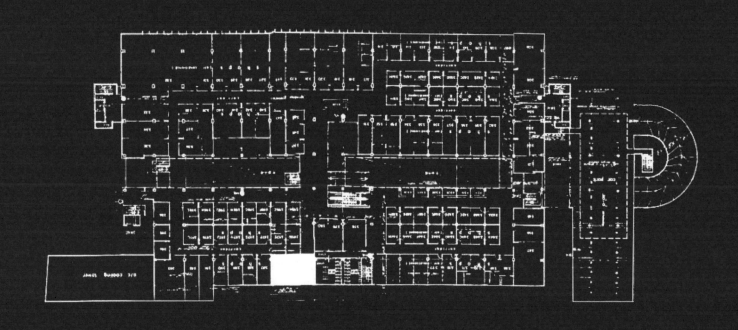

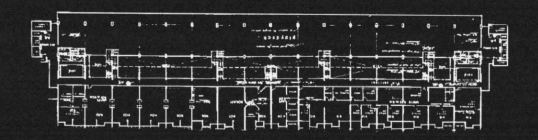

Fumihiko Maki's conceptual
study for the masterplan
for the Shinjuku station area
in Tokyo, 1960.

Courtesy Maki & Associates

built projects. Started as a consultancy to supplement the lack of technical expertise on topics of transportation systems and urban renewal, APAC's ambitions did not materialize in any particular project and the group gradually evolved into a platform for intellectual and cultural exchange similar to Team 10 in Europe. Both APAC and Team 10 transcended the architectural scale, moving towards non-visual or cultural aspects of architecture—the "structure of a community" and the "human character of the built-up environment" respectively. Each member of APAC developed very successful practices within their national domains, but the architectural ambitions of the group evaporated into the all-encompassing scale of humanity, habitation, and the abstract notion of "architectural identity," an idiosyncratic concept for a platform whose members were simultaneously involved with global academic networks and with their respective governments' nationalist agendas at home. Furthermore, all APAC members came from privileged backgrounds, they were educated in the same elite Western universities, and they were often too distant from the society that they wanted to serve.

Back to Singapore, after Lim and Tay left Design Partnership, DP Architects continued experimenting with large multi-use complexes

that made use of internal streets and covered plazas as pedestrian-oriented spaces of social aggregation, but their programs became increasingly more commercial. A direct antecedent to this phenomenon can be found in the work of Austrian émigré Victor Gruen, who worked extensively in the USA and who is commonly credited as the repentant inventor of the American suburban shopping mall. Lim cited the arguments used by Victor Gruen quite extensively in his writings, adopting ideas borrowed directly from Gruen's 1956 Fort Worth Downtown Revitalization Plan.[21] Since encountering Gruen at the First Urban Design Conference at Harvard in 1956, Lim embraced the potential of urban "citadels" with a diversity of functions, where residents and consumers could move about safely through pedestrianized covered streets and multilevel corridors in a temperate environment. This design approach culminated in the collaboration between DP Architects and John Portman for the realization of Marina Centre, a large commercial development conceived in the late 1970s and realized through the 1980s and 1990s.

About twelve years apart from each other, the Golden Mile District and Marina Centre can be read as two phases of the genealogy of bigness as an architectural phenomenon in Asia.[22] This idea was first

Above
Model of the Marina Centre complex by DP Architects and John Portman Associates. The three hotels—Marina Mandarin, Oriental, and Pan Pacific—were connected via Marina Square, a huge covered plaza with an integrated shopping mall.

Below
The 1956 masterplan for Fort Worth, Texas, by Gruen Associates envisioned parking garages on the edges of the city to keep the city center car-free.

Photo: Clyde May© 1981·John Portman and Associates. Courtesy Portman Archives

Courtesy Gruen Associates

introduced by Rem Koolhaas and Bruce Mau in their 1995 book *S,M,L,XL*.[23] Coincidentally, in the book Koolhaas and Mau discuss the work of the megalomaniac architect-developer John Portman in Atlanta, and that of DP Architects in Singapore, in two separate essays.[24] The lineage between the two, however, becomes physically manifest in Singapore in their collaboration for Marina Centre. Marina Centre sits on the single-largest private land-sale site in downtown Singapore. It is a testament to the shift from postwar developmental strategies, as implemented by the UN in the form of economic and technical aid, towards a neoliberal approach to urban development relying on the global circulation of financial and private capital. Marina Centre was Portman's first big foray in Asia. In its original configuration, the development consisted of three hotels—the Marina Mandarin, the Oriental, and the Pan Pacific—all three connected via Marina Square, a central indoor plaza and shopping mall not dissimilar from the classic American downtown. Over the years the project attracted more

investors and more American architects of the level of I. M. Pei, Kevin Roche, Philip Johnson, and John Burgee.[25] Portman's self-contained pedestrian city of the 1980s is a direct descendant of Design Partnership's linear city of the 1970s, albeit this time with a purely commercial program.[26] The Oriental Hotel, for example, shares the familiar slant stepped design of the Golden Mile Complex, but its steps accommodate luxury hotel rooms instead of homes, and the podium is occupied by a spectacular Las Vegas-like lobby space that is directly connected to the Marina Square Shopping Mall via an indoor air-conditioned pedestrian route.

Compared to this, the Golden Mile Complex belongs to an old generation of big, hybrid buildings born from a compromise between the socialist agenda of the Singaporean government and the emergent consumerist economy. Over the years, the internal streets of the Golden Mile Complex came to resemble more and more those of a real city, because—thanks to the strata-title ownership model that the

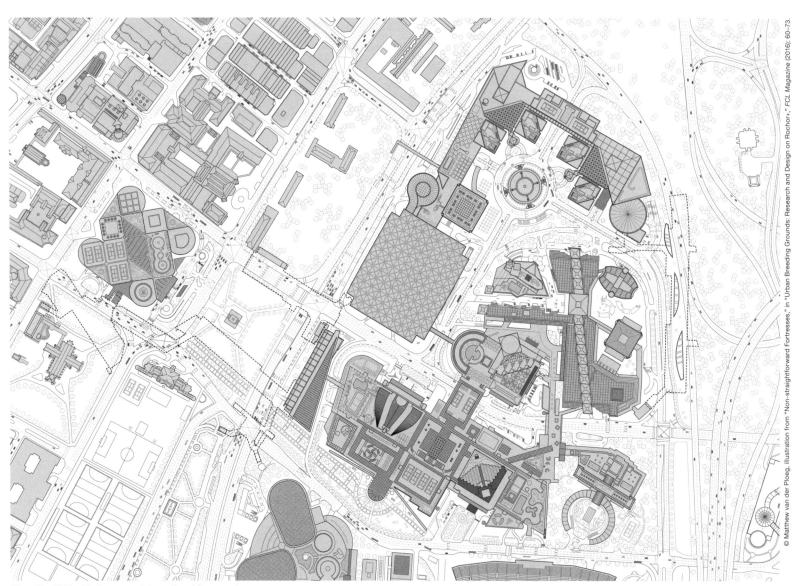

© Matthew van der Ploeg, illustration from "Non-straightforward Fortresses," in "Urban Breeding Grounds: Research and Design on Rochor+," *FCL Magazine* (2016): 60–73.

Since the 1980s, Marina Centre has increasingly been transformed into a fortress of hotels, shopping malls, conference rooms, and concert halls by international firms such as Kevin Roche, John Dinkeloo and Associates, John Burgee and Philip Johnson, and Tsao and McKown Architects.

building pioneered in the 1960s—the commercial space inside it was and remains in the hands of multiple shop owners.[27] This model of collective ownership has produced a very different outcome than the single-developer model of Marina Centre, which, after 30 years, still has the feel of an orderly, generic shopping space. Today, in Singapore, large, uniform shopping malls have replaced the more equitable multi-ownership commercial spaces to the economic advantage of a handful of global investors.

Over the years, APAC and SPUR members gradually became more inward-looking and their personal practices started to carry less sociopolitical agency for architecture. While bigness remains key to the Asian urban context, today it has acquired a different logic from that originally envisioned by the avant-garde groups who first embraced it as the defining feature of an Asian-specific modernism in the 1960s and 1970s. The research of SPUR and APAC, and the ambitious architectural forms they generated in the tumultuous years

of nation-building, with their socially and economic variegated programs, have slowly given way to a more generic idea of bigness, one that has been emptied of its social and political ambitions to better suit the global neoliberal agenda.

This paper was adapted from a shorter paper by the same author, titled "Bigness and the Search for Identity," published by A+U in a special issue on DP Architects in 2019. Additional references were taken from another paper by the same author, titled "An Emergent Asian Modernism: Think Tanks and the Design of the Environment," published in the book Impossibility of Mapping Urban Asia *(Singapore: World Scientific Publishing and NTU Centre for Contemporary Art Singapore, 2020), with thanks to the editors Ute Meta Bauer, Khim Ong, and Roger Nelson. The research benefitted from seed funds from the University of Hong Kong.*

01 The group was founded in 1969 as Asian Planning and Architectural Consultants, but was later renamed as Asian Planning and Architectural Collaboration, which indicated the fact that their scope had become closer to that of a platform for intellectual and cultural exchange, rather than a professional consultancy firm.
02 Howe Yoon Chong, Lim Chong Keat, and SIA Members, "Dialogue Between the Ministry and the SIA," *Journal of the Singapore Institute of Architects*, no. 31 (December 1968): 1–15; SPUR, "Environment Exhibition," *SPUR 65–67* (Singapore: Eurasia Press, 1967), 57.
03 Catharine Huws Nagashima, "Architectural Identity in the Cultural Context: Reporting on a UNU/APAC Meeting in Japan, 1985: A Tribute," *Ekistics* 52, no. 314/315 (1985), 504–6.
04 Fumihiko Maki, Keynote Lecture for the DP50 Symposium, Singapore, Oct 10, 2017.
05 Charles Abrams, Susumu Kobe, and Otto Koenigsberger, Growth and Urban Renewal

in Singapore: Report Prepared for the Government of Singapore, United Nations Programme of Technical Assistance, DESA, 1963. (Charles Abrams Papers and Files, Department of Manuscripts and University Archives, John M. Olin Library, Cornell University).
06 SPUR, "Our Cities Tomorrow: Sky-High Structures May Solve Population Problems," *Asia Magazine* (November 1966): 4–7. Reworked and republished in SPUR, "The Future of Asian Cities," *SPUR 65–67* (Singapore: Eurasia Press, 1967), 5.
07 William S. W. Lim, "Urban Redevelopment: The Humanist Point of View," in *Equity and Urban Environment in the Third World: With Special Reference to ASEAN Countries and Singapore*, ed. Zhuang Weisong (Singapore: DP Press, 1975), 40.
08 SPUR, "The Future of Asian Cities" (see note 6), 9.
09 Ibid.
10 Ibid., 11.
11 Eunice Seng, "People's Park Complex: The State, the Developer, the Architect

and the Conditioned Public, c. 1967 to the Present," in *Southeast Asia's Modern Architecture: Questions of Translation, Epistemology and Power*, eds. Jiat-Hwee Chang and Imran bin Tajudeen (Singapore: NUS Press, 2019), 236–73.
12 To this day, the Singaporean state owns around 80 percent of the land. Time-limited land use rights are sold to private developers via public auctions. Around 80 percent of the population currently lives in apartments developed on behalf of the public Housing and Development Board (HDB) and lease their homes on a time-limited basis, typically 99 years.
13 Chan Sui Him, Interview with H. K. Wee and E. Seng, Singapore, Aug 4, 2016.
14 A strata title is a method of facilitating individual ownership of part of a property, while sharing ownership of the common ground the property is built upon. Strata-leased apartments in Singapore are mainly public housing units with leasehold tenure contracts

of 99 years, where the lessees pay fixed monthly maintenance fees to the town council based on the room types of their strata unit.
15 Singapore Press Holdings, "Unusual Landmark," *The Straits Times*, Property Section (Aug 30, 1971): 14; A. G. Barnett, ed., "Golden Mile Shopping Center," *Asian Architect and Builder* 1, no. 4 (June 1972), Hong Kong, 20.
16 Ibid., 19.
17 Singapore Press Holdings, "Firm Formed to Help in Nation-Building," *The Straits Times* (January 28, 1972): 21.
18 Koichi Nagashima, "Editorial," *Contemporary Asian Architecture: Works of APAC Members, Process: Architecture*, no. 20 (November 1980): 4.
19 Fumihiko Maki, Investigations in Collective Form, Special Publication of the School of Architecture, Washington University, St. Louis, June 1964.
20 APAC, "Objectives," Asian Planning & Architectural Consultants, 12-page brochure.
21 Victor Gruen, "Cityscape and Landscape," *Arts and*

Architecture (September 1955).
22 See Colin Anderson and Ian Choo, *DP Architects on Marina Bay: Evolution of a Civic Downtown* (Singapore: ORO Editions, 2015), 72–77.
23 O.M.A., Rem Koolhaas, and Bruce Mau, *S,M,L,XL* (New York: The Monicelli Press, 1995), 494.
24 Ibid., 832–59; 1008–89.
25 Matthew van der Ploeg, "Nonstraightforward Fortresses: The Development of an Exquisite Corpse of Contiguous Castles," *Future Cities Lab Magazine*, 2016, accessed January 4, 2021, matthewvanderploeg. info/non-straightforward-fortresses-singapore/.
26 Anderson and Choo, DP Architects on Marina Bay: Evolution of a Civic Downtown (see note 22), 75.
27 Ivan Png Paak Liang, "Building Maintenance," Parliamentary Debate, Official Report, Tenth Parliament, vol. 81, Mar 6, 2006, 3, accessed July 19, 2021, www. comp.nus.edu.sg/~ipng/pol/parl_2006/20060306.pdf.

E COMPLEX

DESTINATION

The Golden Mile Complex with the Marina Centre in the background.

Left
A large communal terrace for the residents is located above the commercial zone in the base.

Above
The stepped terraces of the Golden Mile Complex, which overlook Marina Bay, have been extended over time by residents with canopies and enclosed balconies.

Photos: Darren Soh
Text: Mirko Gatti

Completed in 1973, the Golden Mile Complex is one of the first "strata-titled" properties developed under the 1967 Government Land Sales Programme, the pioneering 99-year land lease system that radically transformed Singapore one high-rise after another.[01] In the vision of Design Partnership (today known as DP Architects) the complex was intended to be part of a futuristic linear city of modern apartments, shops, and hotels, rising on a stretch of reclaimed land along Beach Road, which was formerly occupied by beach clubs and small maritime businesses. "This stretch, hitherto a squalid shanty area and dumping ground, will become Singapore's Golden Mile," said Alan Choe, head of the Housing and Development Board (HDB) in 1969.[02]

Designed as a city within the city by Gan Eng Oon, William S. W. Lim, Tay Kheng Soon, and Chan Sui Him of Design Partnership, the Golden Mile Complex was outfitted with all the amenities needed for modern urban life. A mix of offices, shops, kiosks, and cafés is distributed over the three levels of its commercial podium. Above this, twelve levels of residential units are arranged in the distinctive stepped-back design that makes the Golden Mile Complex one of the most iconic architectures of Singapore's post-independence era. The roof deck of the podium, sheltered from the midday sun below a line of majestic pilotis, is accessible to residents for leisure and other outdoor activities. A collective swimming pool is installed above the parking garage, directly connected to the main block via a narrow skywalk. Thanks to the stepped architecture, every apartment benefits from a large individual terrace facing south onto Marina Bay. Over the years, these luxurious hanging gardens were creatively appropriated by the residents, who added canopies and informal winter gardens, turning the building into a vivid realization of one of the adaptive megastructures theorized by Fumihiko Maki in his *Investigations in Collective Form*.[03] Personally and professionally connected to Maki, as well as to other members of the Metabolism movement in Japan, Design Partnership shared the same optimism for technological advancement as their Japanese counterparts and similarly deployed large-scale urban forms as a way to actively reform Singapore's society through architecture. The Golden Mile Complex is internationally regarded as one of the

The shops, restaurants, and cafés in the base zone are spread over three levels.

LING HAIR & BEAUTY

SIRIWAN M   LTD

SINGHA   ข้าวซอย เชียงใหม่

สำนักงานแรงงานในประเทศสิงคโปร์
Office of Labour Affairs, Royal Thai Embassy

ภาพกิจกรรม   ประกาศ

Four monumental floating staircases lead from the commercial podium up to the offices and residential units.

most extraordinary outputs of the Asian avant-garde and as one of the prototypes of the quintessentially Asian modern typology of the commercial podium topped with a tower high-rise. With this work Design Partnership contributed both architecturally and politically to the definition of a new urban paradigm for the modern Asian city.[04]

Now considered obsolete by many, the Golden Mile Complex has been repeatedly threatened with demolition in recent years. Yet, due to the 99-year leasehold of the site, which is only about halfway through, residents must agree to sell all their strata titles *en bloc* for the investors to be able to proceed with redevelopment. In 2020, the Singapore Urban Redevelopment Authority finally announced a conservative redevelopment scheme for the building, stipulating that the original design must be preserved by the new developer who embarks on the project.[05] It remains to be seen whether civic efforts to conserve the building will be limited to the preservation of its captivating brutalist look, or if it will also uphold the legacy of the progressive housing policies that inspired its original design.

01 The sites of the Pearl Bank Apartments and of the People's Park Complex, featured in this issue, were also leased as part of the same program in 1967.
02 William Campbell, "Selling the Golden Mile" in: *The Straits Times* 27 (March 1969).

03 Fumihiko Maki, *Investigations in Collective Form* (St. Louis: Washington University, 1964), 8–13.
04 See Wee H. Koon's article in this issue.
05 See articles by Ho Weng Hin and Johannes Widodo in this issue.

The People's Park Complex, completed in 1973, was one of the first examples of a hybrid podium-tower block typology in Singapore and among the first buildings realized as part of the Government Land Sales Programme offering strata title ownership of home units.
© Darren Soh

ARCHITECTURE DOESN'T MATTER

Tay Kheng Soon is a prominent architect and planner in Singapore, not to mention one of the staunchest critics of its urban development throughout his career over the last 50 years—through the think tank he cofounded, Singapore Planning & Urban Research Group (SPUR), as partner of the architectural firm Design Partnership, or his own firm, Akitek Tenggara. With Design Partnership, he realized the People's Park Complex and the Golden Mile Complex, two of the most iconic modernist buildings in Southeast Asia.

Tay Kheng Soon in conversation with Eduard Kögel and Ho Puay-Peng

EDUARD KÖGEL: How did you start your professional career? **TAY KHENG SOON:** In the 1960s I was very politically active and in 1965, together with William Lim, we set up the Singapore Planning & Urban Research Group (SPUR).

EK: This was even before you founded Design Partnership?
TKS: Yes. Lim Chong Keat, who was one of the most influential architects in Singapore at the time, did not like SPUR because we were very critical of the designs of public housing. At the public exhibition *Singapore's Environment Past, Present and Future*, we showed pictures of apartments realized by the Housing and Development Board (HDB)—the public authority responsible for almost all housing developments in Singapore—side by side with chicken coops. When expansion plans for the old Paya Lebar Airport were announced, in the 1970s, SPUR campaigned firmly against it in the press, saying that it was a disastrous project because it would have destroyed a quarter of the island's surface with its flight paths. The new airport was then moved to Changi, at the eastern edge of Singapore, where it still stands now, occupying a portion of artificial land that has been reclaimed from the sea. These actions upset a lot of people back then. At that time, architecture and planning were generally seen as two separate things; this was absurd to me. With SPUR, I wanted to study the urban and

environmental conditions that are specific to Singapore and apply this knowledge to architecture practice.

EK: The People's Park Complex, completed in 1973, is one of the most iconic housing complexes you designed with Design Partnership. It is a remarkably urban project because it has a multi-level commercial podium that is open to the public with a residential slab on top of it. Was this the first project resulting from your research at SPUR?
TKS: Yes, definitely. The idea for it was also inspired by my personal experience in Tokyo, where I learned that you don't necessarily have to shop on the street level. One of the driving forces behind the project was the idea of working with geometries that invite people to move through the building. That is something I learned from modernist architecture in Israel.

HO PUAY-PENG: When were you in Israel?
TKS: In 1966. During my trip to Israel, I met the architect Alfred Neumann in Haifa, whose handling of geometric building structures made a strong impression on me. On the recommendation of William Lim, I also visited Ram Karmi, with whom he had studied at the AA (Architectural Association) in London. Karmi was working on the construction of the Central Bus Station in Tel Aviv. There I learned how I could get people to move around corners and upstairs

through the precise arrangement of mezzanines, cantilevered volumes, and the like. I wish I had kept some of my early sketches, but I moved several times and threw everything away.

EK: How did the developer react to your programming of the People's Park Complex?
TKS: Willy worked out the economics of the project. We told the developer he could make millions through the sale of separate leaseholds.[01] He said, *"Just go ahead, I don't care what you do, as long as I get the money,"* and so the design was completely in our hands. We even organized the sales program. We had a big public exhibition with models and we did talks, and then the shopkeepers from Chinatown arrived with suitcases full of cash. The idea of multiple ownership was completely new then, there was no strata title back then.[02] I scheduled a meeting with the lawyer Kwa Geog Choo, who was the wife of former Prime Minister Lee Kuan Yew. She immediately understood the problem and said, *"let me do something about it."* The Land Titles (Strata) Act came right afterwards. The problem was how to distribute the maintenance costs, because the value of the apartments above the podium is almost nothing compared to the value of the shops in the mall. Sharing the costs equally places the residents in a bad position. This was a pioneering project, not just in terms of the design but also in

terms of the regulation of mixed-use buildings in Singapore. Through this project we became the go-to architects for shopping malls.

EK: This is a pioneering work in so many ways. It should be preserved, don't you think? This building is a witness to the social and economic changes that new building typologies brought about in Singapore.
TKS: We live in a completely money-driven society. What does an old, run-down building mean today?
EK: Years ago, the old Chinatown, which is right next to the People's Park Complex, was also in very poor condition. It would have been easy to tear it down because it seemed worthless. But today, doing so seems unimaginable.
TKS: Chinatown is the reason why the protection of historic architecture was put in place in Singapore. In the 1980s, people noticed that the tourists didn't come to see the shiny new buildings, but the old ones. That is why Chinatown was preserved. It was for the money, not for sentiment.
HPP: Many years ago, I was invited to a dinner in Hong Kong with former Prime Minister Lee Kuan Yew. When I asked him why Singapore started the conservation of Chinatown, he said, *"I went to Delft. I was very impressed with Delft."*

197

Sectional perspective through the People's Park Complex, with the residential slab block above a commercial podium.

TKS: He also said that Singapore is condemned to build and rebuild forever. This is the reality. There is no sentimental reason, only money counts.

EK: But maybe there is a reason to tell a story about the buildings that is not just about commercial value. It could be about the history of Singapore for example.

TKS: History is all in the books. Especially his story.

EK: Would you argue that this sentimentalism about history is a fundamental difference between Europe and Asia?

TKS: Here history is weak.

EK: In China, there is a growing sensitivity in dealing with historical traces in the urban environment. Even buildings from the 1950s and 1960s are being reassessed today. I have the impression that there is a shift towards material history rather than immaterial memories.

HPP: Maybe it will come to Singapore too, I'm not sure. But certainly not now.

EK: Yesterday, the driver of my taxi pointed at the People's Park Complex and said, *"This is the next one. It's going to be destroyed soon, because Singapore thinks it doesn't need history."*

HPP: This is because the Pearl Bank Apartments (see Ho Weng Hin's article in this issue) are in the immediate vicinity and they have been in the news a lot.[03]

EK: In the case of the People's Park Complex, one could renovate it. The shopping center alone has great commercial potential.

TKS: The color of the complex is terrible today. Originally, it was only natural concrete. Someone asked me to suggest some ideas for the renovation. I proposed to create a Chinese garden on the roof of the shopping center with imported old wooden buildings from China to be used as restaurants. That would be fun, right?

HPP: I hope you do that.

EK: Do you think there is a real chance to renovate or save the building?

TKS: I don't know. It depends on the ownership situation. The current owners don't want to change it because they do good business. But some of the small shop owners want to sell. It's a complex case.

EK: And what is the situation now at the Golden Mile Complex?[04]

TKS: If you preserve a building you also preserve the original floor area ratio. But in the meanwhile, the floor area ratio allowed by law was doubled, and so the private developer—to whom a land-use right is assigned by the State via a public bid—would say, *"I will preserve the building, but only if I can transfer my rights to another site."* But in Singapore you cannot transfer your development rights from one place to another.

The legal system here favors the government and not the developer, because ultimately almost all of the land is public. Singapore is legally socialist but operates in a capitalist mode.

HPP: Like China.

TKS: It appears that China is learning from us.

EK: Do you personally want to see buildings like the People's Park and the Golden Mile Complex preserved?

TKS: I am skeptical about it. The spatial design of the city is much more important than preserving individual old buildings. The evaluation should not be made at the architectural scale, but at the urban scale. The city is not its architectures, the city is a continuous spatial system.

EK: If it were in Europe, the Golden Mile Complex would be repurposed as a hub for the creative industries and start-ups, like they want to do with the Tegel Airport terminal building in Berlin. The government in Singapore is also trying to push start-ups and creative industries. What do you think about this?

TKS: I think that they have all the right words because they all use the same PR consultants from America. The choice of words is very appealing, but it does not reflect the reality at all. People are afraid of new ideas here. There is a bias against new ideas. The government is afraid that creative people are difficult. They see the students in Hong Kong and they are frightened to death. The dilemma is that they want order and control on one side, and yet they want creativity on the other. These are contradictory things I'm concerned with at the moment: how do we switch on creativity? Can buildings do that?

EK: Maybe they can at least offer a space for creativity.

TKS: What I have in mind is not preserving a building for it to be turned into a creative hub, I am thinking of something more ambitious than that: a central nervous system that runs all through the city. All these housing estates, they do not stimulate creativity. The schools are all in the wrong places, they are all in quiet, isolated places—a concept from the 19th century. I propose to demolish all the schools and reconstitute them into a central nervous system, turning the body of a township into a living organism that can process huge amounts of information. The schools should be stretched out as a web into the communities. Imagine schools on the first and ground floors of buildings, together with shops, as well as cultural and civic functions. This is how people learn new things, by experiencing them in their everyday life. If you connect this web from one housing estate to the next, then we could think of Singapore, the whole island, as an organism, in which the synaptic connections make the whole

environment function intelligently. This would bring a million students from all over the world to Singapore and turn the whole island into a campus-city. When our students study together with visiting students, friendships are formed for life. When that happens over the next 10 or 20 years, the glow of this small red dot will spread over the entire region. The smallness of Singapore is an asset and what I propose is doable because the state here owns 80 percent of the land. The urban land reform that took place in the 1960s and 1970s is what makes it possible to plan at this scale. It is fundamental: without land ownership you can't do anything. In India they are completely stuck because the landowners are strangling the whole society. In China they can do it, but there they have other problems like income disparity, geographic distribution, fractionalization, etc.

EK: How is architecture education today in Singapore?

TKS: Very weak. The faculty of social sciences is just across the road from the architecture school, but we don't talk to each other. It's crazy. Everything is prescribed by the Ministry of Education. They just calculate, "we need so many architects, blah blah blah…" But what kind of architects? Architects in their eyes are simply service providers and style mongers, that's all.

EK: Do you think there is a need for more visionary thinkers?

TKS: I'm not talking about visionary thinkers, I have big practical thinkers in mind. What I am talking about is practical. How do you turn this whole place into a brain, that's a practical task. There are three case studies that I am looking at now: one is the Mondragón Corporación Cooperativa, in northern Spain,

the second is the state of Kerala in southwest India, and the third is the island of Bali. Mondragón is a cooperative of 100,000 factory workers who have owned their factories since 1956. They became so successful that they even have their own bank, their own university, and their own hospitals, and nobody ever loses their job. Kerala is a 600-kilometers linear village of little houses surrounded by paddy fields, which are all connected by one road and one railway. It has the highest level of literacy in India and produces a tremendous number of intellectuals. Without Kerala, Bangalore can't function. Three quarters of Bangalore's top computer scientists are from Kerala and there isn't a single big city there. How is this possible? Then there is Bali. In Bali they have the *banjar* system, a peculiar, decentralized community organization system that, combined with a double

Interior view of the shopping center at the People's Park Complex in the 1970s.
© DP Architects

currency system, allows the locals to maintain a degree of financial and political autonomy despite the flourishing global tourism industry. This is possible because they are smart and they retain control of the land. As a foreigner, you are legally not entitled to own land in Bali, you can only obtain a right-of-use contract. In Bali there is a sub-form of collective ownership within the market economy. This is the future. The neoliberal order has reached an impasse, it's fragmenting, it's killing itself. The rich got too rich, and the rest is not rich enough, so now global stagnation is inevitable. We are fighting over the bread crumbs. This is the moment that we should rethink and reengineer our production relationships in a socially sustainable way. It is not communism, it is not capitalism, it is a clever mix. Our role as architects and planners is to find out the connections between these processes of social and physical transformation. This is why we need big and deep thinkers in our schools. Our profession is completely devoid of thinking. We architects have two great skills: we can visualize and we instinctively excel in complexity. We love complexity, but we just don't know enough. The number of dots we want to connect is not enough. We must connect an entire galaxy.

EK: Thinking out of the box is an important issue that needs to be addressed in education. Do we really need more knowledge or do we need to learn where to find it and how to use it creatively?
TKS: I call it the seven Cs. The first are competence and confidence, which bring courage. When you have courage, you dare to ask the good questions, but one also has to be curious and have compassion. With curiosity and compassion, collaboration comes

easy, and so in the end you achieve conviction. If you want to teach creatively, you must start with competence. But what is competence? Different people require different potentialities: babies first lie on their back and then they want to turn over, they want to crawl, sit, get up, walk, run, jump, etc.—each level is driven by an internal process of developing confidence. If any of these steps are prevented, confidence is affected. If you want to design a new educational system, you must reinforce confidence at every step of the educational process. It is not an issue of the curriculum, it is an issue of pedagogy. All the information you need is just one click away, the important part is how to ask the right question, not where to get the answer. For thousands of years men asked the wrong questions: "How do I fly like a bird?" is a stupid question, you will never find an answer to that. But if you ask the question "How does a bird fly?" then you immediately understand aeronautics. Teachers have to teach students how to ask the right question. This is why I think schools should be placed in the central nervous system of the city, because that is where you encounter action and disagreement, and where the right questions come up.
EK: Governments are afraid of new ideas, because new ideas can challenge their own position.
TKS: You see, the left-wing intellectuals in the 1950s and 1960s called the present economy a brothel, because we sell our bodies in this economy. The result was that the PAP government understood the name of the game, and started playing with the international capitalist class.[05] We played very well. Investors came and so we built all the infrastructure, we controlled the trade unions and the minds of the

students, we convinced people that everybody is a service provider, and so our system succeeded. But the greatest achievement of the PAP government is that the state still owns 80 percent of the land, from which it makes huge profits by leasing it to the investors, and so Singapore has now accumulated over one trillion US dollars of reserves. But if no one comes to our island the land value is zero. The simple fact that people come here for business creates land value, nothing else. We accumulated so much over the years that now we could pay each citizen of Singapore 800 dollars a month for doing nothing if we wanted to. The older you are, the more you get. In this situation, more and more people would be free to do

as they pleased. On this basis the whole country could become a network of small and medium-sized enterprises. But the business scope is too small, it must reach the entire region. This is why I am arguing for a central nervous system that pervades the whole island, to bring foreign people and locals together to learn and become friends. This is my model for the future of Singapore.
EK: In this world, all the small countries have to define and redefine their position and cooperation models constantly, otherwise they have no chance.
TKS: My argument is this: we had to prostitute ourselves and this brothel has become very rich. We can change our vocation now, we no longer need to be whores.

01 In Singapore, the state owns around 80 percent of the land. Time-limited land-use rights are sold to private developers via public auctions. Around 80 percent of the population currently lives in apartments developed on behalf of the public Housing and Development Board (HDB) and lease their homes on a time-limited basis, typically 99 years. For this reason, the concept of home-ownership in Singapore is very different from the Western understanding of permanent ownership.
02 A strata title is a method of facilitating individual ownership of part of a property, while sharing ownership of the common ground the property is built upon. Strata-titled properties were intro-

duced in Singapore with the Land Title (Strata) Act in May 1967. Strata-leased apartments in Singapore are mainly public housing units with leasehold tenure contracts of 99 years, where the lessees pay fixed monthly maintenance fees to the town council based on the room types of their strata unit.
03 The Pearl Bank Apartments, designed by Tan Cheng Siong and completed in 1976, was demolished in late 2019. At the time of this interview, there was a debate in the press about whether or not this iconic building should be demolished or preserved.
04 In October 2020, the Urban Redevelopment Authority (URA) recommended that the Golden Mile Complex

be preserved. See Michelle Ng, "Golden Mile Complex Proposed for Conservation," *The Straits Times* (October 10, 2020), accessed July 19, 2021, www.straitstimes.com/singapore/housing/goldenmile-complex-proposedfor-conservation.
05 The PAP (People's Action Party) is the major conservative center-right political party in Singapore. Singapore achieved independence in 1965, and since 1966 the PAP has continuously held an overwhelming majority of seats in the parliament.

View from Chinatown of the People's Park Complex
by Design Partnership.

AN EMBEDDED WORLD-ING
The practice of Lim Chong Keat

In 2014, I visited the office of Architects Team 3 in Singapore, in search of material about the firm's projects since its founding as the Malayan Architects Co-partnership (MAC) in the early 1960s. I was directed to boxes of slides, photographs, sketches, and portfolio sheets, which were about to be disposed of. The significance of the projects realized by MAC and Architects Team 3 across British Malaya have been widely documented, yet the name of its founding partner, Lim Chong Keat (born 1930) is seldom mentioned. As a result, there was little recognition of his pivotal contribution to architectural developments in the region—until the fragmented archive of the two practices finally entered the M+ Collections in Hong Kong.[01]

Text: Shirley Surya

Malayan Architects Co-partnership: Singapore Conference Hall and Trade Union House, Singapore, 1961–65.

From a brochure published by the Singapore Ministry of Culture for the opening of the building on October 15, 1965.

MAC and Architects Team 3 have often been depicted as pioneering architectural practices during the time of postcolonial nation-building in Southeast Asia. This article instead focuses on Lim's own views, in order to highlight the productive tension between his allegiance to local, national, and regional agendas, and his commitment to universalist values that traveled across national boundaries and disciplinary fields. The aim is to explore the intertwining of beliefs embedded within, yet transcending, geographies and disciplines that motivated Lim's principled approach. After the Federation of Malaya became independent in 1957, MAC was one of the first practices established by Singapore- and Malaysia-born architects who had trained in the

international models, but in the creation of new urban patterns based on the "new history" of developing countries.[03]

MAC's founding members first met in 1953 at the Conference on Tropical Architecture held at University College London. Here they learned about the work of British architects in West Africa, which they found very relevant to Malaya's tropical climate conditions, leading Lim to a deeper understanding of the "endogenous" concept—a biological term used to describe a process originating from an internal cause within a system.[04] Lim applied this principle to his first designs, which were developed from and for local conditions. His first built project, a home for Tan Peng Nam completed in 1959 in Singapore, was an

Lim Chong Keat:
House for
Tan Peng Nam,
Singapore 1958/59.
© Lim Chong Keat

United States and in the United Kingdom. The firm's immediate success in winning public competitions—in particular the Singapore Conference Hall and Trade Union House (1961–1965) and the Negeri Sembilan Mosque (1965–67)—was daunting to the more established British expatriate architects who had been dominant in British Malaya until then. Like many architects across South and Southeast Asia, their active role in designing the buildings that came to represent the nation's cultural and political identities was invigorated by postcolonial statecraft. In this light, MAC's work is often perceived as a break from the colonial past, consciously situating the formal language of global modernism within the region's historical and environmental specificities. Nevertheless, Lim's international outlook and his commitment to the region reveal a more nuanced understanding of postcolonial citizenship, one that could not strictly be exercised within predefined borders, nor identified with specifically regionalist or globalist traits. Lim considered his overseas education as a means of becoming "globalized" in the sense of becoming a part of the world, yet interpreting the world in relation to one's own origins with the ultimate goal of being "useful at home."[02] He understood the modern movement in universal terms, while at the same time he confronted the regional context of Asia in social rather than architectural terms. As a result, he did not believe in the application of ready-made solutions from

early exercise in using locally available materials like brick, timber, and mosaic tiles. The home he designed for Dr. Arthur Aeria in Penang (George Town), completed in 1960, with its fair-faced load-bearing brickwork and glass infill, won the Ideal Homes Award of the Federation of the Malaya Society of Architects (FMSA). Not only did this reflect the architects' desire to design modern residences using materials and construction methods suitable to the tropical context, it also reflected the new lifestyle of the emergent middle class. Both houses, with their light-framed construction systems exposed on the facade, show a clear commitment to universal modernist principles of rationality while taking local climatic factors into thoughtful consideration, featuring elements like slated timber screens, grillwork, and overhangs that delicately provide shade, allow natural illumination, facilitate cross-ventilation, and create a smooth transition between inside and outside. Such environmental and material considerations set the tone for MAC's future projects, including some of Singapore's earliest modernist structures that shaped the city's central business district.

Completed in 1965, the iconic Conference Hall and Trade Union House was MAC's first major building commission in Singapore. Its international yet context-specific design was hailed as a symbol of renewed national pride and of the global aspirations of Singapore's

Malayan Architects
Co-Partnership (completed
by Architects Team 3):
Negeri Sembilan State
Mosque, Seremban,
Malaysia, 1965–67.

new political leaders. MAC's sensibility for the climate is evident in the building's east-west orientation, the cantilevered roof slabs, the lofty, cross-ventilated lobby, the openings atop the windows designed to allow natural airflow, and the use of vertical louvers made of locally sourced tropical hardwood.[05] Equally important is the fact that the design is based on modernist ideals of openness and access, enhancing human interaction and setting the building apart from the enclosed and severe colonial architecture of the past. The extensive multilayered lobby space encourages movement, while the huge glass facade visually connects it to the street, making a spectacle of the building's public function. The Conference Hall and Trade Union House embodies Lim's articulation of a regionalist form of modernism in Malaya, which was not to be seen merely as a "stylized expression" of a postcolonial identity based on the "myth of cultural independence,"

but was the result of practicing architecture as a socially "progressive discipline" offering "newer and better technological and aesthetic solutions."[06] The Malaysia Singapore Airlines Building (1965–67), the Jurong Town Hall (1967–74), the Development Bank of Singapore (1969–75), and the United Overseas Bank (1971–74) are all landmark buildings whose design is driven by concerns for structure, materials, technology, total environments, as well as for the development of new urban patterns. Lim once described MAC's projects as Singapore's "native modern" buildings, not just for their formal expressions but also as eminent proof of the ability of local architects and builders to improve their own country's urban and social conditions.[07] But while his generation was greatly inspired by nationalistic and anticolonial sentiments, Lim was not opposed to the idea that foreign architects from the colonial establishment would continue to practice in

Singapore or Malaysia. On the contrary: Lim's sharpest criticism was directed at the lackadaisical attitude of local architects who, instead of developing their own knowledge and skills, pursued the replication of international models that were not suitable to the local context.[08] Addressing the Malaysian Institute of Architects (PAM) on the topic of architectural education, Lim called for "national architectural professionals to stand on their own feet," and to reappraise the advantages and disadvantages of their colonial legacy so as to develop their own learning frameworks and drive the country's own development instead of remaining "in the backwash of postcolonial trends."[09] He dismissed the concept of the masterplan, which he deemed "oversophisticated" for Singapore's "new pragmatic dynamism," and merely a legacy of technical aid between "developed" and "underdeveloped" countries that would produce a form of neocolonialism. Lim differentiated between relevant and indiscriminate transfers of ideas, embracing, for example, Otto Koenigsberger's concept of "action planning"—the idea that parts of the city should be built incrementally based on progressively gained experiences,[10] a method that Lim applied in the design of the KOMTAR complex, built from 1974 to 1988. The KOMTAR high-rise was conceived in response to a growing demand for civic, commercial, residential, and administrative facilities in the central area of Penang, combined with a desire to preserve the historical urban fabric of George Town. After close observation of local demographics, Lim proposed a 65-story office tower atop a podium, rising above existing fabric, with a combination of commercial and public uses, including a shopping arcade and a multipurpose event hall.[11]

Lim's aversion to the use of indigenous architectural forms for their nationalistic, regionalist, or touristic appeal stemmed from his own longstanding ethnological studies. His involvement in the Southeast Asia Habitat research project was the result of the conviction that a true identification with the region should be manifested in the documentation and appraisal of local cultures "for their own sake," and not for deriving architectural forms from them. His research revealed how indigenous architectural forms were designed with a sense of scale and proportion integral to each community's way of life, to their "endogenic self-sufficiency of skills and materials," and to their "inherent symbolism and cosmology." These elements could not be reconstructed outside the community, nor copied into eclectic derivations, be it a *kampong* house[12] or a historical timber palace with a curved roof made of reinforced concrete.[13] In his view, the adoption of "historical antecedents" under "artificial circumstances" was merely a form of "synthetic nationhood."[14] Lim's research instead shows an uninhibited understanding of the Malayan identity that was shared by many architects in the first decade after independence, as expressed in a widely disseminated discussion on "What Is Malayan Architecture?".[15] For Lim's generation it was futile to construct a single Malayan identity through particular vernacular forms. Instead, they opted for designs based on multiple factors like climate, local materials, and structure, as well as models from other tropical regions. It is to this openness and multiplicity of perspectives on cultural identity that Lim attributed the success of the Negeri Sembilan Mosque project in Seremban, something that was only possible before the politicization of the idea of a "Malayan" style.

Realized between 1965 and 1967, the mosque is based on a nine-sided polygonal floor plan representing the nine districts of the Negeri Sembilan state. In place of the conventional round dome, an umbrella-shaped roof made of nine concave vaults rises above the prayer hall, which is enclosed within glass walls. Nine slim minaret-like structures stand at every intersection of the vaults. The mosque's structural

lightness and aesthetic simplicity, resulting from the delicate composition of curved load-bearing concrete surfaces and the absence of any gilded ornamentation, set this design apart from traditional mosque typologies. It was Malaysia's first competition for a mosque organized by the Federation of Malaya Society of Architects. Lim described it as a "completely universal" design with an emphatically contemporary approach. It was the last mosque commissioned to non-Muslim architects before the onset of conservative Islamic nationalism in Malaysia.[16]

Lim's universalist approach to design and identity was rooted in his "awareness of the world as a whole," with its specificities, diversities, and interdependences. This was an awareness that he shared with American architect, inventor, and philosopher Buckminster Fuller.[17] Fuller and Lim had many exchanges during Fuller's trips to Southeast Asia. Lim emphasized that both he and Fuller had a "mutual empathy for ethnology" but without trying to exploit it or utilize it in their work.[18] Instead, they often looked for parallels across various cultures. For example, Fuller conceptually linked the three-way weave basketry craft of Southeast Asia with his worldview and with his theorization of the geodesic dome,[19] while Lim looked for "historical interweaves" and "ethnographic interactions" in languages, arts, crafts, techniques, and building features resulting from migratory patterns and cosmopolitan trades within, and beyond, Southeast Asia.[20] These observations are at the basis of Lim's view that "culture has no boundaries" and that one's commitment to national and international causes does not need to be mutually exclusive but interrelated for the collective growth of the profession.[21] In the post-independence years, there was a widespread sentiment that only Singaporeans should design buildings in Singapore. At a conference addressing architectural identity, Lim noted how even if key architects across Southeast Asia—namely Sumet Jumsai in Thailand and Leandro Locsin in the Philippines—employed "world building techniques" and "un-self-conscious international design criteria" when they undertook projects in other parts of the world, they were not "transient foreigners" but "nationals in residence," who took their urban responsibilities very seriously. This also applied to Lim's own practice, which was primarily rooted in Malaysia and Singapore, yet unbounded in terms of how and where ideas were sourced. Lim's only three overseas projects were a residence for Singaporean shipping magnate Robin Loh in Hong Kong, the Bank of Ceylon Headquarters in Colombo, and the US Geodesic Dome Botanical Pavilion in Bangkok, co-designed with Sumet Jumsai.[22] A Malaysian citizen, Lim regarded "both territories [Singapore and Malaysia] as one" and was actively involved in educational institutions, national professional bodies, and high-level policy-making for Singapore's public housing and city planning schemes.[23] Lim encouraged the Malaysian Institute of Architects, Pertubuhan Akitek Malaysia (PAM), to think beyond the nation-state by engaging in regional cooperation. He took the Regional Board of Architectural Education of the Commonwealth Association of Architects[24] as an example of a regional network whose scope was to avoid a "one-way traffic of 'experts' and 'expertise' from the developed world to determine how architectural education, research, and the profession should be run elsewhere."[25] He called for developing professional expertise to meet global standards through regional interdependence, as opposed to postcolonial self-reliance—a view that reflected his understanding of Fuller's work as the exercising of "comprehensive global design responsibilities, beyond national or regional divisiveness" in order to pursue a "common fulfillable destiny for humanity on earth" and "a world for you *and* me, not you *or* me."[26]

Architects Team 3: Development Bank of Singapore (DBS), Singapore, 1969–1975.

Lim's resonance with Fuller's comprehensivist stance was not only about exercising design responsibilities in a culturally and geographically indivisible world, it went "beyond conventional architecture to the inexorable integrity of human science and art."[27] On one level, this is demonstrated by an approach to architectural practice encompassing other disciplinary fields, while reaffirming the architect's distinct contribution and responsibility. On another level, Lim's design approach is undergirded by particular universal principles of integrity. He believed that "interest in culture, art, and music is integral to designing a building."[28] His own interest in music and acoustics was crucial to the design of the auditorium for the Singapore Conference Hall. As a major supporter of the Singapore artist cooperative Alpha Gallery, Lim is known for his vested interest in the visual arts, which he expressed with the integration of several artworks and sculptures specifically commissioned for his buildings. Lim emphasized that even if architecture and the fine arts shared a common denominator in the search for "aesthetic implications" of form-making, this was only one of the architect's "repertoires of concerns," which also included the responsibility for providing "a comprehensive set of design solutions to a particular environmental need."[29] Lim's interdisciplinary engagement is thus rooted in his comprehensive views. Just as

"synergy is to energy what integration is to differentiation," for Lim the "creative aspect of architecture lies in its integration process" of form, structure, space, materials, engineering, services, and economy of construction.[30] From residences to office towers, Lim was concerned with the entire design process: negotiating with the client, developing the concept, realizing the drawing, and supervising the site. He worked across such fields as interior design, furniture, carpet design, wall hangings, light fittings, and even designed details like ashtrays. At the same time, he was also concerned with the planning of entire environments, a task that requires absolute clarity in terms the architect's social and political responsibilities inasmuch as it affects the future of urban patterns. This is something that particularly emerges in his design of Singapore's earliest high-rise structures. The Malaysia Singapore Airlines (MSA) building for example—with its podium of three stories instead of the two stories originally stipulated by the government—set the ideal proportions of the typical podium-tower typology that came to define the commercial district between Robinson Road and Shenton Way. This was also the first building in Singapore to use the slip-form construction method, and to have an underground car park and a landscaped roof garden on the podium. For the Development Bank of Singapore, instead of occupying a long site with three towers,

Malayan Architects Co-partnership (completed by Architects Team 3): Malaysia Singapore Airlines Building, Singapore, 1965–67.

© Architects Team 3 Pte Ltd, Singapore

as originally proposed by the developer, Architects Team 3 delivered three blocks of varying heights and volumes, including the slim and elegant 50-story office tower, which was Singapore's tallest building at the time. Breaking the overall volume into three different blocks reduced the impact on the skyline and on the adjacent buildings, creating a variety of spaces accessible to the public, including an auditorium, exhibition facilities, restaurants, and a shopping arcade. These were all functions that were not in the original brief but became common features of office complexes in Singapore.

Lim saw architecture as inseparable from universal humanist principles. A manifestation of physical and metaphysical integration of the arts and humanity, architectural design was to be exercised as a form of conscious learning and not as the mere expression of stylistic influences. This view parallels Fuller's concept of comprehensivity as the capacity of seeing the "great patterns or order in the total experience to cultivate the ability" to comprehend the universe and become transcendent.[31] Between 1975 and 1983, Lim and Fuller co-organized the Campuan World Meetings, a series of informal workshops held in Bali and Penang, during which participants from

different fields explored various manifestations of "integrity."[32] For Lim, concepts like identity or style were rooted in the idea of "aesthetic durability," which requires a basic literacy in the universal language of geometry.[33] In this respect, two of the most frequently elements of Lim's architecture are the preoccupation with the geodesic dome—the embodiment of a transcendent "universal structure"—and his prismatic approach to design. Fuller's contribution to spherical geometry and his championing of the geodesic dome as a means to enclose the maximum space with the greatest economy of effort was fundamental to Lim's own understanding of comprehensive architecture. During Fuller's visit to Singapore, Lim arranged for students to construct domes. At the second Campuan World Meeting in Bali, he tested the universality of the structure by building a dome from bamboo. Lim genuinely embraced Fuller's radical notion of structural economy and incorporated domes into his own designs, including a 44-meter-high dome for a multipurpose event space at KOMTAR; Fuller participated in its realization as a consultant. KOMTAR's dome and polygonal tower represented the deliberate use of a culturally transcendent, universal geometrical language at a time when identifiably regionalist

© Architects Team 3 Pte Ltd, Singapore

Architects Team 3:
Lobby of the United Overseas Bank (UOB), with a geodesic dome in the back, Singapore, 1971–74.

Right
Paul P. Blackburn, Sumet Jumsai, and Lim Chong Keat (left to right), in front of the Geodesic Dome Botanical Pavilion commissioned by the US Embassy in Suan Luang Rama IX Park in Bangkok, Thailand, 1987/88.

Below
Gathering in a bamboo geodesic dome during the second Campuan World Meeting, co-organized by Lim Chong Keat and Buckminster Fuller in Bali, Indonesia, 1977. Sumet Jumsai was among the guests.

© M+ Collections, Hong Kong. Donated by Sumet Jumsai, 2018

© M+ Collections, Hong Kong. Donated by Sumet Jumsai, 2018

Architects Team 3:
KOMTAR complex under
construction, George
Town, Penang, Malaysia,
1962–86.

forms were preferred in Malaysia. The United Overseas Bank in Singapore and the Bank of Ceylon in Colombo, both nascent urban sites situated in historic cultural and financial districts, were designed with a similar prismatic approach as a form of "prototypical inventiveness." Through the application of careful three-dimensional studies, both buildings relate to their environment by presenting the same polygonal facade from every angle.[34] On the question of whether such a geometrical approach negates originality, Lim emphasized that consistency with regard to environmental integrity trumps originality, especially when the design of different buildings requires similar solutions to similar programs, and when a design could impact adjoining buildings.

Lim's universalist approach to architecture best emerges in his design for the residence of Robin Loh, in Hong Kong. Like a futuristic spaceship perched on a hill, the house is composed of overlapping cantilevered trapezoidal volumes supported by six gigantic circular columns, with sloping smoked glass windows and a green rooftop. Although Lim considers it a "dream building," its strong form is not grandiose but highly functional, even economical, with multipurpose service spaces such as an elevator, staircase, and bathrooms embedded within each of the six columns.[35]

In light of today's increasing nationalist-regionalist hubris and self-serving nature of the architectural profession, Lim's approach—characterized by twin ideals and complementary polarities of universality and specificity[36]—is worth reevaluation, as it probes how architectural production in Southeast Asia can manifest itself and be historicized through the lens of embeddedness locality and discipline, while still being globally porous and all-encompassing in scope.

Architects Team 3: Model of the Central Area Redevelopment Plan for Penang (KOMTAR), George Town, Malaysia, 1962–86.

01   The Malayan Architects Co-partnership (MAC) was founded in 1961 by Lim Chong Keat, Chen Voon Fee, and William S.W. Lim. It was succeeded by Architects Team 3 in 1967, founded by Lim Chong Keat, Baharuddin Abu Kassim, and Lim Chin See.

02   Two interviews with Lim Chong Keat, Hong Kong, May 19, 2017; and Kuala Lumpur, April 22, 2018.

03   Fred Parish, "New Face of Singapore," *Free World – Horizons* 19, no. 5 (1969): 10–15.

04   Interview with Lim Chong Keat, Hong Kong, May 19, 2017.

05   Ibid.

06   Lim Chong Keat, "Cultural Development," paper delivered at the Conference of Commonwealth and Overseas Architectural Societies, 1963, RIBA Archive, 12.2.8 box 1, 9.

07   Interview with Lim Chong Keat, Hong Kong, May 19, 2017.

08   Ibid.

09   Lim Chong Keat, "The Role of the Professional Institute in the Development of Architectural Education," *Journal of the Singapore Institute of Architects*, no. 83 (July/August 1977): 6–11. Originally presented to the Malaysian Institute of Architects (Pertubuhan Akitek Malaysia, PAM) in November 1976.

10   Lim Chong Keat, "Regeneration of the City: The Planning Crossroads in Singapore," *Journal of the Singapore Institute of Architects*, no. 35 (July/August 1969): 6–22.

11   Interview with Lim Chong Keat, Hong Kong, May 19, 2017.

12   *Kampong* means "village" in Malay.

13   Lim Chong Keat, introduction to *Habitat in Southeast Asia: A Pictorial Survey of Folk Architecture* (Kuala Lumpur: National Art Gallery, 1986), 2–4.

14   Arthur M. Foyle and A. Adedokun Adeyemi, eds., *Conference on Tropical Architecture, 1953: A Report of the Proceedings of the Conference Held at University College*, London, March, 1953 (London: George Allen and Unwin, 1954), 77.

15   Kington Loo, ed., "What is Malayan Architecture?", *PETA: Journal of the Federation of Malaya Society of Architects* 3 no. 4 (August 1961).

16   Interview with Lim Chong Keat, Kuala Lumpur, April 22, 2018.

17   Fong Peng-Khuan, ed., "An Earthonaut Assessed: Lim Chong Keat on Fuller," *Pacific* 11. no. 1 (1982): 60–61.

18   Interview with Lim Chong Keat, Kuala Lumpur, April 22, 2018.

19   Lim Chong Keat, "The International Context for South East Asian Architecture," in *Architecture and Identity*, ed. Robert Powell (Singapore: Concept Media/Aga Khan Award for Architecture, 1983), 25–29. Part of the conference proceedings from a regional seminar organized by the Aga Khan Award for Architecture, held in Kuala Lumpur, Malaysia, 1983.

20   Lim Chong Keat, introduction to *Habitat in Southeast Asia: A Pictorial Survey of Folk Architecture* (see note 13).

21   Lim Chong Keat, "The International Context for South East Asian Architecture" (see note 19).

22   Lim's overseas projects resulted from his personal and professional network: the Bank of Ceylon (BOC) Headquarters was commissioned through the recommendation of Sri Lanka's first city planner, Oliver Weerasinghe, who met Lim at the United Nations State and City Planning Review Panel; and the US Geodesic Dome Botanical Pavilion in Bangkok's Suan Luang Rama IX Park resulted from Lim's connection with USIS (United States Information Service) officer Paul P. Blackburn.

23   Interview with Lim Chong Keat in Hong Kong, May 19, 2017.

24   The Regional Board of Architectural Education of the Commonwealth Association of Architects was initiated by ARCASIA (Architects Regional Council Asia), which Lim cofounded.

25   Lim Chong Keat, "The Role of the Professional Institute in the Development of Architectural Education" (see note 9).

26   Lim Chong Keat, *In Memoriam RBF*, July 1984.

27   Lim Chong Keat: "The International Context for South East Asian Architecture" (see note 19).

28   Interview with Lim Chong Keat, Hong Kong, May 19, 2017; and Kuala Lumpur, April 22, 2018.

29   Ken Yeang, ed., "Interview No. 1 Lim Chong Keat – The Designer," *Majallah Akitek* 2, no. 78 (June 1978): 12–17; Lim Chong Keat, "Free Form in Contemporary Architecture: A Study of the Roots and Characteristics of Plasticity in Architectural Design" (MArch diss., Massachusetts Institute of Technology, 1957), 1–6.

30   Richard Buckminster Fuller, "What is the Purpose of Man's Life," *Ekistics* 26, no. 155 (October 1968): 344–46; Fred Parish, "New Face of Singapore," *Free World – Horizons* 19, no. 5 (see note 3).

31   Ibid.

32   *Campuan* means "confluence of rivers" in Balinese.

33   Ken Yeang, ed., "Interview No. 1 Lim Chong Keat – The Designer" (see note 29).

34   Ibid.

35   Interview with Lim Chong Keat, Hong Kong, May 19, 2017.

36   Lim Chong Keat, "Free Form in Contemporary Architecture" (see note 29).

Architects Team 3:
House for Robin Loh,
Hong Kong, 1973.

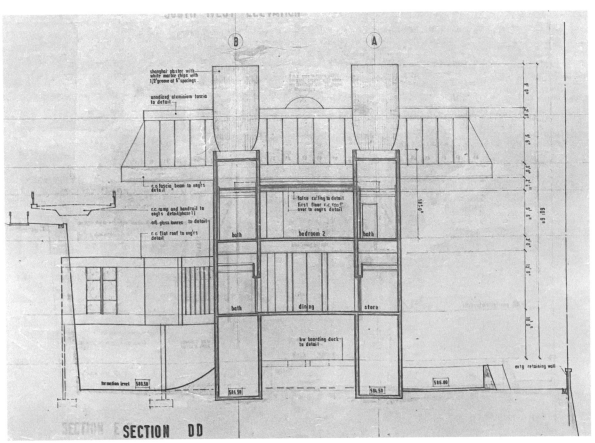

Longitudinal section.

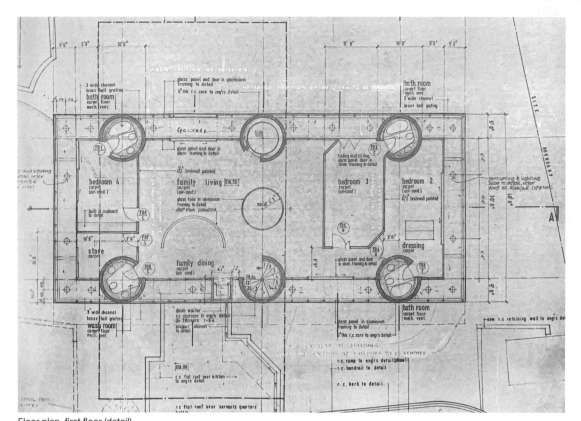

Floor plan, first floor (detail).

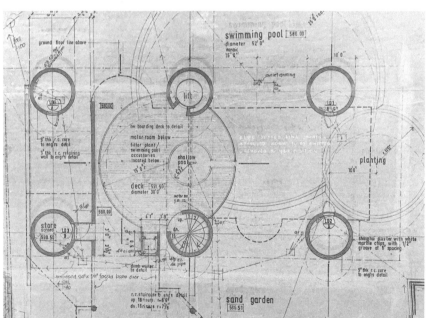

Floor plan, ground floor (detail).

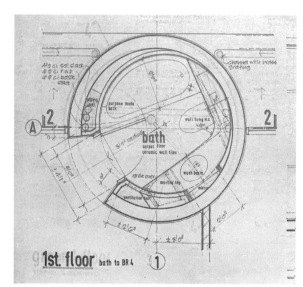

Floor plan of the bathroom,
which is integrated into
one of the six round pillars
(detail).

SOUTHEAST ASIA AS A "GEOCULTURAL PROBLEM"
Ute Meta Bauer, founding director of the NTU Centre for Contemporary Art (CCA) in Singapore, in conversation with Moritz Henning, Christian Hiller, and Eduard Kögel

CHRISTIAN HILLER: In 2013, you became the founding director of the NTU Centre for Contemporary Art (CCA) at the Nanyang Technological University in Singapore. Prior to that, you held various positions in cultural and educational institutions around the world, including head of the program in Art, Culture and Technology (ACT) at the Department of Architecture at MIT in Cambridge, Massachusetts. What prompted you to go to Southeast Asia, and more specifically to Singapore, and take over the director position of the CCA?

UTE META BAUER: It wasn't a plan I'd been mulling over for a long time, but was much more a spur of the moment decision. I've always found this region very exciting. In 2005, my first year at MIT, I went to China with the architect Yung Ho Chang—our chair at the time—to visit the Shenzhen Biennale for Urbanism and Architecture, which he launched and curated. By

then I already knew this metropolis quite well, having already been there on trips to Hong Kong and Guangzhou, beginning in 1998. I was fascinated by how quickly everything was changing and modernizing, but still keeping traditions and local cultures visible. This parallelism of different temporalities and time layers is characteristic of many Asian cities even today.

In 1993, I traveled to Beijing and Bangkok for the first time, followed by journeys to Hanoi and Singapore in 2004. Shortly after the 3rd berlin biennale for contemporary art, where I was artistic director, I was invited by Singapore's Ministry of Culture to join curators of different biennials in sharing our experiences, since Singapore was planning its own biennial at the time. So I got to know some people back then, with whom I stayed in contact over the years. These included the art critic Lee Weng Choy, the artist Lim Tzay Chuen, the curators

June Yap and Ahmad Mashadi, and the art historian and curator Eugene Tan. From Weng Choy, I heard about plans to develop an internationally oriented art quarter in Gillman Barracks, under the overall project management of Eugene Tan. There were also two Berlin galleries involved in that project.[01] The NTU Centre for Contemporary Art Singapore was planned as a partnership initiative between the country's Economic Development Board (EDB) and Nanyang Technological University (NTU). I found the idea of a new hybrid institution very exciting, something between an art gallery, academic research, and education. Together with Weng Choy, who was to be the deputy director, we talked about what contribution the CCA could make to the local and regional art scene at this location.

It sounded almost too good to be true: to get to build up an institution combining exhibitions, artistic and curatorial research, as well as a residency program for artists, curators, and researchers from all over the world, in a region that has always been very appealing to me, and with a reasonable budget.

CH: The aforementioned ACT program at MIT resulted from the 2009 merger of the Visual Art Program, which you previously headed, and the Center for Advanced Visual Studies (CAVS). The program pursued a fundamentally interdisciplinary approach, linking together art, culture, and media technology, along with architecture and urban planning. To what extent did this interdisciplinary and transdisciplinary work also feed into the agenda for the CCA in Singapore?

UMB: You should know that CAVS was founded in 1967 by György Kepes, a Hungarian exile. Before he was appointed to MIT's Department of Architecture in 1945, as its first art professor, he

had taught, along with his wife Juliet Kepes, at the New Bauhaus in Chicago, at that time directed by László Moholy-Nagy. When Kepes retired in 1974, the German artist Otto Piene took over as the head of CAVS. Piene had become well known in the 1960s for cofounding the artist group ZERO in Düsseldorf. So actually, this center was interdisciplinary from the start. In general, the Bauhaus had a very substantial influence in Cambridge. Walter Gropius and Marcel Breuer moved from Europe to Massachusetts before the Second World War to teach at the GSD, the Harvard Graduate School of Design.

From Cambridge, connecting lines also stretch across to southeast Asia, for example through the architects William S. W. Lim and Lim Chong Keat, and the artist and curator Choy Weng Yang, a former fellow at CAVS. Buckminster Fuller was a major influence on Keat, an MIT alumnus

based in Penang, Malaysia (see Shirley Surya's article in this issue). So it is not so unusual for the CCA to build on these linkages.

CH: At a presentation of the CCA you once said that one of its main features is the residence program. It is particularly important that artists not only come to Singapore, but also always have an opportunity to travel on to another Southeast Asian country, in order to bring the whole region closer together. The exhibitions you are doing also aim for strong involvement of artists and cultural workers from all over Southeast Asia. What is your general take on networking within the region?

UMB: First of all, concrete historical events formally contribute to stronger networking across the countries of Southeast Asia. In 1967, Thailand, Indonesia, Malaysia, the Philippines, and

Singapore founded the Association of Southeast Asian Nations (ASEAN), and were later also joined by Brunei, Vietnam, Myanmar, Laos, and Cambodia. Together, these countries now form an economic area similar to the EU, which not only benefits from coordinated economic cooperation, but also has common guidelines on questions of safety and environmental policy. Another important historical anchor, which we addressed in our last exhibition *Non-Aligned* (2020), is the Bandung Conference of 1955 and its geopolitical influence. At that time, 29 (post-)colonial states from Asia, Africa, and Latin America met in Bandung, to push to maintain their territorial sovereignty, and to bring an end to imperialism and other forms of colonial rule. In 1961, the Non-Aligned Movement of Non-Aligned States emerged from this alliance. These countries declared their neutrality in the East–West conflict,

John Akomfrah: *The Unfinished Conversation*, 2012. Exhibition view, *Non-Aligned*, NTU Centre for Contemporary Art Singapore, 2020.

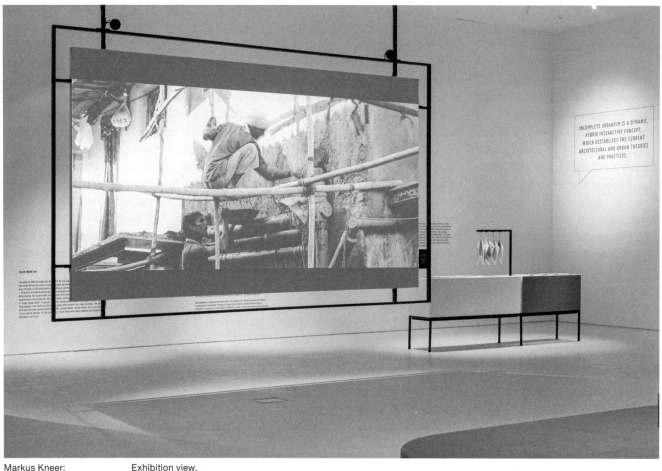

Markus Kneer:
Mumbai: Maximum City
Under Pressure, 2013.

Exhibition view,
*Incomplete Urbanism:
Attempts of Critical
Spatial Practice,* NTU
Centre for Contemporary
Art Singapore, 2017.

and spoke out in favor of the disarmament of the two military blocs.

Today in the region, people are increasingly looking to the Western world. There is also an underlying tension and competition among the various Southeast Asian states. Southeast Asia is a relatively recent name for this region, coined after the Second World War, offering a kind of geographic orientation between South Asia [south of China] and East Asia [east of India]. The Second World War Allies used the term to describe a region which was then mostly occupied by Japan, and had to be reconquered. So the basic question arises as to whether and to what extent the name makes any sense today. Given the very heterogeneous structure of the region—in cultural, religious, political, and economic terms—

can we speak of a unitary construct called "Southeast Asia" at all? In this context, the art historian T. K. Sabapathy has also spoken of the "geocultural problem" of Southeast Asia. This is because most of the nation states that emerged from decolonization were new creations, some arising from political calculation or from the political situation after the colonial occupation, and some have a certain degree of arbitrariness.

EDUARD KÖGEL: Against this backdrop, we should take a closer look at Singapore's particular role. Viewed from the West, Singapore shines as a modern high-tech metropolis. But what is the view of Singapore from inside the Southeast Asian context? Isn't it much more critical, also given

the competitive conditions that you mentioned earlier?
UMB: It is a complicated constellation, because these competitive relationships are also based on interdependence. Singapore isseen as an important global financial metropolis, politically stable and open to the West. Many international companies have their Southeast Asian headquarters in Singapore, and some even have their entire Asian headquarters there. Singapore is also an important strategic trading partner for neighboring countries. A large part of imports and exports with the West go through Singapore. This role is, of course, closely related to Singapore's development, since colonial times, as one of the most important trading ports. The country has a very favorable geostrategic

location, and is not directly affected by tsunamis or earthquakes. This wealthy city-state is now a multiethnic, multireligious nation with four official languages: Malay, English, Chinese, and Tamil. However, the financial strength of countries like Indonesia or Malaysia is easy to underestimate, since wealth is so unevenly distributed there. Singapore's neighbors increasingly have high strategic market importance for Europe and the USA. Not only that, they also play an important role in relation to China, in terms of military strategy and security policy.

MORITZ HENNING: To what extent does this also have an impact on cultural and political issues?
UMB: On this question, it is interesting to look back. One of my

doctoral students, a Singaporean, is researching the Cold War and the influence of the United States after the Second World War, through cultural activities like exhibitions in Southeast Asia. I hadn't been aware of that, and find it fascinating.

CH: You are now addressing the "postcolonial situation." What role do postcolonial discourses play in Singapore today?

UMB: Of course, people do know about them here. A few years ago, the Getty Foundation gave financial support to "Ambitious Alignments," a major research project involving the Power Institute Foundation for Art and Visual Culture at the University of Sydney, the National Gallery in Singapore, and the Bandung Institute of Technology. The project's name makes reference to the Non-Aligned Movement that I mentioned earlier. Its aim is a scholarly analysis of artistic developments during the Cold War; questions of decolonization and the associated struggles for independence and democracy were central here. The word "Ambitious" in the project's name definitely has an empowerment agenda: instead of focusing on the differences between the ASEAN countries during that period, it aims to trace the connections and networks between them at the time. In retrospect, what is the common history that can be told today? There were many similar approaches, especially in the architecture and building cultures of the various countries. This is definitely something worth exploring further.

In addition to this debate, there is also a strong interest, especially among younger generations, in looking ahead and developing their own perspectives, independent of Western theory. In 2017, for example, young art scholars from the region founded the magazine *Southeast of Now*. They are now quite confidently saying: we will no longer only publish in the West, we are publishing among ourselves, for ourselves, and who knows, maybe then, conversely, we can have an influence on the West. Despite this existing critical discourse, which of course often takes place under very privileged conditions, and in very particular spaces, we also have to see that there is still a thoroughly ambivalent relationship to colonialism here, not an undisputed one at all. In 2018, Singapore hosted a commemorative year for the British imperialist Stamford Raffles, who took possession of the island 200 years earlier, in what some now see as the birth of modern Singapore. A well-known Singaporean sociologist mentioned at a university conference that there is hardly a country other than Singapore that celebrates the anniversary of its colonization. The postcolonial situation is complex and complicated here, as is the postcolonial self-image. There are quite different perspectives, depending on who you are talking to. In this sense, we see the CCA as a platform for staging these discourses in order to expand them, to look beyond the respective postcolonial formations of the individual countries, and ask: how can a common perspective on postcolonial Southeast Asia be established today? ASEAN is usually about economic cooperation, or about expanded political and military cooperation. But could we promote cultural understanding and cooperation and nuances—can a critical regional discourse be established?

CH: The architect William S. W. Lim is of central importance to your work at the CCA, but also beyond that. Born in Hong Kong in 1932, Lim studied architecture and urban planning at the Architectural Association in London and at Harvard University, where he also met the Bauhaus people we mentioned earlier. In the 1950s, he went to Singapore and founded DP Architects with Tay Kheng Soon and Koh Seow Chuan: this was the firm that designed the People's Park Complex (1973) and the Golden Mile Complex (1973). In 2017–18, for Lim's 85th birthday, you dedicated an exhibition to him with the title *Incomplete Urbanism: Attempts of Critical Spatial Practice*. What particular role does William S. W. Lim play for you?

UMB: When I moved here, William Lim and his wife Lena Lim were among the first people I was introduced to. Lena had cofounded the critical publishing house Select Books in the 1970s, and she and Willy ran a kind of salon in their apartment, where people from very different disciplines came together. They opened up their living room, an unusual thing to do in Singapore, and welcomed so many people, including me. That was special because there are hardly any public spaces here where you can exchange ideas and network on a regular basis.

These meetings with Willy and Lena Lim were an important entry point for me in understanding, the Singapore context that I am now a part of. Lim is blunt in his evaluation of what is happening in the country, views which have unquestionably cost him a number of building contracts. But Lim isn't just someone who designed buildings, he was always involved in a variety of ways. For example, he founded the Singapore Planning Urban and Research Group (SPUR) in 1965, the Singapore Heritage Society in 1987, and launched many other international research networks (see Wee H. Koon's article in this issue). He was also involved in the groundbreaking exhibition *Cities on the Move* (1997–99), curated by Hans Ulrich Obrist and Hou Hanru, which for the first time tried to understand the rapid architectural and cultural development of Asian cities in the late 20th century. As with many other architects who studied at Harvard or MIT and then returned to Southeast Asia, for Lim the question of tropical modernism was a crucial one. In 2003, he founded the Asian Urban Lab, with the aim of investigating and reconfiguring the question of socially fair spatial planning, often associated with modern architecture, but doing so with specific reference to the various specificities of local Asian conditions. He conducted research on this topic by traveling to many different locations in Asia, finally incorporating his experiences and impressions into his concept of "Incomplete Urbanism," the title of the book he published in 2012. That was an important foundation for our exhibition, which had the same name.

CH: What exactly is meant by Incomplete Urbanism?

UMB: Lim's book is subtitled *A Critical Urban Strategy for Emerging Economies*. It refers to the political dimension of his considerations with reference to the economy. Incomplete Urbanism is a critical analysis of the global-capitalist world order, with its power shifts and its crisis-ridden dynamics, which is deeply inscribed in how cities are planned around the world today. For Lim, spatial justice cannot be created through rigid top-down planning; it should include strategies of "post-planning" (Hou Hanru) or "incomplete urbanism," meant to create open, permeable, and changeable spaces, allowing for participation and encouraging action, while taking into account local conditions and the needs of urban society. Without residents or users, architecture is really nothing. In 1967, Singapore's first prime minister, Lee Kuan Yew, presented his Garden City concept, which envisaged extensive greening and afforestation in Singapore—from a "garden in a city" to a "city in a garden." The annual Tree Planting Day was launched by the government; ideas such as urban gardening or urban farming were introduced here early on, albeit from the top down. Lim was also very interested in these practices, but more from the aspect of space which is public and thus remains open to appropriation.

CH: Does the principle of participation in urban development even play a role in Singapore today? The city seems to have been planned and designed from top to bottom.

UMB: Space is indeed very well designed here. Public space is highly regulated and controlled. Regina Bittner, head of the Academy of the Bauhaus Dessau Foundation, has researched so-called void decks, the public ground-floor zones in state-owned HDB housing complexes in Singapore. These

supposedly open zones are subject to strict planning and supervision, and if, for example, artists want to present their work there, they must first obtain approval from the appropriate state authority. Public housing complexes being built today have considerably reduced the amount of common areas they provide. Another example of the ever-increasing regulation of public space in Singapore is hawker centers: semi-open, roofed-over buildings featuring small food stalls. These were planned by the government back in the 1970s, in order to remove food stalls from the streets, which were considered dirty and unhygienic. Hawkers now sell their food at assigned stands, and in some cases have to pay high licensing fees. In fact, today

the hawker centers are being increasingly replaced by air-conditioned food courts in privatized shopping centers, which restricts the accessibility of these places for small businesses even more dramatically. There is little free urban space left in Singapore. In Johor Bahru in Malaysia, or Ho Chi Minh City in Vietnam, or in Jakarta things look quite different. There, the population relies much more on self-organization in everyday life. Administrative structures in megacities like that are usually so overloaded that many things are handled informally.

MH: The need for new initiatives can also be seen in the arts. In countries like Cambodia and Indonesia, many artist groups have developed in recent

years, for example Sa Sa Art Projects or the Vann Molyvann Project in Phnom Penh. Other small subgroups and projects have now emerged alongside these, creating a new infrastructure on their own initiative, as well as new formats for art promotion and mediation. The Gudskul initiative by ruangrupa in Jakarta is another example. The alternative art scene is developing new educational systems and learning infrastructures on non-academic, non-institutional levels.

UMB: That's right. In recent years, a lot of theoretical and practical formations have been established there; they produce knowledge at the site itself, from the community. They are well networked and operate internationally. In a few years, we will see

Trinh T. Minh-ha: *The Fourth Dimension,* 2001. Exhibition view, *Trinh T. Minh-ha: Films,* **NTU Centre for Contemporary Art Singapore, 2020.**

Foreground: Irene Agrivina: *SOYA C(O)U(L)TURE* (detail), 2014.
Back wall: Marjetica Potrč: *The Earth Drawings*, 2009–19.

Exhibition view,
*The Posthuman City:
Climates. Habitats.
Environments*, NTU Centre
for Contemporary Art
Singapore, 2019.

the fruits of this. These bottom-up structures are very vital, but also very sustainable. Many of them have existed for more than two decades. It is impressive to see what is happening here in the countries of Southeast Asia, in terms of architecture, but also in other fields—there is a lot to look forward to.

CH: You were part of the selection committee that commissioned members of ruangrupa and Gudskul to take over the artistic direction of documenta fifteen, which will take place in 2022. Within the context of documenta, what kind of dynamic can unfold from the idea of personal initiative as the basic principle of these alternative institutions? How will they manage the

balancing act as curators anchored in local communities, on the one hand, and serving the global institutional system of documenta, on the other? Will ruangrupa make documenta more accessible to a non-art audience? It will be interesting to see the reactions when usual expectations of "seeing art" are challenged, and visitors end up in a kind of learning environment instead.

UMB: Yes, I'm curious about that too. When I was part of the curatorial team for Documenta11 under the leadership of Okwui Enwezor in 2002, a clear opening up and reorientation of documenta was already happening. It was moving away from Eurocentric discourse and classic art presentation, toward postcolonial issues and more global perspectives.

Nevertheless, artists from all over the world were represented by their own works of art. That is going to change with ruangrupa; they want something completely different. They are interested in local structures that stand up for social justice, the right to education, and the right to creativity. The central point for them is how this can be demanded by civil society and through activism, and how it can be implemented in practice. Current social movements and grassroots movements, situated in different geopolitical contexts, will serve as an important frame of reference for documenta fifteen. At least, that is what I assume will be the case.

01   Galerie Michael Janssen and Galerie Matthias Arndt, both of which are based in Berlin.

BENJAMIN BANSAL
is an economic historian based in Thailand and Germany. He co-authored the *Yangon Architectural Guide* (with Elliott Fox and Manuel Oka, 2015), which builds on a research project he conducted on Myanmar architecture. He holds a PhD in development studies from the National Institute for Policy Studies in Tokyo with a focus on postwar Tokyo. Currently he works as a development specialist with various international financial institutions.

UTE META BAUER
(born 1958) is the founding director of the NTU Centre for Contemporary Art, Singapore, and a professor at the School of Art, Design and Media at Nanyang Technological University of Singapore. Previously, she was an associate professor in the Department of Architecture at the Massachusetts Institute of Technology, where she also served as the founding director of the MIT Program in Art, Culture, and Technology (2005–13). She has curated exhibitions worldwide, including Documenta11 (2002, co-curator), the 3rd berlin biennale for contemporary art (2004), and the US Pavilion for the 56th Venice Biennale (2015). She is currently co-curator of the 17th Istanbul Biennial (2021) and a working group member of the Sharjah Biennial 15 (2023).

SALLY BELOW
is an urbanist and curator with a focus on sustainable urban development projects, interventions in public space and exhibitions, as well as discourse formats that contribute to a constructive engagement with current issues in the urban fabric. The cooperative transformation of intellectual and real spaces is one of her concerns. She advises ministries, municipalities, and organizations on the development and implementation of urban and cultural projects.

D-ASSOCIATES
is an architectural office in Jakarta, founded in 2001 by Gregorius Yolodi. Maria Rosantina joined the firm two years later as a partner. With projects such as the Tamarind House in South Jakarta and the DRA House on Bali, they also became known outside of Indonesia. In the run-up to the 2018 Asian Games, they were commissioned with the renovation of the iconic Gelora Bung Karno Sports Complex in Jakarta.

DESIGN PARTNERSHIP
was an architectural firm launched in 1967 in Singapore by William S. W. Lim, Tay Kheng Soon, and Koh Seow Chuan. It was responsible for the design and realization of some of the most iconic buildings from Singapore's post-independence era, including the People's Park Complex and the Golden Mile Complex. In 1975, Design Partnership was dissolved and reformed as DP Architects Pte., a global architecture corporation that has since realized numerous large commercial developments worldwide.

MICHAEL FALSER
(born 1973) is an art and architectural historian based in Vienna. As project leader in the Cluster of Excellence "Asia and Europe in a Global Context" (Chair of Global Art History) at the University of Heidelberg, he wrote the two-volume monograph *Angkor Wat: A Transcultural History of Heritage* (2020). He is currently a fellow in the DFG Heisenberg Programme at the Chair of Theory and History of Architecture, Art and Design at the Technical University of Munich (TUM), with a focus on German colonial architecture in Africa, East Asia, and Oceania.

MIRKO GATTI
(born 1987) is a freelance architect, and has been an editor, project manager, and curator at ARCH+ since 2014, where he worked on the projects *An Atlas of Commoning* and *1989–2019:*

Politics of Space in the New Berlin, among others. He studied architecture in Milan, completed a MA at Goldsmiths, University of London, and was a research fellow at ETH Zürich. While his interest in architecture encompasses such fields as critical theory and political activism, his approach remains highly practical.

MORITZ HENNING
is an architect and writer based in Berlin and one of the artistic directors of the project *Encounters with Southeast Asian Modernism* and *Contested Modernities*. He studied architecture at the Technical University of Berlin. Besides working as a freelance project manager for a number of Berlin architectural firms he has been increasingly active in research and writing. His work currently focuses on postcolonial modernities and contemporary architectural developments in Southeast Asia.

CHRISTIAN HILLER
(born 1975) is a media scientist, curator, and writer. He has contributed to international exhibitions, events, and research projects and written widely on topics at the intersection of architecture, urbanism, art, and media. Since 2016, he has been an editor at ARCH+, where he has led research and exhibition projects. Most recently he was a member of the curatorial teams of *An Atlas of Commoning*, *Contested Modernities,* and *Cohabitation*.

HO PUAY-PENG
is head of the Department of Architecture at the School of Design and Environment, National University of Singapore (NUS). He studied architecture at the University of Edinburgh and received a PhD in Art and Architecture History from the School of Oriental and African Studies (SOAS), University of London. Prior to joining NUS, he was a professor of Architecture and an honorary professor of Fine Arts at the Chinese University of Hong Kong (CUHK), where he served as university

dean of students, director of the School of Architecture, and head of the Department of Architecture.

HO WENG HIN
is a senior lecturer at the Department of Architecture, School of Design and Environment, of the National University of Singapore (NSU). He studied architecture at NUS and at the University of Genoa, Italy. He is a founding partner of Studio Lapis, an architectural conservation consultancy, a founding member of ICOMOS Singapore, a voting member of the International Scientific Committee on 20th Century Heritage, as well as member of the DoCoMoMo Singapore Working Party. Weng Hin Ho has coauthored several books, including *Our Modern Past: A Visual Survey of Singapore Architecture, 1920s–70s* (2015).

HUN SOKAGNA
is an architect and researcher based in Phnom Penh. She is the finance and administration manager for New Khmer-Architecture (nk-a), a nonprofit association that emerged from the Vann Molyvann Project, whose aim is to promote critical thinking and dialogue on modern and contemporary design, architecture, and urbanism. In 2016, she cofounded the Roung Kon Project, an initiative dedicated to support and document cinemas in Cambodia that are threatened with demolition.

EKKEHART KEINTZEL
(born 1960) is an architect and photographer. He studied architecture at the Technical University of Vienna and has lived in Berlin since 1993. In his photographic work, he investigates the representation of urban space, urban landscape, history, and transitory urban processes.

EDUARD KÖGEL
(born 1960) studied at the Faculty of Architecture, Urban Planning and Landscape Planning at the University of Kassel. His research focus is the history of architecture and urban planning in Asia. From 1999 to 2004 he was an assistant professor at the Technical University in Darmstadt. In 2007, he finished his dissertation at Bauhaus University in Weimar. He is also a research consultant and program curator for ANCB The Aedes Metropolitan Laboratory Berlin, and project manager at chinese-architects.com.

LIM CHONG KEAT
(born 1930) studied at the University of Manchester and the Massachusetts Institute of Technology, and is cofounder of Malayan Architects Co-Partnership and its successor, Architects Team 3. Lim played a formative role in the shaping of Singapore's urban developments in the 1960s and 1970s as President of the Singapore Institute of Architects, founding Chairman of Architects Regional Council Asia (ARCASIA), board member of Singapore Housing and Development Board and United Nations Review Panel for State and City Planning of Singapore. In the 1970s, Lim, together with Buckminster Fuller, co-organized the Campuan World Meetings in Bali and Penang.

LU BAN HAP
(born 1931) was one of the most important architects and urban planners in Cambodia in the 1960s. He studied in Paris from 1949 to 1959, graduating from the École Spéciale d'Architecture. Upon returning to Phnom Penh, he was commissioned to set up and direct the Department of Town Planning and Housing, where he was responsible for all areas of planning and building in the capital. In parallel, he ran his own office. In 1975, he fled from the Khmer Rouge with his family to Paris, where he still lives today.

MAM SOPHANA
(born 1936) studied architecture at Miami University in Ohio and became one of the most important protagonists of New Khmer Architecture after his return to his home town, Phnom Penh, in 1965. In 1974, he fled with his family to Singapore, where he stayed until 1993 and worked as an architect. Back in Phnom Penh, he again founded his own office and advises the Cambodian government on urban planning issues.

ALFRED (AL) MANSFELD
(born 1912, died 2004) was born in Saint Petersburg, studied at the Königlich Technische Hochschule zu Berlin until 1931, and then moved to Paris, where he graduated from the École Spéciale d'Architecture under Auguste Perret in 1935. In the same year, he emigrated to the British Mandate Territory of Palestine, ran his own office and taught at the Technion Israel Institute of Technology in Haifa for over 40 years from 1949, chairing its Faculty of Architecture and Town Planning from 1954 to 1956.

ANDRA MATIN
(born 1962) graduated in architecture from Parahyangan Catholic University in Bandung in 1981 and founded his office Andra Matin Architects in 1998. As one of the founders of Arsitek Muda Indonesia (Young Architects of Indonesia), he is a key figure in contemporary Indonesian architecture. Matin has designed and built over 100 projects throughout Indonesia, notably the AM Residence (Jakarta, 2007–13), EH House (Bandung, 2014), IH Residence (Bandung, 2015), and the renovation of the Aquatic Center at Gelora Bung Karno Sports Complex for the 2018 Asian Games in Jakarta.

ANH-LINH NGO
(born 1974) is an architect, author, and publisher of ARCH+. He cofounded the international initiative projekt Bauhaus (2015–19), which critically examined the ideas of the Bauhaus. From 2010 to 2016, he was a member of the Art

Advisory Board at the Institut für Auslandsbeziehungen (ifa), for which he co-curated the touring exhibition Post-Oil City (2009) and An Atlas of Commoning – Places of Collective Production. He is a member of the board of trustees of the IBA 2027 StadtRegion Stuttgart and co-curator of the exhibition Cohabitation (2021).

PEN SEREYPAGNA
is a freelance architect, urban researcher and executive director of the Vann Molyvann Project in Phnom Penh. He holds a Bachelor of Architecture and Urbanism from the Royal University of Fine Arts, Phnom Penh, and a Master of Architecture from London Metropolitan University. In 2010, he founded Lumhor Journal, an online platform for architecture and urbanism in Cambodia.

POUM MEASBANDOL
is an architect, researcher, and illustrator based in Phnom Penh, where he documents and graphically reinterprets New Khmer Architecture and the modernist architectural heritage of Cambodia. His illustrations were included in the exhibition Folding Concrete in Phnom Penh (2019).

FARID RAKUN
trained as an architect at the University of Indonesia in Jakarta and Cranbrook Academy of Art in Detroit. He is a visiting lecturer in the Architecture Department of University of Indonesia and part of the artist collective ruangrupa, with whom he cocurated Sonsbeek 2016 TRANSaction in Arnhem, and is overseeing the artistic direction of documenta fifteen (2022) in Kassel. Since 2013, he has worked for the Jakarta Biennale in different capacities and currently serves as its interim director.

RUANGRUPA
is a Jakarta-based collective established in 2000 that produces collaborative works in the form of exhibitions, festivals, workshops, research projects, as well as books, magazines, and online publications. ruangrupa has been involved in many exhibitions such as the Gwangju Biennale (2002, 2018), the Istanbul Biennial (2005), the Asia Pacific Triennial of Contemporary Art (Brisbane, 2012), the Singapore Biennale (2011), the São Paulo Biennial (2014), and the Aichi Triennale (Nagoya, 2016). In 2018, in Jakarta, together with Serrum and Grafis Huru Hara, ruangrupa co-initiated Gudskul, a horizontal learning institution established to practice an expanded understanding of arts and collective values. ruangrupa is overseeing the artistic direction of documenta fifteen (Kassel, 2022).

FRIEDRICH SILABAN
(born 1912, died 1984) studied at the Koningin Wilhelmina School in Batavia (colonial Jakarta), and at the Amsterdam Academy of Architecture. He worked as architect and engineer for the Dutch Army, and for the cities of Batavia and Bogor. A key figure in the realization of president Sukarno's vision for a newly independent Indonesia, Silaban realized some of the most representative buildings in Jakarta in the 1950s and 1960s, including Istiqlal Mosque and the National Bank of Indonesia.

GIOVANNA SILVA
(born 1980) is a freelance photographer and editor based in Milan. She also teaches photography at NABA in Milan, IUAV in Venice, and ISIA in Urbino. She cofounded Humboldt Books and San Rocco Magazine and regularly collaborated with the magazines Domus and Abitare from 2005 to 2011. Among her many publications are Mr. Bawa, I Presume (2020), Imeldific (2020), Tehran (2019), 17 April 1975: A Cambodian Journey (2018), Afghanistan: 0 Rh- (2017), and Syria, A Travel Guide to

Disappearance (2016). Her work *Nightswimming: Discotheques in Italy From the 1960s to the Present* (Bedford Press) was featured at the Venice Architecture Biennale in 2014.

DARREN SOH
(born 1976) is a sociologist by training and began working as an architectural photographer in 2001. His personal works are an extension of his curiosity about how we live and the spaces we create as well as leave behind. His personal mission is to document places that are in danger of disappearing. He is particularly interested in modernist and vernacular architectures that are deemed too banal or insignificant to be noticed.

SETIADI SOPANDI
studied architecture in Bandung and Singapore and cofounded the architectural firm Indra Tata Adilaras in Bogor in 2003. He currently teaches Indonesian architectural history at the School of Design at Pelita Harapan University in Karawaci, Tangerang. His independent research, writing, and archival work focuses on architects and architectural works from 20th-century Indonesia. He has been a contributor to the modern Asian Architecture Network (mAAN) since 2007, and to the modern Southeast Asian architecture project (mASEANa) since 2015. He is the author of *Sejarah Arsitektur: Sebuah Pengantar* (Architectural History: An Introduction, 2013), and the biography *Friedrich Silaban* (2017). He has co-curated several exhibitions, including the Indonesian Pavilion at the Venice Architecture Biennale (2014), *Tropicality: Revisited* at the German Architecture Museum (DAM) Frankfurt (2015), and *Friedrich Silaban, 1912–1984* at the National Gallery of Indonesia (2017). In 2017, he launched the virtual museum arsitekturindonesia.org with Avianti Armand, Nadia Rinandi, and Ria Febriyanti.

SHIRLEY SURYA
is curator for Design and Architecture at M+ in Hong Kong. She has contributed to the shaping of the M+ permanent collection through her research and acquisition of works, which engage with plural modernities as well as transnational and interdisciplinary knowledge networks in greater China and Southeast Asia. She received a BA in Media Studies at the University of California, Berkeley, and an MA in the History of Design from the Royal College of Art in London.

TAY KHENG SOON
(born 1940) is an architect, urban planner, and associate professor at the National University of Singapore (NUS). He cofounded the Singapore Planning & Urban Research Group (SPUR) in 1964–65, was partner in the architecture firm Design Partnership from 1968 to 1975, and has run his own firm, Akitek Tenggara, since 1976. Tay Kheng Soon is involved in the Future of Singapore citizens' forum, whose discussions on issues of economics, social and global industrial policy, education, culture, urban planning, and land policy will culminate in the People's Plan for Singapore.

U SHWE
(born 1939) studied architecture at the Maebashi Municipal College of Technology in Japan and returned to his native Burma in 1972, where he taught at the Rangoon Institute of Technology until his retirement in 1990. Parallel to teaching, he ran his own architectural practice, with which he realized various buildings. He has written about architecture and translated short stories from English and Japanese into Burmese.

U SUN OO
(born 1955) founded Architect Sun Oo and Associates in Yangon in 1979. Today, he runs the architectural firm Design 2000, is an honorary professor at the

Department of Architecture of Yangon Technological University, and a visiting professor at the Architecture Department of Mandalay Technological University. He is also president of the Association of Myanmar Architects (AMA) and of the Myanmar Architect Council (MAC) in the Ministry of Construction, Vice President of International Council of Monuments and Sites (ICOMOS) Myanmar, and a member of the Committee for High-rise and Public Buildings in the Ministry of Construction.

VANN MOLYVANN
(born 1926, died 2017) studied architecture at the École Supérieure des Beaux-Arts in Paris and returned to Cambodia in 1956. In 1962, he became director of Urban Planning and Housing as well as Secretary of Public Works and Telecommunications. In 1965 he became rector at the Royal University of Fine Arts in Phnom Penh and in 1967 was appointed Minister of Education and Fine Arts. In 1971, he fled Cambodia for Switzerland, where he worked as a consultant for the United Nations Centre for Human Settlements, among other positions. In 1991 he returned to Phnom Penh and became Minister of State for Culture, Urban Planning, and Construction (1993–98) and Director of the APSARA Authority in Siem Reap/Angkor (1995–2001).

WEE H. KOON
researches on the sociopolitical and urban effects of industrialization and modernization in Asian cities in the 20th century, and on the transnational formation of Asian modernism in architecture and urbanism. This knowledge connects with the experimental architectural practice SKEW Collaborative, where he is a principal. His recently authored and edited books include *Singapore Dreaming: Managing Utopia* (2016) and *The Social Imperative in China: Architecture & the City* (2017). Koon is the founding

director of the University of Hong Kong Cities in Asia Summer Program, and an assistant professor at its Department of Architecture.

JOHANNES WIDODO
(born 1960) is the director of the Architectural Conservation program at the National University of Singapore. He studied architecture and urban history at Parahyangan Catholic University, Bandung, and Katholieke Universiteit Leuven, and received his PhD in Architecture from the University of Tokyo. He is founder of mAAN (modern Asian Architecture Network), founder and director of DoCoMoMo Macau and Singapore, director of the International Network of Tropical Architecture, and an active member of major international heritage networks, such as ICOMOS Singapore and the UNESCO Asia Pacific Heritage Awards.

In 2019, **ARCH+** joined forces with Birkhäuser
to publish and distribute an annual English edition,
in addition to the quarterly German issues.

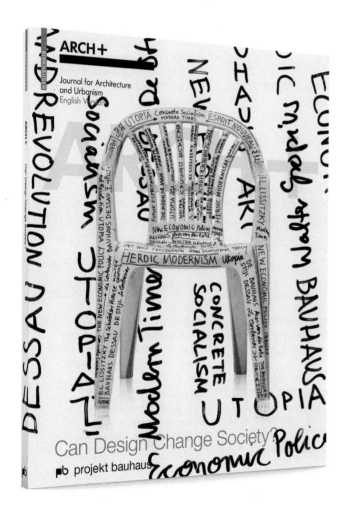

The Property Issue
Politics of Space and Data

"Who owns the land?" is a central question because space is a
resource as vital as air and water. Today, however, data ownership
has become just as relevant as the question of land ownership
in the context of urban planning. This issue, co-edited by ARCH+,
Arno Brandlhuber, and Olaf Grawert of station+/ETH Zürich,
discusses the politics of space and data; the real and virtual assets
of the city of the future.

projekt bauhaus:
Can Design Change Society?

How can design still become effective as a political project? What
are the possibilities and problems encountered by universal
design in the age of globalization? Can the emancipatory potential
of technology still be activated in a digitalized world? *project
bauhaus*, an international group of experts from a wide range of
disciplines, searched for answers to these questions.

ARCH+

Further English publications by ARCH+
can be found here:
www.archplus.net/english-publications

archplus.net
birkhauser.com

ARCH+
Journal for Architecture and Urbanism

Publishers
ARCH+ / Birkhäuser Verlag GmbH

Editor
ARCH+ Verlag GmbH
Friedrichstr. 23a, 10969 Berlin, Germany
Phone: +49 30 340 467 19
verlag@archplus.net

Advisory board
Beatriz Colomina, Arno Brandlhuber,
Philipp Oswalt, Stephan Trüby,
Mark Wigley, Karin Wilhelm, Georg
Vrachliotis

Editor-in-chief
Anh-Linh Ngo*

Editorial team
Nora Dünser*, Mirko Gatti*,
Christian Hiller*, Sascha Kellermann,
Melissa Koch*, Alexandra Nehmer

Guest editors
Sally Below, Moritz Henning,
Eduard Kögel

Head of research and exhibition
projects
Christian Hiller*

Art direction
Mike Meiré*

Design
Charlotte Cassel*, Jeremias Diekmann*,
Meiré und Meiré

Creative direction
Max Kaldenhoff*

Managing editor
Nora Dünser*

Managing editor English edition
Mirko Gatti*

* Editorial team for this publication,
which is based on the German issue
ARCH+ 243: *Contested Modernities –
Postkoloniale Architektur und
Identitätskonstruktion in Südostasien*
(Autumn 2020)

Copy editor
Alisa Kotmair

Translations
Brían Hanrahan (pp. 12–25, 50–63,
86–87, 122–23, 150–59, 214–19), Alisa
Kotmair (pp. 01, 04–11, 26–49, 64–85,
88–111, ARCH+ features, 114–21,
124–149, 160–213, 220–22, 224)

Proofreading
James Copeland

Prepress
max-color, Berlin

Printing
Medialis Offsetdruck GmbH, Berlin

Direct orders
of ARCH+ English editions:
archplus.net/english-publications
birkhauser.com

Subscriptions
ARCH+ magazine in German:
archplus.net/abo

Head of communications & marketing
Barbara Schindler

Ambassador
Christine Rüb

Advertising
anzeigen@archplus.net
archplus.net/mediadaten

ARCH+ gGmbH (non-profit
organization)
ggmbh@archplus.net
Director: Arno Löbbecke

Donation account
GLS Bank
IBAN: DE47 4306 0967 1229 2768 01
BIC: GENODEM1GLS
archplus.net/nonprofit

Bibliographic information published by
the German National Library: The
German National Library lists this
publication in the Deutsche National-
bibliografie; detailed bibliographic data
is available online at dnb.dnb.de.

Library of Congress Control Number:
2021945512

ISBN 978-3-0356-2453-3 (Birkhäuser)
ISBN 978-3-931435-66-0 (ARCH+)

This publication is part of the international exhibition and discourse project
*Contested Modernities: Postcolonial
Architecture in Southeast Asia*. The
project is a continuation of *Encounters
with Southeast Asian Modernism*,
which began in 2019 in several countries
in Southeast Asia and is now being
discussed in a German context.

**Contested
Modernities**
Postcolonial
Architecture in
Southeast Asia

Initiators & artistic directors
Sally Below, Moritz Henning,
Christian Hiller, Eduard Kögel
Visual identity & exhibition design
Constructlab – Peter Zuiderwijk,
Alex Römer
Project management & communications
sbca – Sarah Reiche, Amelie Schulz,
Hanna Köhler, Laura Hermlin-Leder

In addition to this ARCH+ publication,
Contested Modernities includes a
discourse program and an exhibition
with the following contributions:

Folding Concrete, curated by Pen
Sereypagna and Vuth Lyno, Phnom
Penh, Cambodia

Housing Modernities, curated by Ho
Puay-Peng with Nikhil Joshi and
Johannes Widodo, Singapore

Occupying Modernism, curated by
Avianti Armand and Setiadi Sopandi
with Rifandi Nugroho, Jakarta,
Indonesia

*Poelzig's Legacy and the Prefab in the
Tropics: German Influences* curated
by Sally Below, Moritz Henning,
Christian Hiller, and Eduard Kögel,
Berlin, Germany

Synthesis of Myanmar Modernity,
curated by Pwint (†) and Win Thant
Win Shwin, Yangon, Myanmar

*Visualization of the National History:
From, by, and for whom?*, curated by
Grace Samboh, Hyphen —, and
ruangrupa/Gudskul, Jakarta, Indonesia

www.seam-encounters.net

Contested Modernities is funded by

Partners and supporters
Senate Department for Urban
Development and Housing, Berlin
The Governing Mayor of Berlin,
Senate Chancellery
Goethe-Institut Myanmar
Goethe-Institut Singapore
Haus der Statistik
stadtkultur international ev

This issue is supported by

Goethe-Institut Indonesien

Embassy
of the Federal Republic of Germany
Singapore

EMBASSY OF THE REPUBLIC OF INDONESIA
BERLIN